THE MOMENTS
and other pieces

BOOKS BY J. B. PRIESTLEY

FICTION

Adam in Moonshine
Benighted
The Good Companions
Angel Pavement
Faraway
Wonder Hero
Laburnum Grove
They Walk in the City
The Doomsday Men
Let the People Sing

Blackout in Gretley
Daylight on Saturday
Three Men in New
　Suits
Bright Day
Jenny Villiers
Festival at Farbridge
The Other Place: short
　stories

The Magicians
Low Notes on a High
　Level
Saturn Over the Water
The Thirty-First of
　June
The Shapes of Sleep
Sir Michael and Sir
　George
Lost Empires

PLAYS

The Roundabout
Duet in Floodlight
Spring Tide
Mystery at Greenfingers
The Long Mirror
The Rose and Crown

The High Toby
Bright Shadow
Dragon's Mouth (with
　Jacquetta Hawkes)
Private Rooms
Treasure on Pelican

Try it Again
Mother's Day
A Glass of Bitter
Mr Kettle and Mrs
　Moon

COLLECTED PLAYS

Volume I	Volume II	Volume III
Dangerous Corner	Laburnum Grove	Cornelius
Eden End	Bees on the Boat Deck	People at Sea
Time and the Conways	When we are Married	They Came to a City
I Have Been Here	Good Night Children	Desert Highway
Before	The Golden Fleece	An Inspector Calls
Johnson over Jordan	How are they at Home?	Home is Tomorrow
Music at Night	Ever Since Paradise	Summer Day's Dream
The Linden Tree		

ESSAYS AND AUTOBIOGRAPHY

Talking
Open House
Apes and Angels
Midnight on the Desert
Rain upon Godshill

The Secret Dream
Delight
All About Ourselves and
　other Essays (chosen
　by Eric Gillett)

Thoughts in the
　Wilderness
Margin Released
The Moments and
　other pieces

CRITICISM AND MISCELLANEOUS

Brief Diversions
The English Comic
　Characters
Meredith (E.M.L.)
Peacock (E.M.L.)
The English Novel
English Humour
　(Heritage Series)
The Balconinny

English Journey
Postscripts
Out of the People
British Women Go To
　War
Russian Journey
Theatre Outlook
The Olympians (opera
　libretto)

Journey Down a Rain-
　bow (with Jacquetta
　Hawkes)
Topside
The Art of the
　Dramatist
Literature and Western
　Man
Man and Time

THE MOMENTS
and other pieces

J. B. PRIESTLEY

HEINEMANN · LONDON

William Heinemann Ltd

LONDON MELBOURNE TORONTO

CAPE TOWN AUCKLAND

First published in Great Britain 1966

© J. B. Priestley 1966

Mr J. B. Priestley made an outright gift
of this book to Oxfam. The publishers are
making a contribution to its cost.
Printed in Great Britain by
Western Printing Services Ltd, Bristol

PR
6031.
R6M6

Contents

[v]

Preface

APART FROM THE vanity and exhibitionism inseparable from authorship, my chief reason for reprinting these periodical pieces is as follows. People will keep on writing for copies of pieces they have particularly liked, often from very distant places and usually months and months after the pieces have first appeared. (The *New Statesman* especially seems to wander round the globe.) So now instead of laboriously explaining that I have no copies for distribution, I can refer them to this volume—on a postcard. And I have decided to leave the pieces exactly as they were, not tinkering with them to make them look clean up-to-date, if only because in essence they are not topical journalism, I believe. They are mostly from the *New Statesman* but I have collected a few others from elsewhere, and I take this opportunity of thanking all the editors concerned for the hospitality of their columns.

J.B.P.

The Moments

ALL MY LIFE, I now realize, I have been nourished and secretly sustained by certain moments that have always seemed to me to be magical. If I have completed the tasks and shouldered the burdens all the way, finishing the marches without handing over my rifle and pack or dropping out, it is neither conscience nor energy that has kept me going but the memory and the hope of this magic. It has visited me before; it will come again. Sooner or later I would taste the honey-dew once more. And if this is to have a romantic temperament, then I have a romantic temperament. If there is immaturity here, then I am still immature in my seventy-first year.

But here I shall fire a few rounds in the direction of the enemy camp. People who in their confident maturity reject this magic, who have instant 'nothing-but' explanations of everything, are either kept going by their vanity—and the vanity of severely rational persons is astounding—or not sustained at all, existing hungrily in despair, seeking power at all costs, trying various brutal excesses, or stiffening into automata. I can imagine an age, in which this magic has been explained away, that would cover the world with zombies all manipulated and directed by power-maniacs. In such an age, power and organization and machinery would be everything, poetry would be nothing. How far off is it?

Sometimes I have wondered if the seemingly in-explicable *rages* of the young, violently destructive now in so many different countries, might not be ex-plained by the non-arrival of these magical moments. Something expected, promised at birth, is missing. Where among all these prompt deliveries of Grade-A pasteurized is the milk of paradise? However, it is true that for one lad who is breaking windows there are a hundred, not mentioned in the papers, who never pick up a brick. And it is not for me to say that our Pop culture never brings its magical moments. But what is certain is that it does not attempt the grand and sublime, which is what we cry out for in our youth. On the other hand, it is equally certain that whenever the Eroica or the Choral Symphony is being performed, the cousins of the brick-throwing lads will be there, if necessary standing for hours. The contemporary scene is now so wide and complicated that anything can be proved from it. I must return to myself.

Describing an innings by Jessup, Neville Cardus wrote: 'He at once took the game out of the prison of cause and effect.' That is what these moments have always done for me. That is why they are magic. 2 and 2 suddenly make 25. In a flash they add another dimension to existence. They award us, for as long as they last, a bonus, huge, irrational, glorious. We win a prize from God knows where. It isn't earned and deserved; that would be justice or fair-dealing, a decent cause producing a satisfactory effect; whereas this is magic. It belongs to the fairytale world, in which the idlest of the three lads in the forest meets

[2]

the princess, and hardly anything that happens could be explained by experts writing in the weekly journals. Indeed, the moments are entirely beyond the reach of experts, who, I am convinced, never experience them. They favour the woolly-minded, of whom, I am proud to declare, I am one. Brush away all wool, give yourself a first-rate razor-sharp intellect, and you will go far, and probably a hell of a long way from this magic. This is one reason why men who have arrived where they have always wanted to be are impressive but not much fun to be with, so that their women so often look depressed. Whatever they may say, women believe in a magical world. They are seen in the prison of cause and effect only on visiting days.

It is my experience that these moments arrive as and when they choose. They cannot be summoned, nor even induced, beckoned. But of course some circumstances are more favourable than others. It is just possible I might be visited by one of these moments while reading a report on the tinplate industry, or a list of arthritic patients in Bedfordshire, but all odds are heavily against it. On the other hand, I have found the arts most generous with these magical moments, and this is one good reason—there are several others, mark you—for hanging around with them. If this last phrase suggests an absence of painstaking study, anxious application, then it is doing what I intended it to do. I suspect—though of course I am writing within the limits of my own temperament—that you have to hold yourself a bit loosely, not bothering about cultural improvement, for the magic to work.

In the long run, which is where I am now, music has worked best for me, though when I was younger I think literature and drama were neck-and-neck with it. The visual arts have given me enormous enjoyment—and indeed I am a bit of a holiday painter myself—but for some reason obscure to me they have rarely brought me these magical moments. Perhaps my ear provides a shorter cut to enchantment than my eye. Certainly music may do the trick when it is far below its highest level. Let nobody imagine I have to wait for Bach's B Minor Mass or Beethoven's late quartets. To give the first example that occurs to me —and I could offer dozens—in the opening movements of his Cello Concerto and his D Minor Symphony, Dvorak makes his woodwind trail after his main themes—they are like sunlit wisps of dissolving cloud—and to this day the magic has not utterly faded from them. Again, listening recently to a new recording of Elgar's First Symphony (which I had long thought I didn't care for), I found that with the muted trombones at the end of the third movement, the *Adagio*, the sudden magic seemed almost numinous, as if the gods walked the earth again. Enough, enough!

How far and with what complexity and depth the arts interact with life, we do not know, though some brave writers—Proust, for instance—have refused to avoid the subject. It may be that people who know and care nothing about the arts have known as many magical moments as the rest of us have—perhaps even more if they happen to be introverts living in lonely places. (But probably far fewer if they happen to be ambi-

[4]

tious politicians, editors of sensational newspapers, brisk salesmen, New York taxi-drivers.) There seems to me no difference in quality between the moments coming by way of the arts and those that arrive, quite unexpectedly, in our ordinary daily life. These are more remarkable than the immensely heightened moments of travel, of which most of us could furnish examples—and perhaps too often do. In my life I have suddenly known the greatest happiness always when *there was no apparent reason for it*—when out of nowhere there came floating up the great blue bubble. I shall never forget walking once, some years ago, along Piccadilly and across Leicester Square in a blinding snowstorm, which made walking difficult and did not seem to me at all picturesque and romantic, and yet I walked the whole way in a kind of ecstasy, as if in another world, magical and immortal. And there was no reason for it at all, not the tiniest scrap of any possible cause.

It is the same, at least in my experience, with personal relationships. I have never needed any help from manuals on how to get rich in the private commerce between the sexes; but even so, I think we are now inclined to make too much out of the bedroom scenes in our love stories. It is my experience that even in love the magical moments come when they please, often when we are wearing all our clothes and are far from the bedroom. I can remember a moment of complete insight and perfect understanding, as if one had been given the freedom of a strange continent, that arrived in a dreary little teashop near the ministry from which I had extracted the lady of my choice. There were not even any words, just a meeting of eyes above the teacups, but a magical meeting, in which there was the promise of many happy years, an unearned bonus if there ever was one.

So long as we experience these moments, we live in a magical world. (And don't let anybody talk you out of it, boy.) I was arguing the other day with a clever young man who said that we are machines—extraordinarily elaborate, intricate, delicate, subtle—but machines. I said that we weren't so long as we remained open-ended, with one end open to the collective unconscious, the whole heritage of earth life, and the other open to influences beyond our understanding. And perhaps it is when we are suddenly opened a little more at either end that 2 and 2 seem to make 25, another dimension is added, we taste the honey-dew, and all is magical. Of course the moments do not arrive as often as they did, but I soldier on in the belief that I have not yet used up my ration, that there are still a few more to come.

Ambience or Agenda?

TO SAVE TIME in what follows I shall describe as *ambience* or *atmosphere* the total climate of values, ideas, opinions, fears and hopes, in which we live. And by *agenda* or *programme* I mean of course a party's specific proposals, the political *table d'hôte* offered to the electorate. Now what I ask here is which is more important, which ought to be put first—agenda-programme or ambience-atmosphere?

Our lives may depend upon the answer. So indeed may our whole civilization, which I must confess often seems to me to be preparing for its end. (Mircea Eliade has suggested that our deepening interest in the past might be compared to a drowning man remembering in a last few seconds the whole of his life.) For at the heart of the nuclear quarrel is the division between agenda-planners and ambience-changers.

You meet a multilateralist expert, humane, not stupid, no death-wisher, but a 100 per cent agenda man. He says you are just tub-thumping and showing-off; you are incapable of getting down to work on all the problems of disarmament. He has written a book of 600 pages that you must read, if only to prove you take the subject seriously. But what he will not see is that in this particular ambience, which he and his like do nothing to change except for the worse, no disarmament is possible. They cannot even stop the arms race for a while in order to look around and take a few deep breaths. Every time the expert finished

[7]

another 100 pages of disarmament programme, he could have observed that we were all in a worse situation than when he began them. The atmosphere was thicker, nastier, less in favour of life. What can he do about this? Nothing except help to make it worse.

Any attempt to clear and purify the atmosphere involves not only an effort but a risk. If our species had always preferred apparent security to any risk, we would probably never have got out of the mud. To want security at any price, as so many people seem to do now, means sooner or later dallying with ruin, pestilence and death. This is a universe of curved tracks and irony. Take no risks, ask for security first of all, being ready to sacrifice honour, decency, our common humanity, and you will arrive not merely at the old insecurity, the one men have always known, but a new and appalling one specially designed for you, all life depending on a switch or a button.

This is the wider atmosphere in which we live now, poisoned by the fear it generates. But take a risk that might begin to clear and purify it? 'Oh no!' cry the sane, sound, level-headed agenda men, seemingly no longer conscious of the existence of any ambience. Shrugging away the crackpots once again, they return to their serious disarmament agenda work, like a tribe in the Sahara planning an ice palace.

If Labour had taken the unilateral risk, not only would it have had a better programme but, what is far more important, it would have begun to change the atmosphere. And unless it can do this it will spend a long time shuffling shadow cabinets, handing to Brown the large lump of nothing taken away from

[8]

Jones. It has now plenty of agenda men, ready to work overtime, but where are the ambience changers? In whose belly is the fire? 'Bring me'—it ought to be singing now—'my miniature token bow of lukewarm silver-gilt.'

Now not only have the Tories more money to spend on advertising and image conjuring. Not only have they on their side the Establishment, which in recent years seems to me to have had a lot of steel and reinforced concrete plugged into it from foundation to apex. But they know—and indeed have always known —that ambience is more important than agenda, that if you can create the right atmosphere, then the programme can look after itself. This is sound political strategy. But of course an atmosphere that is right for an election may not be life-enhancing afterwards. After a time it may prove to be unhealthy even for those robust men seeking high office or power, money, privilege, honours and titles. High office may turn into a headache; power and money may be threatened; privilege may be questioned, derided; honours and titles may begin to look tawdry. There may be cracks even in that reinforced foundation of Topside.

I often wonder what our ministers and our spokesmen of sound opinion think and feel when they find themselves awake at three in the morning? It should be obvious by now that we English, for all our capacity for self-deception, have lost any good image of ourselves. Where is the prestige abroad for which we adopted the Bomb, sacrificed moral leadership, alienated the best minds everywhere? Who admires, who praises us? How contemptibly we have so often

[9]

behaved, in these last years, as a nation? And are we any happier with ourselves at home? Does it never occur to us that our life as a people may be now running down? Do we never feel a lack of vital creative energy in our community, as if the atmosphere were short of oxygen?

Programmes must be planned sometimes, agendas set out, but first things first, I say, and this means changing the ambience, clearing the 'atmosphere'. And this is now not the easy but the hard part. A Left that insists upon behaving pedantically and peevishly has not a hope.

Labour has already made three huge and tragic mistakes. It came to victory in 1945 in a certain ambience, which had in fact been created for it during the war. Once in power, it made no effort to keep this atmosphere. Its second mistake was to accept instead of rejecting the nuclear deterrent, which may now be seen protecting the hard core of capitalism, casting a shadow in which what we may call the liberal Left apparently cannot exist. Its third mistake was to allow its leaders to campaign violently and often unscrupulously against unilateralism, to the admiration and applause of its enemies. Not much ambience-changing, atmosphere-clearing, there!

Let me give an instance of what seems to me political folly, an obvious lack of any intuitive understanding of our situation. Now Michael Foot is a man I like, but he is far from being a close friend and in fact I rarely set eyes on him. If I mention him here it is because he provides me with an example I need. And it seems to me that to proscribe Foot in any way is to sit in a desert pouring water into the sand. In the situation in which we find ourselves now, he is worth 50 docile mumbling back-benchers. For he belongs to the ambience-changers, the atmosphere-clearers, the bringers of fire and water. I do not know whether he can plan a programme or not, and I do not care. What I do know is that, unlike so many of his fellow members, he can help to create an atmosphere in which plenty of good programmes can soon be planned. Not to understand this, deliberately to go the other way, seems to me an open confession of a lack of political insight: it is the Left trying too hard to be safe and right.

By staying with the deterrent, Labour seems to me to have created a situation here as unhealthy as our present ambience. I am not considering now the fact, already mentioned, that the liberal Left cannot flourish in the shadow of the deterrent. (They belong of course to two different worlds of thought and feeling.) I am thinking about the distribution of political forces on the ground. Towards the right, where political machines and men are massed, there is hardly room to move. But towards the left, not over where the communists are but where the rebellious young radicals may be found, there is so much vacant ground that anything may happen, not immediately but fairly soon. It is there that doctrines of 'direct action', and not simply against the Bomb, are being preached.

An impatient radicalism, despairing of what Labour seems to represent, may soon want not only to bypass but even wreck the machinery of parliamentary government. And here I must add that, although I

[11]

am myself by temperament an impatient radical, I am not in sympathy with such aims and methods. But there is that large empty space, to which more and more of the liveliest youngsters may soon find their way, and where sooner or later a demagogue or two with a touch of genius may start shouting. Then ballot boxes might go up in flames.

Even without disorder on a very large scale, I say that in the atmosphere in which we exist now, in an ambience that will certainly not be irradiated by membership of the Common Market, the reaction of the Right could be very sharp indeed. We could in fact discover that for the sake of law and order we had been taken over by a bowler-hat-and-umbrella fascism. But what do I mean by this? I mean state action on behalf of big money, now with the lid off, no more clap-trap about freedom. And I am afraid I believe now that what the West wants to deter is any menace to money—and not to freedom. (Look at its allies!) It is not when personal liberty is in danger, but when the big money is threatened, that the West spurns an ally. Freedom is a rare plant; I cannot see it flourishing in a soil watered and manured by tough tycoons, politicians under pressure, political inquisitors, hush-hush men and security experts. We know in fact what has been happening to it ever since we began deterring.

Probably I shall now be told that swift and fairly ruthless reaction from the right could not succeed here, the trade unions being too strong. I hope so. But I must point out that it is the unions, by reversing their decision about the nuclear deterrent, who moved out of that space I have already mentioned, leaving so much ground politically vacant that anything might happen in it. And this is the situation here and now: an unhealthy atmosphere, a bad ambience, too many programmes and agendas without life and hope in them, and a distribution of political forces and machinery that is asking for trouble.

All right, I am no prophet, do not pretend to be. But about one thing I am certain, that ambience is more important than agenda, that you change the programme by changing the atmosphere. Remember America's New Deal and this country in 1945. Research teams and cautious pamphlets are all very well, but do not come first if the light is failing, the oxygen going. If Labour really wants to save this country, it should stop trying to swallow the deterrent and should spit it out. It should turn its back on the traditional hocus-pocus, the Establishment, Topside, and become fiercely radical. It should stop draining off its energy by proscriptions and expulsions, and all this melancholy clowning of distributing ministries it has not got.

What we need is a new way of life, not a possible new Parliamentary Under-Secretary for Fisheries. It should turn and look at that great stretch of ground where rebellious energies it needs so badly are going to waste. It should run out there, roaring at the top of its voice. Ambience before agenda, friends! Change the atmosphere, the programme will follow.

Tobacco

I HAVE JUST realized that I have been smoking a pipe for half a century. I grew up among pipe-smokers; my father was one and so were most of his friends. Fifty years ago in the north there were still some real tobacconists, who knew how much Latakia and Perique to add to Virginia, who did not earn a living by hiring girls to push packets of cigarettes across the counter. In those days men offered their tobacco pouches to one another. Some of them in the north may still do it, but not for years and years have I given or received a fill. Perhaps I don't live right.

To this day you will find pipe tobacco improves as you move up the map. It is better in the north of England than it is in the south. In Scotland it is better still. The Scots like to boast, but it is strange they never mention the debt owed to them by the world's pipe-smokers. There is some good tobacco in Ireland too. On the Continent, especially in the northern half, there has been some improvement since the war; but most of it, now got up to look British, is still very poor stuff. Most American pipe tobacco is too sweet, as if meant for eating not smoking. I remember that George Doran, the publisher, used to smoke a Los Angeles mixture that had a chocolate flavour. If any pipe-smoking reader is planning to stay in America, he should make a note of a mixture, medium and broad-cut, that comes from St Louis and is called Hayward Mixture. I have carried yellow pound tins of it into almost every state of the Union. Sometimes when I wondered if I was going out of my mind, a few pipes of it have restored my sanity.

When I started smoking a pipe, 50 years ago, I bought Cut Cavendish from Salmon and Gluckstein at 3½d. an ounce. It was very strong, and there were times when, after puffing furiously as youngsters nearly always do, I felt queasy and my surroundings began to shift about and dissolve. Since that hard beginning, I have been able to smoke anything, though not of course always with enjoyment. But I would rather have bad tobacco than no tobacco. In Egypt, earlier this year, I was compelled to smoke some of their local muck, wondering as I coughed and cursed why the United Arab Republic, which you are never allowed to forget for a moment, did not make sure that Syrian tobacco reached Egypt. Probably President Nasser does not smoke a pipe.

Those people now ready to write and tell me I am a slave to a dirty habit need not waste time, paper and stamps. I admit I have been long enslaved by tobacco. But all men are enslaved by something, and there are worse masters than the weed. By encouraging me to reflect, at the same time freeing me from spiritual pride, it has kept me from more dangerous forms of slavery. Nor have I ever been able to see that smoking is a particularly dirty habit. It is absurd of course, this continuous puffing out of smoke, but no dirtier than most of our habits. You have only to be sufficiently fastidious, and life itself is one huge dirty habit. Purity is reached only in the crematorium.

We are told, usually by people who dislike tobacco, that smoking injures the health. That may be so, though it is worth pointing out that the contributions to a world civilization of men careless of their health far exceed those of the health-seekers. (*Fit for what?* still seems to me the best joke *Punch* ever achieved.) There may be something in this lung cancer idea. Yet when I was young, and good tobacco was far less than a tenth of the price it is now, I was surrounded by heavy smokers, but nobody seemed to be suffering from lung cancer.

I suspect a good deal of disguised puritanism among medical men, especially in America. They denounce various forms of enjoyment but never suggest that the whole modern way of life is idiotic. A man who sits with ten telephones in Wall Street, desperately trying to outwit his competitors, might be healthier if he did not smoke, did not drink, ate no fats. He would be healthier still if he got to hell out of Wall Street and forgot the rat race.

But look at the money we waste on tobacco. No, madam, in Britain we are not spending all that money on tobacco, but on taxes. If we all stopped smoking tomorrow, several hundred million would have to be found elsewhere, for rockets that must never be fired and other imbecilities. The ever-increasing duties on tobacco, making its price about 12 times what it was when I started smoking, show our Establishment at its worst—uncreative, lacking all ingenuity, lazy-minded, mean and callous. I am not thinking of myself now, when I call this completely inequitable taxation mean and callous. I am thinking of men of my generation trying to keep going among the never-had-it-so-goods on wretched tiny pensions.

You are 70 and have always enjoyed a smoke. Now, no longer active and with a lot of time on your hands, you enjoy a smoke more than ever. To ponder and remember over a pipe is probably now your greatest pleasure. So what do they do to you, these smirking Chancellors of the Exchequer, with their annual Budget performance, these first-class minds of the Treasury, the pick of Oxford and Cambridge? Every time they need more money, they empty your tobacco pouch, robbing you of the last enjoyment life offers you. There is no fire in the grate, the cupboard is nearly bare; the road at the end of the street is noisy and dangerous with cars; your friends are dead or dying; so they screw another sixpence out of you, before you are carted away to rot in an over-crowded under-staffed hospital; and if you haven't the sixpence then you suck an empty pipe while you read, in the paper you borrowed, all about the tax-free millions that have been made out of property deals.

In restaurants all pipe-smoking is sharply discouraged, not because of the food, cigar smoke being even stronger, but probably because there is no profit to be made out of it. (The profit on cigars is fierce.) It is the banning of the pipe from aeroplanes—and I bet the British started that—which has brought me hours of misery. Only on the old Stratocruisers could one go below to the little bar and light a pipe, and more than once I have bumped across the Atlantic, reading and smoking the night away while all the other passengers were asleep. On one flight, without the little bar below, I was able to smoke my pipe all the way to Montreal, but that was because I had deliberately chosen a Friday the 13th and had the plane almost to myself. This does not mean I am not superstitious. I was born on a 13th and so feel free of its sinister influences.

Pipes of course can smell foully, though the worst of them are probably more easily endured than the reek of the last inch or so of soggy cigars. To my mind the gravest offender is that favourite of all authorities —the cigarette. It is not the tobacco but the paper that is so offensive. A room crowded with cigarette smokers is like a papermill on fire. Again, it is not the cigarette that is being smoked that afflicts eyes, nose and throat, but the cigarette smouldering in the hand or on the ashtray, the Virginian joss stick. The behaviour of cigarette smokers has always puzzled me. Why, for example, do they want to light up ten seconds before a meal, then puff again between meat and pudding? Many of them, I feel, do not consciously enjoy smoking, as I most genuinely do, but wish to avoid the pain of not smoking. I do not include them among the friends of tobacco.

Cigars can be things of beauty, works of art, but on this level they are harder and harder to find, evil entropy being at work here as elsewhere. (This is called by my friends Iris and John Bayley 'Jack's Law'.) On a much lower level I would now just as soon smoke a Jamaican cigar as a Havana; and I have spent many a pleasant hour abroad—never finding them in London—with those large black Brazilian cigars, banded a threatening scarlet and emerald green, that are so surprisingly mild and friendly, as if some flashing-eyed Carmen in a gipsy cave came across, took your hand, and talked quietly and sensibly.

A cigar rounds off a substantial meal, but when, being short of pipe tobacco in distant places, I have found myself compelled to smoke them all day, I have soon got tired of them. Perhaps if Sir Winston, round about 1944, had taken to a pipe, we might have all been living today in a happier world. But the pipe-smoker's appearance of solidity and wisdom is of course illusory. Some of the biggest chumps I have ever known have had pipes stuck in their faces. Even so, I fancy they were great re-lighters and puffers and knockers-out of dottle, and perhaps never filled a pipe when they were by themselves. There is a kind of pipe-smoking that belongs to actors on the stage and clergymen having a jolly good yarn with the chaps.

It is just possible that a few readers may decide either to try smoking a pipe for the first time or, what is more likely, to have yet one more shot at it. To them, after this half-century, I venture to offer some advice. Many men have defeated themselves as pipe-smokers. They start the wrong way. They buy a small light pipe and probably fill it with some rubbed-out yellow flake, at which they puff away. In a few minutes they have a furnace in their hands and too much saliva in their mouths; there is no fragrance, no flavour; the pipe, almost too hot to hold, begins to gurgle disgustingly; so they decide pipe-smoking is not for them—'Tried but can't manage it, old boy—wet smoker.' I would be one as well with that equipment.

To begin with, do not buy one pipe but at least

three. If you cannot afford pipes by well-known makers, do not buy cheap imitations but search the tobacconists' for throw-outs. Some of the best pipes I have ever had I have picked out of the baskets of throw-outs. Here I must add, after my 50 years, that just as you choose a pipe, so a pipe chooses you. I have had as presents magnificent pipes, cut from the finest straight-grain brier, that never gave me ten minutes satisfactory smoking. Either they were not right for me or I was not right for them. There is something like a personal relation here. And until you are used to smoking a pipe, avoid small thin light pipes: they get hot too quickly. You will be happier at first with fairly large pipes, even if they seem too heavy. And do not scrape out all the carbon, for it keeps the pipe cool.

But why three pipes? Because you must never refill a warm pipe: it is precisely this that has left us pipe-smokers in bad odour. I have watched with horror men smoking the same pipe hour after hour, smelling like gardeners' bonfires. Always I carry three pipes in my pocket. On my desk there may be a dozen or more. I buy and use a great many pipe cleaners. On the other hand, I remove from all pipes any aluminium tubes or similar devices. I have been sent pipes that had most ingenious arrangements for collecting nicotine, but they always seemed to me to taste nasty. The pipe, I suspect, is an enemy of gadgetry.

Now for the tobacco. Do not make a start with light Virginia leaf or mild mixtures. They can easily be hot and tongue-burning. Try a darker flake or a mixture with a fair amount of Latakia and Perique in it. Out of the strong comes forth sweetness. Fill your pipes carefully, using the third finger not the first to complete the filling. The trick then is to keep the tobacco smouldering, smoking as slowly as possible, for the hotter it is the worse it tastes and smells.

A cool clean well-packed pipe that is just being kept alight pleases the smoker and any body who comes near him. All over the world people have said to me 'What wonderful tobacco you must be smoking!' I have even gone through Customs (but not in England) on fragrance alone—when in fact there was nothing remarkable about the tobacco itself: it was being treated properly.

If I were a youth today perhaps I would never start smoking, if only to thumb my nose at these appalling prices. But after 50 years of it, I regret nothing. Man, the creature who knows he must die, who has dreams larger than his destiny, who is for ever working a confidence trick on himself, needs an ally. (Woman I include here in Man.) Mine has been tobacco. Even with it I have too often been impatient and intolerant. Without it I should have been insufferable. You may retort that I am insufferable anyhow, but, with a pipe nicely going, I do not believe you.

Dark Junction

IT IS A cold wet day and the light is going. You are a
woman with two small children and a baby, a heavy
suitcase, one of those baskets that young mothers
always seem to need, and a carry-cot. You are travelling by train from Wabbleton to Wobbleton, which
you must do by way of Wibbleton. But the line from
Wibbleton to Wobbleton has been closed. You have
no private car at your disposal; you cannot afford to
take a taxi 15 miles; you must go by bus. Has Mr
Macmillan or Mr Marples or Dr Beeching ever tried
boarding a bus with two small children and a baby, a
suitcase, a basket and a carry-cot?

They have not, of course, and for that matter
neither have I. But at least I can imagine the experience;
they do not seem to have any imagination at all. And
it is this lack of imagination, the sheer inability to put
yourself into somebody else's place, that explains the
decision to cut railway services and close for ever some
of the pleasantest little stations in the country.

I do not blame Dr Beeching—though my heart does
not leap up when I behold him—but the politicians
who told him to go ahead and behave as if he were
still helping to run ICI. And this of course is ridiculous because British Railways and ICI do not exist in
the same world. ICI has to make a profit. British Railways have not to make a profit. They are part of the
public services of this country, for which we pay our
taxes. I do not like paying taxes, and as I have not

retreated to the South of France or Switzerland or Bermuda, and I am not a limited company, and I am not a City millionaire but a hard-working professional man (and it is our noses that are held most firmly to the grindstone), I seem to pay my share of them. Even so, I feel ready to shoulder a certain amount of loss on these little stations and lines now under sentence of death. Compared with so many things we spend public money on, they seem to me pretty good value.

For instance, I caught a glimpse on TV not long ago of a new nuclear-powered submarine that has cost us £20 million. I would prefer to lose a little money on Wincanton Station, which is more useful than the submarine, more fun, far more likely to add value to people's lives. What the hell can we do with this submarine, anyhow? As soon as it can be used to hunt other submarines, we are in a major war, and after the first morning we shall not be here to learn if the submarine is doing any good or not. And I refuse to believe its mere existence can act as a deterrent. So as far as I can see, that £20 million has gone down the drain. And hundreds of millions have gone down the same drain. And—to change the imagery—if we still have money to burn, I should like to see some of it keeping Wincanton Station warm.

There are of course some commonsense arguments against driving more and more people and goods off the railways and on to the roads. We have the railways, all set up, whereas we shall have to build new roads, at a stupendous cost and murderous to our landscape. (An England that is a network of huge 'motorways' will have been ruined for ever.) This island is not another America, and what suits it best is not private but public transport, in which I believe railways take first place. Why, some of my most rewarding hours have been spent on sleepy little trains going nowhere in particular. If they now lose money, very well they lose money. After all, so do many other things that I for one never want to see again.

It seems to me, however, that we must go deeper than this kind of argument. Behind the idea that public services should show a profit, and must be curtailed if they don't, are other and even more important ideas that seem to me wrong, so profoundly wrong that I feel the politicians who cherish them are no longer fit to hold office. Now I know that the country must earn its living, pay its way, balance imports and exports, and so forth. I am not an economist, but I believe my Labour friends when they tell me that even on this ground the Tories, who hate to plan because they receive so much support from uncontrolled private enterprise, have done us far more harm than good. And I do not need to be an economist to know that the government's quick-change attitudes towards the Common Market have never made sense.

Now where these politicians go wrong is in assuming that, because the country has its economic responsibilities, it is really some kind of commercial concern, a larger ICI. And it is not. It is our home. We don't just work here, we live here. This seems obvious enough, yet I believe that the men who demand that public services should show a profit have forgotten that we live here. The quality of the life we lead, here in our home, need not, they feel, be any concern of theirs. Their idea of a good government is one that cuts losses and begins to show a profit. It is business on a national scale.

I will agree that a case can be made out for a government that has no concern whatever with the quality of its people's life. Let them raise their own standards of living, paying for any fancy work they feel they need, while the government simply governs, keeping order, minding its own business. But this kind of government, known to our forefathers, did not employ hundreds of thousands of civil servants. Under this kind of government, income tax would be threepence in the pound, tobacco ninepence an ounce, and whisky five shillings a bottle. And clearly we are not under this kind of government, and never will be. Expensive and ubiquitous government has come to stay. Whatever party may be in power, we now have no alternative.

If we believed the Tories when they are orating, we should imagine that after 12 years of their rule only a few large buildings would be occupied by state employees, civil servants becoming older and older and fewer and fewer. But the truth is of course that now even a Tory government is willy-nilly a kind of socialist government. The very men who tell us they believe only in private enterprise are in fact making use of public enterprise all day long. If Tory ministers were consistent they would be always publicly boasting how little their departments did and how they were dwindling every year. To enlarge those departments to increase their power and scope, is not to Keep Out

Socialism but to bring it in. But there must be sops for the rugged individualists, especially when election funds are needed, so we have these idiotic and callous proposals to make public services show a profit. And we have expensive and ubiquitous government that shirks its essential responsibility, that of steadily heightening and deepening the quality of life in this island.

There seem to me two important differences between Mr Harold Macmillan and Mr Harold Wilson. Mr Macmillan has to run—he cannot help it—a kind of socialist government while believing it ought to be something quite different. He has to step backward and forward at the same time, which helps to explain some of his extraordinary contortions. He has to be Blue on the platform and Pink in Downing Street, whereas Mr Wilson can remain one colour and instead of being condemned to a swaying motion he can move straight forward.

The second difference returns us to a point I made earlier, namely, that this country is our home, we live here. Now it seems to me that Mr Wilson and his friends live here in a sense in which Mr Macmillan and his friends don't live here. These Tory grandees live in a very tiny Britain all their own, in which, for example, it is not of the least importance if a railway junction might soon be dark and empty, and any talk of the quality of living, what ordinary people might get out of life, is regarded as the sort of hot air to be expected from long-haired writing types, and of course the kind of funeral that France gave Braque a few weeks ago is just tomfoolery. I wish these gentlemen no harm; for all I care they can enjoy their club smoke-rooms and grouse-moors a few years longer. But for Heaven's sake, and all our sakes, including that woman with two small children and a baby, let us hurry them away from the seats of power as soon as we can!

Conjuring

I AM A bad conjurer. I haven't the hands for it, the speed, the skill, the cheerful impudence. But even now, though God knows I am old enough to know better, I hanker after conjuring, not of course for any public performance but only in private. The other day, telling myself I was only going in search of toys for my grandchildren, I cut the time needed to buy the right train sets and wooden circuses and sidled into the magical department. After all, there would be grand-children here over Christmas and they would like some entertainment. So I bought some odd tricks and a very large cardboard box emblazoned with 'Magic'.

This box contains a lot of tricks, but too many of them are feeble, and in my hands would be feebler. There is nothing here as neat, well-made, convincing, as the tricks I had before the war. (I think it was late in 1939 when I distributed them among my children, who soon—as we conjurers say—'vanished' them for ever.) I remember even now with affection the cigar-ette, which I could puff at for a second or two, that turned into a couple of matches; the beautiful little metal box that I could show to be empty over and over again and yet produce from it coloured silks and indignant-looking flowers; and the 'sand-frame', as we fellows call it, which, after being covered by a handkerchief, displayed as if it had been there for years like an old family photograph, the two of diamonds or knave of spades chosen at random from 20 or 30 cards, all of them—between ourselves—either the two of diamonds or the knave of spades.

I inquired about these particular tricks and was told they are no longer obtainable. (It is this experience, repeated all too often, that inclines me towards a gnostic view of this world, now under the domination of some evil demiurge.) However, I shall assemble a few tricks—including my old friend, that wizard pack which has a secret I shall not reveal here—and perhaps on Christmas evening, when everybody is still heavy with pudding, will then, as we like to say, 'endeavour to entertain' a small but extremely mixed audience. As usual, the young children, with their fixed round stare, will not be deceived. Nor, I fancy, will one or two simpler adults there. It is the clever people who will be most easily foxed, for it is they who lend themselves to misdirection. Kindly remember that, my friends: *it is the clever ones who are so often misdirected*. Even a bad old conjurer knows that.

'Mystify your friends with this little baffler!' is the cry in the catalogue of 'Magic', clearly aimed not at men of my age and weight but at schoolboys. I realize I should have retired from this company many years ago. But there it is—I still hanker. And not simply to be a performer. I delight—or did when I had the opportunity—in watching real conjurers. How happy I was in the Thirties when, on sombre winter afternoons, I could take the children to Maskelyne and Devant, who offered us then a large but cosy cave of magic, where pretty girls were sawn in half and even men on motorbikes suddenly vanished. (How often since I have wished I knew that trick!) How well I remember, with gratitude, the suave and high-toned Maskelyne, the laconic sorcery of Oswald Williams.

But then, going back half a century, I remember the regal David Devant himself, the Zanzigs and their thought-reading act, Chung Ling Soo, whose real name was Robinson and who was killed by a bullet he should have caught on a plate, and 'The Great Lafayette', the German illusionist whose scenery caught fire in Edinburgh and burned him to death—he was unable to escape because he always insisted upon the passdoors to the auditorium being locked. Probably the most remarkable of them all was Houdini, who could escape from anything; but his was a dull act on the stage, for you stared for 10 minutes or more at the screens enclosing his box or barrel, and listened to the band playing the same little tune over and over again. But that time, perhaps because of its innocence and modest public technology, was the great age of conjurers and illusionists. Afterwards, when political leadership, mass imbecility and some wooden-headed generals had made whole divisions disappear into the mud, it was never quite the same.

It is certainly not the same now, though there are still a few good conjurers about, because I watch the tricks only on television, through a glass darkly. I do not really feel they are happening and that I am there. A few of those shadowy, bloodless girls being sawn in half means nothing. They would have to take a circular saw to Dimbleby, and do it full colour, before I would sit up and stare hard. Seeing an illusionist on television is rather like reading a novel about a novelist; the whole thing suggests an illusion anyhow, as if all the life it pretends to capture were a flickering dream; it is conjuring without marvels and bright objects, and with pompous patter.

I no longer know where the good conjurers perform on stages, as distinct from television studios; there do not seem to be any left for them. If I were dictator I would provide them with halls of their own again, more magic caves to take children to on winter afternoons. Conjuring appeals to two different sides of our nature, one very old, the other more recently acquired. The old one is our capacity to wonder. This may be childish but unless, at any age, we keep it alive, we are beginning to die. We should try to work, think and live rationally, sceptical of political, economic and social miracles, then satisfy our ancient appetite for marvels out of hours, with the conjurers. It is not the advertising agencies but the honest, self-styled illusionists we should applaud. It does us no harm and perhaps much good to watch pretty girls, whom we shall see later bringing on tables and top hats, vanishing in mysterious cabinets. This is much better than watching cabinets making millions of our money disappear, after asking for our applause for their sound common sense. I am a bad conjurer but these fellows, with their planes and rockets stuck in their sleeves, are a great deal worse.

Moreover, about some of the best conjurers there is a fine prodigality that costs us not a penny more in taxes. Like fairy-tale characters, they seem to exist outside the economic structure. They pluck from the air packs of cards by the score; they litter the stage with cigarettes from which they have taken only a puff or two; out of one jug they pour every kind of drink, from iced champagne to hot coffee, like party hosts gone berserk; they fill the stage with ribbons, flags, flowers, bon-bons, sausages, eggs, bottles, doves, rabbits, all pulled out of one hat or small box, and with never a recession, credit squeeze, wages policy, in sight. And all they ask, their dress collars now limp with sweat, is that we should clap our hands at their entertainment. They do not pretend, even in fun, to be better, wiser, nobler than we are; they ask for no grouse moors, hat-touching, titles; they wipe off their perspiration and grease paint, pack up their gear and go home contentedly to steak and chips and bottled beer. They have given our sense of wonder an airing. And it is as important for us to live in a fairy tale on occasional Saturday nights as it is for us to refuse to live in one, after we have looked at the papers on Monday morning.

Then there is the other side of our common human nature to which the conjurers appeal. This is far newer, being intellectual and scientific. We ask ourselves how they do it, where we have been deceived. Here, as an old hand, no matter how clumsy, I will venture a tip. Almost always when a conjurer makes elaborate preparations to prove he is not deceiving you, he has already begun to deceive you. (And he is not the only one who does this.) At the ingenious mechanical devices of the more ambitious illusionists, I can only stare and wonder, not having that sort of mind; but in most smaller tricks, not involving extraordinary sleight of hand, I can generally spot the cunning elements of misdirection and false choice—'Take any card you please, sir.' How like life, which seems to offer us a full pack to choose from —yet the same old cards turn up, that two of diamonds, that knave of spades! And how we keep on *misdirecting ourselves*, turning doves and rabbits back into boxes of sawdust!

If I had had a much better visual memory and more impudence, I would never have bought a trick: I would have concentrated—all for private performance, of course—on a bogus mind-reading act. These acts require little or no apparatus, no dress coats with odd pockets and elastic up the sleeves, no manual dexterity. And what they do demand—a quick sure memory, plenty of solemn patter, sheer cheek—I do or did have a little of. For example, take that impressive piece of thought-reading done with books or, in my version, with telephone directories. Members of the audience choose one out of several directories; another member writes down the number of any page he fancies and the number of any line in the first column of that page; then the magician hands this folded note to the people who have chosen the directory they prefer, asks them to find the page and count down from the top, and then, even while they are doing this, he writes on a blackboard or boldly announces the telephone number, name and address they will find. 'It baffles science,' as W. C. Fields used to exclaim when he was showing the Smallest Giant and the Tallest Midget in the world. And I can do this trick, or at least I could do it, having worked it out for myself; I have left some good minds bewildered by it. And as I *did* work it out for myself and I am not a member of the Magic Circle, I will admit—and this is the clue—that the words above, *this folded note*, are not to be taken as strictly accurate.

But where is the harm in 'forcing' and false choices and misdirection and bland impudence when nothing more than innocent entertainment is intended? The conjurers feed our wonder and exercise our wits. And if the Tories, as members of the Magic Circle or the Variety Artists' Federation, were attempting their grand illusion, *The Modernization of Britain*, candidly on a stage, I would be one of the first to applaud them. It could be a great show. Heath producing employment, Joseph houses, Boyle new schools, all out of hats. Thorneycroft and his Vanishing Shield! Marples not mentioning himself! Butler sawing Hogg in half! And then the final magnificent effect—*Britain Modernized* —when after Sir Alec has pointed his wand and there has been a gigantic thunder-flash—the smoke clears to show us that he and his friends have disappeared for ever!

Wrong 'Ism

THERE ARE THREE ISMS that we ought to consider very carefully—regionalism, nationalism, internationalism. Of these three the one there is most fuss about, the one that starts men shouting and marching and shooting, the one that seems to have all the depth and thrust and fire, is of course nationalism. Nine people out of ten, I fancy, would say that of this trio it is the one that really counts, the big boss. Regionalism and internationalism, they would add, are comparatively small, shadowy, rather cranky. And I believe all this to be quite wrong. Like many another big boss, nationalism is largely bogus. It is like a bunch of flowers made of plastics.

The real flowers belong to regionalism. The mass of people everywhere may never have used the term. They are probably regionalists without knowing it. Because they have been brought up in a certain part of the world, they have formed perhaps quite unconsciously a deep attachment to its landscape and speech, its traditional customs, its food and drink, its songs and jokes. (There are of course always the rebels, often intellectuals and writers, but they are not the mass of people.) They are rooted in their region. Indeed, without this attachment a man can have no roots.

So much of people's lives, from earliest childhood onwards, is deeply intertwined with the common life of the region, they cannot help feeling strongly about it. A threat to it is a knife pointing at the heart. How can life ever be the same if bullying strangers come to change everything? The form and colour, the very taste and smell of dear familiar things will be different, alien, life-destroying. It would be better to die fighting. And it is precisely this, the nourishing life of the region, for which common men have so often fought and died.

This attachment to the region exists on a level far deeper than that of any political hocus-pocus. When a man says 'my country' with real feeling, he is thinking about his region, all that has made up his life, and not about that political entity, the nation. There can be some confusion here simply because some countries are so small—and ours is one of them—and so old, again like ours, that much of what is national is also regional. Down the centuries, the nation, itself so comparatively small, has been able to attach to itself the feeling really created by the region. (Even so there is something left over, as most people in York-shire, or Devon, for example, would tell you.) This probably explains the fervent patriotism developed early in small countries. The English were announcing that they were English in the Middle Ages, before nationalism had arrived elsewhere.

If we deduct from nationalism all that it has borrowed or stolen from regionalism, what remains is mostly rubbish. The nation, as distinct from the region, is largely the creation of power-men and political manipulators. Almost all nationalist movements are led by ambitious frustrated men determined to hold office. I am not blaming them. I would do the same if I were in their place and wanted power so badly. But nearly always they make use of the rich warm regional feeling, the emotional dynamo of the movement, while being almost untouched by it themselves. This is because they are not as a rule deeply loyal to any region themselves. Ambition and a love of power can eat like acid into the tissues of regional loyalty. It is hard, if not impossible, to retain a natural piety and yet be for ever playing both ends against the middle.

Being itself a power structure, devised by men of power, the nation tends to think and act in terms of power. What would benefit the real life of the region, where men, women and children actually live, is soon sacrificed for the power and prestige of the nation. (And the personal vanity of presidents and ministers themselves, which historians too often disregard.) Among the new nations of our time innumerable peasants and labourers must have found themselves being cut down from five square meals a week to three in order to provide unnecessary airlines, military forces that can only be used against them and nobody else, great conference halls and official yachts and the rest. The last traces of imperialism and colonialism may have to be removed from Asia and Africa, where men can no longer endure being condemned to a permanent inferiority by the colour of their skins; but even so the modern world, the real world of our time, does not want and would be far better without more and more nations, busy creating for themselves the very paraphernalia that western Europe is now trying to abolish. You are compelled to answer more questions when trying to spend half a day in Cambodia than you are now travelling from the Hook of Holland to Syracuse.

This brings me to internationalism. I dislike this term, which I used only to complete the isms. It suggests financiers and dubious promoters living nowhere but in luxury hotels; a shallow world of entrepreneurs and impresarios. (Was it Sacha Guitry who said that impresarios were men who spoke many languages but all with a foreign accent?) The internationalism I have in mind here is best described as world civilization. It is life considered on a global scale. Most of our communications and transport already exist on this high wide level. So do many other things from medicine to meteorology. Our astronomers and physicists (except where they have allowed themselves to be hush-hushed) work here. The UN special agencies, about which we hear far too little, have contributed more and more to this world civilization. All the arts, when they are arts and not chunks of nationalist propaganda, naturally take their place in it. And it grows, widens, deepens, in spite of the fact that for every dollar, rouble, pound or franc spent in explaining and praising it, a thousand are spent by the nations explaining and praising themselves.

This world civilization and regionalism can get along together, especially if we keep ourselves sharply aware of their quite different but equally important values and rewards. A man can make his contribution to world civilization and yet remain strongly regional in feeling: I know several men of this sort. There is of course the danger—it is with us now—of the global style flattening out the regional, taking local form, colour, flavour, away for ever, disinheriting future generations, threatening them with sensuous poverty and a huge boredom. But to understand and appreciate regionalism is to be on guard against this danger. And we must therefore make a clear distinction between regionalism and nationalism.

It is nationalism that tries to check the growth of world civilization. And nationalism, when taken on a global scale, is more aggressive and demanding now than it has ever been before. This in the giant powers is largely disguised by the endless fuss in public about rival ideologies, now a largely unreal quarrel. What is intensely real is the glaring nationalism. Even the desire to police the world is nationalistic in origin. (Only the world can police the world.) Moreover, the nation-states of today are for the most part far narrower in their outlook, far more inclined to allow prejudice against the foreigner to impoverish their own style of living, than the old imperial states were. It should be part of world civilization that men with particular skills, perhaps the product of the very regionalism they are rebelling against, should be able to move easily from country to country, to exercise those skills, in anything from teaching the violin to running a new type of factory to managing an old hotel. But nationalism, especially of the newer sort, would rather see everything done badly than allow a few non-nationals to get to work. And people face a barrage of passports, visas, immigration controls, labour permits; and in this respect are worse off than they were in 1900. But even so, in spite of all that nationalism can do—so long as it keeps its nuclear bombs to itself—the internationalism I have in mind, slowly creating a world civilization, cannot be checked.

Nevertheless, we are still backing the wrong ism. Almost all our money goes on the middle one, nationalism, the rotten meat between the two healthy slices of bread. We need regionalism to give us roots and that very depth of feeling which nationalism unjustly and greedily claims for itself. We need internationalism to save the world and to broaden and heighten our civilization. While regional man enriches the lives that international man is already working to keep secure and healthy, national man, drunk with power, demands our loyalty, money and applause, and poisons the very air with his dangerous nonsense.

The Mad Sad World

OUR MORE SENSIBLE and sensitive film critics have already told us that *It's A Mad, Mad, Mad, Mad World* is not really funny at all, but violent and cruel. I believed them but I felt I had to see it for myself. Having seen it, I have now reached the conclusion that it must be the oddest example of film-making there can ever have been. I never remember before sitting in a place of entertainment and feeling at such complete cross-purposes with the providers of the entertainment. It is as if we belonged to different planets.

The programme, which cost a steep five bob at the Coliseum, is full of information about how the film was made. From its conception to its release, we are told, it took three and a half years, 166 shooting days, 636,000 feet (approximately 125 miles) of exposed film, finally reduced to 21,939 feet—a 'running time of 210 minutes, including intermission'. Some 1,700 drawings, blueprints and models of the exterior and interior settings were needed. There were 217 items of special effects—'a conglomeration of unworldly devices such as pemberthy siphons, gun powders, squibs and squib hooks, dynamite caps, pulleys, cranes, compressors, popping matches, air rams, hydraulic rams, smoke pots, smoke blowers, cables and wires and opaque paint.' For one effect alone, a car going off a cliff in the opening sequence, they had to have 'a radio-controlled pilot put together with bits and pieces

[41]

of electronic equipment they acquired from the laboratories of the California Institute of Technology and nearby aerospace plants.' Here, we may say, was our new technological age, nowhere better represented than in Southern California, happily at play. The backroom boys were having fun. And the result is murderous.

Stanley Kramer, the producer-director, is an experienced and courageous film man. He is quoted as saying: 'Bill Rose's script was the funniest ever written. If the motion picture isn't the funniest ever made, the fault will lie with the man I see in the mirror.' (An odd but perhaps significant way of putting it, for in the mirror we see our outward selves, embodying *our conscious intention*.) We read that:

> He sought to brew an unheard-of mix of onscreen chicanery, calamity, disaster and suspense, requiring more performing talent and behind-the-camera artistry and cunning than any entertainment recipe ever before devised, and to come up with an explosive celluloid of belly-laughs. He aimed to fashion a giant blend of slapstick and whimsy to the end that audiences of all ages, lands and mores would find delirious divertissement.

Even the writer of the programme, we feel, is straining so hard that he may rupture himself.

William Rose, responsible both for the original idea and the final script, is a writer of very considerable talent, an American who spent some years over here and gave us *Genevieve*, surely one of the best comedy films made in this country. Moreover, the cast reads like a convention of film and TV comedians. Never since Hollywood began have so many funny men been assembled by a film producer. And never have funny men been less funny. They all work like whipped blacks at it, and hardly raise a smile. There are some laughs of course, but they are mostly of the shocked nervous sort, in response to yet another realistic catastrophe on the huge screen and a new barrage of amplified sound. We never find ourselves chuckling. Strictly speaking, there is no humour.

Now what can have happened? Where did these experienced film makers, with so much talent and time and money at their command, go wrong? How could they set out to achieve the funniest film ever made and end with something that leaves us stunned, repelled, saddened? What became of all the fun that they and we were going to enjoy? To what desert did the river of laughter find its way, thinning out and drying up and vanishing in the hot dust? Why is it that the slapstick films of 35 to 50 years ago are still a joy—often making us laugh more now than they did when we first saw them—when this immensely ambitious new attempt at a comic masterpiece fails so dismally?

Before trying to answer these questions, I will make a point in passing. A few years after the war, a company that not only produced films but that could also distribute them, offered me the chance of writing and co-producing a feature-length slapstick film. Delighted, I said I would do it, and then I retired to the country to consider what I would do. Some days later, I found myself declining the offer. I realized that such a film, to succeed, would have to create for itself an artificial world in which everybody and everything would be ridiculous, as they were in the genuine old slapsticks, in which the very roads and trees, automobiles and trains, were comic characters. I was neither clever enough nor, what was even more important, sufficiently strong-willed and ruthless to create, simply for one film, such a world, so different from ours. Many thanks but nothing doing!

Now this is the trap into which Messrs Kramer and Rose and their colleagues have rushed headlong. Not only have they not attempted to re-create the old artificial world, the dream empire of slapstick, populated entirely by clowns, but they have been at the greatest possible pains and expense, calling on our new technology for all its formidable resources, to show us—in panoramic breadth and full colour—our actual world as it exists today in Southern California. It is there to the smallest puff of dust and can of orange juice. I know that region fairly well, and as soon as the film began, with wide shots of the twisting desert roads, like tape tossed on a moulting hearth rug, I was back there. And I knew that the MAD-4 boys were stuck with it; they could never come out laughing.

Then—at least this is my guess—something else happened. I think they worked so hard and so long at this Super-Jumbo-Comedy that, without being aware of what was happening, they began dredging up out of the dark of their minds more and more disgust and contempt and hatred. A sardonic lama and a communist intellectual, collaborating to attack contemporary American life, could not have done a more ruthless job. It is Southern California on the rack and having its bones broken. It is the American Way drenched in wormwood solution and sulphuric acid. There is in it not a glimmer of affection for anybody or anything. All its huge explosions and bashings are not so much overdone attempts at slapstick as they are the outward and exaggerated expression of an unconscious violence, of disgust and contempt and hatred, once concealed, now boiling over. What it offers us is no 'giant blend of slapstick and whimsy', but a savage rejection of contemporary American society and its values and status symbols.

All the people, condemned from first to last to a frenzied chase, are moved by nothing but greed, the hope of getting money without working for it, the fear of missing a soft buck. If all these comedians are never funny (and they aren't) it is because they are not allowed time and space in which to deploy themselves; they are tied to a story-line that is really a fizzing string of fire-crackers. The characters are all contemptible people, inevitably doomed to disaster. They are all screaming their heads off for something they will never be allowed to have and that would do them no good even if they had it. They are loveless, without dignity and self-respect, suspicious and treacherous and stupid; and any society breeding more and more of such creatures is moving away from any true civilization.

Machinery and property are held in high respect in the American way of life, seen near its peak in Southern California. So in this savagely violent film, more machinery and property are wrecked than ever before. Automobiles, no longer sacred objects, clash against one another, lose wheels and other essential parts, run off the roads, tumble down gorges, fall off cliffs. Aeroplanes are bashed about as if they were cheap toys. A whole filling station is reduced to a heap of boards. Neat rows of canned merchandise, fit for any supermarket, are hurled from their shelves, split open, ruined. The mere existence of a wall, any wall, is a signal for somebody or something to come crashing through it. Nothing is safe from this appalling violence and explosiveness. Even the things that normally try to save life are here a menace to it, so that in the last sequence a gigantic firemen's ladder is transformed by some evil magic into a monstrous catapult, hurling one character after another through doorways and windows far below. And everything that had a kind of dreamlike comic innocence in the old slapstick films now seems menacing, relentless, cruel. This is the world of the nuclear deterrent trying to have fun. It is the high jinks of a ruthless technology. Behind my shrinking gaze and battered hearing, my blood ran cold.

I cannot help suspecting that many of the episodes were chosen not for their comic possibilities but as symbolic presentations of our various predicaments. (In this department it is far superior to the film made out of Kafka's *The Trial*.) As disgust and contempt, hatred and despair, came boiling up from the unconscious, such symbolism was inevitable. It explains the long and wearing adventures of the pair who found themselves locked in the basement of the ironmonger's, together with enormous stocks of explosives, fireworks, fuses and blow-lamps. It explains the episode of the two idiotic youths in the fine private aeroplane, whose owner, a drunk, was unconscious; they did not know how to fly it; while the men in the control tower of the airport were themselves no longer in control. It explains why the good old honest cop (Spencer Tracy, no less) was the craftiest crook of them all. I could go on and on; but why should I? Either you have seen the film or you haven't.

As an attempt not merely to revive but to enlarge, magnify, lengthen and strengthen and bring bang-up-to-date the old slapstick film, demanding a maximum of 'belly-laughs', *It's A Mad, Mad, Mad, Mad World* seems to me a huge and appallingly expensive flop, wasting more comic talent than any film has ever done before. But as a savage satire of the kind of society, really a sort of Hell, we are striving so hard to maintain, prepared if necessary for its protection to turn the world into a radio-active cinder, it is in an eye-straining, ear-battering, nerve-shattering class of its own. It makes the blackest of the avant-garde Theatre-of-the-Absurd playwrights seem like tepid protesters playing at charades. And what I wonder now is whether Stanley Kramer and William Rose and their colleagues can go on making motion pictures in Southern California. Purged, purified, free to meditate in peace, they ought to be making arrangements to enter Tibetan monasteries or caves in the Indian forest.

The Blue Yonder Boys

A FEW SUNDAYS ago, on BBC television, there was a discussion on 'Advertising and Society' that seemed to me unusually good; and ever since then various thoughts about advertising have been plaguing me. All but the last, a conclusion of some importance, are commonplace enough; but they are worth stating briefly, if only to clear the ground.

The defenders of advertising, who claim that it is primarily informative, seem to me to be disingenuous. They are in the business and so must know even better than we do that the really big money is not spent giving the public information. This line of defence is impudent humbug. It could be adopted only by men who are secretly convinced that we are all stupid.

Naturally we objectors do not oppose every form of advertising. When I have a play running or have just published a book, I welcome a few advertisements of that play or book, to give playgoers or bookbuyers a nudge or two. But though I am generally pleased with my own handiwork, I think I would be distressed if large striking advertisements of it appeared, suggesting that families buying Priestley would be transported at once to some domestic Nirvana.

Some defenders of advertising—especially the smooth pseudo-scientific types who pretend to be detached—tell us that if we protest then we are underrating (in our intellectual conceit) the powers of judgement and discrimination of ordinary people, who are quite capable of taking care of themselves and their purses. But this does not seem to me to make sense. If people cannot be dazzled and bewitched out of their rational judgement, then why should millions be spent dazzling and bewitching them?

Then again, why does almost everything we read about large-scale advertising contradict what is told us by its official apologists. I am not thinking now simply of books like *The Hidden Persuaders* or *The Affluent Sheep*, but also of all the novels I have read about advertising from the inside, especially those stories of frenzied agencies in Madison Avenue. And it is no use anybody telling me that those are American and we are British, because in fact our advertising is now largely American. In *The Affluent Sheep* we read: 'The president of a top Canadian agency has predicted that British advertising will be fully controlled by the men from Madison Avenue by 1963.'

Incidentally, Mr Robert Millar, the author of *The Affluent Sheep*, rebukes me for writing, more than 25 years ago, that advertising men were clever but quite unscrupulous. He says that most advertising agents he has met 'sincerely believe in their work'. They may believe in their skill and what it can produce, but do they sincerely believe in the truth and real value of the claims they make on behalf of their clients? If they do, then a lot of books, both fiction and non-fiction, coming out of Madison Avenue and its equivalent here, have been crammed with lies and libel. And this I doubt.

Moreover, since I made that observation 25 years

ago, a number of men educated, often at the public expense, in psychology and sociology have been employed by the agencies in the business of 'motivational research'. And it seems to me that, if these men offer their services to anybody willing to pay their fees, without regard to the value of the merchandise to be sold or to the ultimate effect on the public of these researches, then they are engaged in a form of prostitution. They are tarts with degrees. Science is now street-walking and soliciting.

Now I will pass over all the expensive and wasteful 'brand image' nonsense, the attempts to prove there is an enormous difference between kinds of stuff that are in fact all alike. I will ignore the false pseudo-scientific claims that are as indefensible as the three-card trick, I will merely salute in passing the creation of demands through irrational fears, and the bullying and manipulation of the potential consumer. I will come at once to what seems to me the greatest disservice to our society for which the advertising agencies must be held responsible.

This is nothing less than a steadily increasing creation of dissatisfaction. Nobody who takes a good wide look at our famous Free Society, our Affluent Society, our Never-had-it-so-good Society, can fail to notice this dissatisfaction. It pouts and shrugs and spits from here to Seattle. Compared with the people of the hungry continents, we would seem to lead the life of demigods. Yet in fact more and more of us are clearly dissatisfied, behaving as if we had just been cheated at a gaming table. The new good life, with its higher wages and shorter hours, its labour-saving devices, its technological marvels, its 'fabulous' holidays, somehow seems to be a fraud. We pity our grandparents until we remember their states of mind, and then we begin to wonder.

Now of course there are many reasons why ours is a society of profound feelings of frustration, and I doubt if anybody wants me to climb into the pulpit to repeat them. But one I have not mentioned so far in these columns has to do with advertising and the highly skilled techniques of what I will call its Blue Yonder Boys. It is a mistake, and a dangerous mistake, to imagine that we ourselves are proof against the Blue Yonder sorcery and spells. No doubt on a low level—say, that of TV advertising, in which a breakfast food or a bar of chocolate sends whole families into ecstasy—we can resist them; but the boys, with their magic arts, will reach us somewhere. And the result is just the same.

There, if only we buy something, is the Blue Yonder. There is the enchanted life we have always felt we deserved to enjoy. So far we have always just missed it, but now—with 'Boojum' or whatever they are trying to sell us—it is here at last, the Happy Land where tall distinguished-looking men, who have just been drinking an assortment of magnificent liquors, tenderly regard the upturned radiant faces of slender golden girls; where airplane meals no longer seem to be made of cardboard; where a certain coat or skirt is a wonder and a joy; where eyes sparkle not only at the sight of Hongkong or Bermuda, but just because livers and kidneys are well flushed and content; where headaches vanish in 10 seconds and a cup of something leads to success in banking, general commerce and all the arts. Just a tin, a packet, the payment of a small deposit, and Successful Living, Gracious Living, Casual Living, the lot, are within our grasp.

When in America, I have spent weekends out of New York and almost at once have felt there was something curious, puzzling, in the atmosphere of the party. There was about it, you might say, a kind of empty expectancy, as if we were waiting for some final guest, a gigantic personality. Then I would realize what was happening, no such guest being expected. We were waiting to be summoned to the Blue Yonder. All the right clothes, all the new expensive accessories were there, ready for superb Casual Living, but somehow we did not find ourselves yet in the Happy Land. And the fact that most of us were obviously the wrong shape hardly troubled us at all, so powerful are the enchantments of the Blue Yonder Boys. We had between us most of the *things* that would provide us, they had promised, with the magical transport. So we waited, and waited in vain.

Now it is all very well for cynical, thick-skinned old codgers like me to laugh at these confidence tricks; but I can remember what I was like 50 years ago, a youth innocent as an egg, and I thank Heaven that most of the Blue Yonder boys were not even born then. If I had spent my teens under these pressures, as the youngsters do now, I do not know what lights I would have followed into the bog. For not only is Blue Yonderism extremely artful, far more so, I believe, than most intelligent people imagine (chiefly because it seems so contemptible on its lower levels), but also it has caught us at a very bad time. Not only has our 'Free Society' no obvious goals—and it no longer cares very much about freedom—but it is also busy substituting dubious secondary satisfactions for primary ones, those demanded by our psychic inheritance. The *chimera* of that Happy Land is about all we have left. So what we are really manufacturing, at the highest possible rate of productivity, is disappointment, followed by disillusion and frustration.

It is a mistake, in my view, to denounce all this as 'materialism'. The Americans, who created Admass, which in turn has been responsible for Blue Yonderism, are in fact less genuinely materialistic than most western Europeans. It is dreamers of dreams, idealists on the wrong track, who spend more and more trying to reach the Happy Land. It is people still haunted by a vision of the good life whom the advertising agencies bamboozle. This is why youngsters are so vulnerable; they grow up with great expectations. 'You have a dream,' the Blue Yonder boys tell them, 'and you have only to earn and then spend a little more money and then, without any further effort, your dream will come true.' And it is all a lie.

As an old square, I dislike the appearance, the jargon, the manners and style of life of beatniks, hipsters and the rest; but I do understand what it is that moves them. It is a contemptuous rejection of the whole Blue Yonder confidence trick. They are looking for their own Happy Land, though I do not think they will find it by way of 'kicks' and 'giggles'. But at least they are not going to wear themselves out chasing

[53]

the electric hares of Admass. And it is significant that this revolt began where the Blue Yonder boys are princes of sorcery—in America. And now, we read, they are about to take us over entirely, so that more and more of us will be Blue Yondered out of our wits.

This need not happen. But do not expect any help from these Tories, these Olde Englishe country gentlemen, always ready, as soon as the toastmaster has cried 'Pray, silence', to orate about our splendid traditions and our glorious heritage. It is these bogus Yeomen of the Guard who have opened the gates to Admass, who have encouraged Blue Yonderism, who have dangled before us the tickets and passports to the Happy Land, where nothing flourishes except sales figures and agency percentages and disappointment, disillusionment and frustration.

Giving up Conferences

FOR ALL I know other people may turn down more invitations to conferences than I do. However, their percentage of refusals cannot be higher during these past few years because mine is one hundred per cent. Down they are turned, these invitations, one after another, *flat*.

Not that I am rude about them. I always offer an excuse. I am not very well, I have other long-standing engagements, I am wrestling with some great opus. I bring in a lot of reluctance, am filled with regret. But I make it quite plain that I am not going. And here I behave better than some of my distinguished colleagues, who accept such invitations, allow their names to go into print, and then never turn up. This is bad. I am ashamed of such distinguished colleagues and sometimes doubt (*a*) if they are all that distinguished and (*b*) if they really are colleagues.

But before I explain why I do not attend them, let us be clear about these conferences. They are apparently on a high, wide and handsome level. I am not concerned here with a week-end in Wolverhampton in August or three nights at Worthing in February, with delegates arriving by bus and being sent to a Youth Hostel or the Gladstone Temperance Hotel. Any man over thirty and in his right mind will refuse that sort of invitation.

Most of these conferences I turn down are international, and fares will be paid to Switzerland, Italy, the Island of Rhodes. Rooms have been booked at the Bristol or the Grand. There may be sight-seeing tours laid on, to say nothing of official luncheons and cocktail parties and seats at the opera. They look like Continental holidays for nothing. Why should a man boast (it is a weakness of mine) of turning them down? Is he trying to suggest that he is *so grand* that he can afford to refuse—and even sneer—at such magnificent invitations?

No, madam. (For it is about thirty to one that the last query was feminine.) It is the old hand in me that writes the refusals. I have had my share of these doings. And now I know—and it is high time I did—the limitations of my own temperament and tolerance. Lady, I know what it will be like, and probably you don't. Just listen now.

In the ten years following the War, when public spirit still moved in me, I attended a number of international conferences. On several occasions I was actually the Chairman. This is, I must admit, not as bad as it sounds. In fact I would rather 'chair' a conference than simply attend one as a delegate. My method as a chairman was to make a speech, brief but rousing, at the opening session, make another, just as brief, at the closing session, and during the three days in between do nothing official and boring at all, having divided the work between all the other people, who would be toiling over resolutions and amendments and final reports while I was sitting at ease in the nearest bar. But with whom, you may ask. The answer is—with a few rebellious and choice souls who had marched out of their sub-committees or working parties. And sometimes that is how the real work of the conference was done, well away from the conscientious gasbags.

My first complaint against international conferences is that there are so many foreigners attending them. I have a great store of international goodwill except when I am surrounded by foreign delegates, who suddenly seem altogether *too foreign*, as if they were playing irritating character-parts. Some I don't mind —usually, the Scandinavian, the Dutch, the Swiss, the Austrian. The worst of the Europeans—and I say this with regret, being a greedy man and fond of France— are the French. M. Toulemonde and his delegation from Paris are conference-wreckers to a man. (They never used to send any women in my time.)

To begin with, they always pretended not to under- stand a word of English, fighting a rearguard action for their own language. On being introduced to them, you would mutter a few words of your own miserable French, and then later they would corner you and pour out floods of rapid and idiomatic French, which you nodded and muttered at, hoping they were com- plaining about the Grand or Bristol Hotel food. After- wards, to your horror, you would discover, at some plenary session, that you had apparently already given your support to some monstrous proposal of theirs. Their other trick was to arrive late, in a body, at some meeting, insist upon discussing something not on the agenda, and then depart furiously in a body if they were called to order. No wonder they have to have a de Gaulle.

Delegates from much further afield usually be- longed to one of two groups. Either they spoke little but when they did speak could not be understood at all, or they were orators and went on and on and on. Many South Americans, in my conference time, were capable of wasting hours and hours, chiefly for the benefit of the reporter from the *Uruguay Gazette* they had persuaded to attend the session. In Paris once, as Chairman, I was challenged to a duel by one such orator, whom I had accused of wasting our time. And if this seems a bit much, I must add that once as Chairman in the Central Hall, Westminster, I had fireworks thrown at me, even though I was not rebuking anybody.

Even apart from the boredom of most of the procedure, I have never been able to escape feeling a fool at most of these conferences. There is, I think, something silly about us, the way in which we all arrive together, hand in our names (though I have never yet worn one of those badges they give out) and queue up for programmes, tickets, labels, time-tables, city plans and guides, like sheep who have suddenly developed a taste for print. I may have been too self-conscious and over-sensitive, but I always felt that the other people in the hotels and the local citizenry regarded us as so many self-important asses. Moreover, I always had a suspicion that the hotels and restaurants, the ones in which we dined en masse, had earlier been beaten down to their lowest possible prices, so that we figured in their eyes as a miserable lot of cut-rate guests who did not deserve much attention.

And the receptions by the Minister, the Burgomaster, and the rest, did nothing to restore my self-esteem. I felt that in their eyes we were just part of yet another official chore. 'What have I to do to-night?' they probably asked. 'Oh—those fellows. No way of getting out of it, I suppose?' If they hadn't said anything like that, they always seemed to me to look as if they had. After all, who in his senses wants to Welcome A Conference? What is there to say that would not be better left unsaid? What sane man (I am not sure about women) enjoys routine official hospitality?

Not I, for one. Coming close to my idea of hell is the official diplomatic life, with its endless luncheons, cocktail parties, dinners, receptions, suppers, all packed with the same people saying nothing in particular. It is boring to receive such hospitality, and it must be still more boring to give it. You cannot even drink yourself out of tedium, because either the booze is not strong enough (that thin white wine that does not seem to come from anywhere) or, if potent, then there is not enough of it. And when there are a hundred or so of you—and there can easily be far more at a big conference—all wearing badges and fixed grins, then everything is much worse. The tipple may easily be one part of cheap Barsac and one part of Riesling to four parts water. The only conference guest who has a chance is the Chairman, who, if he knows what's what, may escape to a back room and whisky.

Then there is that *Morning* or *Afternoon Sight-seeing*, with which the trap is so often baited. Anything is probably better than listening to men droning on and on in a stuffy room, until you have covered your agenda with doodles, but I am not one who enjoys an official tour of the city and its environs accompanied by special guides who let you off nothing. 'This book,' said the little girl when returning it to her teacher, 'tells me more about penguins than I want to know.' And guides are like that. I took to painting partly in order to avoid sight-seeing when on holiday. And this was private and conjugal sight-seeing, whereas on conferences there may be three or four coach loads of you, yawning and yawning or wondering what could have been wrong with the *fruits-de-mer* served at the cut-rate lunch.

As for those free seats at the opera, it depends where you are. In Vienna—fine! But in Boojum or Snarksy, you may be in for a terrible evening—and five hours of it too. And if the alternative is the Municipal Theatre, it is ten to one they will be doing, specially for you, a very long and quite incomprehensible historical play ending about quarter to twelve, by which time you would be ready to rat on the conference's chief resolution if anybody offered you cold beer and hot sausages.

Finally, there is too often about the conference's whole proceedings an air of futility. Gasbags, who love these affairs, will have nearly asphyxiated you. *Point-of-order* sticklers will have infuriated you. Chairmen (not me) will have said nothing in longer and more pompous terms than you have ever known before. Final resolutions, adopted in despair after the last oxygen has left the room, will seem quite meaningless. And—but here I exclude scientific and technological conferences—instead of feeling more optimistic about international co-operation, you may now have lost all belief in it.

Certainly, madam, I am exaggerating and I am being unfair and it can't be as bad as I say it is. The fact remains though, I turn the invitations down *flat*, even though they come from Venice, Ascona, Dubrovnik, Stockholm. I'm not going. I've given it up.

The Music Halls

VARIOUS TV PROGRAMMES, the popular clubs and singing rooms in the North, certain ventures in the West End (and I enjoyed the variety at the Prince Charles Theatre), all suggest a reawakening of interest in music-hall shows. I was not aware of this when I decided to write *Lost Empires*; most of the evidence has drifted in since then. However, I did spend a lot of time in music-halls during the years 1909–14, when they were still in their glory, and such impressions of them as remain in my mind might interest younger readers. Moreover, unlike most elderly men, I will try hard to tell the truth.

Now in my opinion, most of the acts or *turns* were boring. They would have been intolerable away from the halls themselves. But then the halls themselves, all these Empires, Palaces, Hippodromes, made an enormous contribution to the evening. To begin with, they were just the right size—not too big, like the Coliseum or even the Palladium; not too small, like the Prince Charles. They were plushy, glinting with gold, smoky, rather boozy (though the bars were outside the auditorium, they never seemed far outside); they created an atmosphere unlike any other, of innocent wickedness.

Their orchestras helped to create this atmosphere. If any reader is thinking of reviving variety, I implore him to engage an orchestra, no matter what it costs. An evening is ruined for me as soon as I see two

pianos and drums. They can't make the right noise—
but then, for that matter, neither can a band lug-
ubriously swollen with saxophones. Sixteen was the
average number of instrumentalists, except in the big
London halls, and I fancy that the whole lot, plus the
conductor, probably cost under £100 a week. They
didn't play badly—and would tackle anything—but of
course the strings, except in soft passages, for ever
took a beating from the brass and wood wind, and the
result was a curious tone that I came to love—and
would love again tomorrow night if somebody was
brave enough to install an orchestra in place of those
damnable pianos. I remember now some friends of
my parents, the kind of family that managed mills and
banks, who had produced one black sheep, poor W.
who 'couldn't carry corn' etc., and after being given
chances of this and that sank to playing the 'cello in
one of the local music-halls, probably for four pounds
a week and a lot of beer. He had married, too, on that
sluttish low level. And he seemed to me beyond any
doubt the happiest member of that family.

Next in importance to atmosphere, in the old music-
halls, and always delighting my friends and me, was
incongruity. A man wearing a red wig and the uniform of the Ruritanian Navy would balance himself on
top of a swaying ladder and would then sing about his
mother. A family of Latins, grave as cardinals, would
arrive in evening dress in front of an incredible Bay of
Naples backcloth, and would then begin turning
somersaults. A pale silent fellow would be discovered
in bed; an alarm clock would ring and he would take a
hammer from under his pillow to stop it ringing for

ever; he would then get up to juggle with scores of plates but after a few minutes would walk away, turning the stage into a shambles of broken plates; he would then return with the hammer and bash any plates still unbroken. A quick-change artiste would advance to the footlights in evening clothes and accept a bouquet, with which somehow he turned himself at once into a Viking. Why a Viking, why a bouquet, why the hammer, why the plates? Reason supplies no answers. We are beyond the rational order of things.

This incongruity, this unfailing daftness, delighted me then, 50-odd years ago, and would probably delight me now, even though the world outside is obviously getting dafter. But I took no pleasure at all in some of the most admired and highly-rewarded star turns. Prominent among these were the so-called male impersonators, who sang songs, intolerably long, about soldiers and sailors and Charlie-Brown-out-on-the-spree, but neither looked nor sounded like soldiers and sailors and Charlie Brown, drunk or sober. Did these Charlie Browns, always in white tie and tails and for ever going to Piccadilly with a few old pals, really exist? I often wondered, never having seen any. The only variety swells I liked were the broken-down ones, with tattered gloves and spats, with spotty fronts but no shirts, who sang *They built Piccadilly for me* or *My people are well-off, you know*. Though I had never seen one of these either.

In most of the TV attempts at variety shows, we are always offered chorus singers. But most of these were boring too. There were the sentimental girlish types, like Gertie Gitana, though I must admit that Kitchener's Army, when in drink, would howl her choruses for hours. There were the naughty-naughty girly-girly types, though again I must admit that one of them, just one, had a touch of genius. She was a little redhead called Madie Scott—*For you don't know Nell as well as I do, Said the naughty little bird on Nelly's hat*. Marie Lloyd—alas!—I never saw and have only heard on some scratchy old records of hers that I possess, in which you can just hear, out of a vanished London, a saucy Cockney ghost in some spectral pub.

The male vocalists were usually either horrible or tedious. Among the horrors were adenoidal Irish tenors with an Oedipus complex. (Old Irish mothers and General Buller always got a round. God knows why.) Hardly more sufferable were the patriotic baritones, with their *Boys of the Old Brigade* as a 'song-scene', in which they would introduce genuine veterans, at one-and-six a night. Then there were the dandy 'light comedians', like George Lashwood (the only star turn, as far as I know, to retire with a fortune), who sang about spooning in the park and girls-with-their-curly-curls. There were also the singers of 'coon songs' who could never arouse my slumbering enthusiasm, though I could enjoy Eugene Stratton, perhaps because his favourite songs had been composed by Leslie Stuart. The latter, the master of a subtly modulated melodic line, died comparatively young—and bankrupt—and any comparison of his work with that of our new pop composers would show us what progress we have made—in publicity, earning power and the transformation of composers into limited companies.

The star illusionists, to whom I was devoted, were unlucky too. The Great Lafayette died in a fire in Edinburgh; Chung Ling Soo (whose real name was Robinson) was shot while pretending to catch bullets on a plate; and the greatest of them all, David Devant (he has almost been deified by the Magic Circle), was compelled to retire because he suffered from—of all things—*paralysis agitans*. Houdini, who could escape from anything, was a remarkable man but a boring turn, simply because after he had been roped, hand-cuffed, nailed down, he disappeared behind screens (perhaps to eat steak and chips in his dressing room) and then the band played the same little tune for 15 minutes until he appeared again.

I had a weakness for all the acts that heightened the incongruity and general daftness. So I remember R. A. Roberts, so incredibly fast at changing wigs and cos-tumes that he could play all the characters in a sketch about Dick Turpin, and a man called Selbit who of-fered us 'spirit paintings'. And the Brothers Egbert who gravely nodded a balloon pig at each other. And Cinquevalli for serious juggling and W. C. Fields, not as ripe then as he became afterwards, for comic juggling. And Joe Jackson, who did an act in dumb-show simply about a tramp finding a bicycle, an act so beautifully timed, so rich in perfect little touches, that it remained an enchantment. He did it for years and years of course. This is the trouble with TV clowning, all rushed on for one night, with nobody bringing an act close to absolute perfection.

The comics were my meat, but only the best of them. I cared little for the grotesques who belted out songs, like T. E. Dunville and Mark Sheridan (who both committed suicide), though I had a weakness for Wilkie Bard, who, about to sing a ditty *I'm Here if I'm Wanted*, would be discovered as a policeman sitting on a swing. (Charlie Austin and, later, Robb Wilton were good as policemen apparently running an independent force.) The cross-talk comedians were tedious, with the possible exception of a pair called Farr and Farland, who suggested two men in a golf club bar so unable to communicate properly that they were going mad.

My favourites, whom I would see over and over again, were Grock (wistful, hopeful, from another planet), Little Tich (all insane energy), Harry Tate (incredulous, furious, in a surrealistic world), George Robey (ripe as old blue cheese) and an indescribable comedian called Jimmy Learmouth, who only played the provinces, and died young, and was perhaps the funniest man I ever saw on the stage. These giant drolls didn't buy a lot of gags and learn them off by heart; they were richly comic in themselves, all compact of drollery, and with a gesture, a look, could command great roars of laughter. With them, also anticipating surrealism, I would set the mad sketches, largely in dumbshow, about bricklayers or bakers, or acts like *The Mumming Birds*, in which Chaplin played for years. These acts, essentially English, toured America, and when the slapstick silent films came along, performers like Chaplin and Stan Laurel took part in them.

[67]

So what had been originally created largely by and for the English industrial working class, especially in the East End and the North, finally went a long, long way, its Empires outposts of an empire far larger than the one we were always colouring red. Variety might often consist of a lot of stupid turns applauded by a lot of stupid people, trying to forget for two hours their dreary work and dark streets; but the best of it was both enchanting and seminal; and the whole of it existed in an atmosphere, and offered a daft incongruity, that some of us sadly miss. I am looking now at the programme of the first (1912) Royal Command Variety Performance. It includes among many others *Humpsti Bumpsti* (a wonderful clown act with scores of chairs), Cinquevalli, Harry Tate, Little Tich, Arthur Prince (the best ventriloquist), Alfred Lester (a melancholy wisp of a comic), George Robey, David Devant, Wilkie Bard, Anna Pavlova, Harry Lauder, and that superb mimic, Cecilia Loftus. It makes our most recent Royal Command Performance look like something got up for teenagers in a village hall. We have the technology but not the talent. Ah well!

Morgan in a Mirror

FOR OVER 30 years I was acquainted with Charles Morgan, meeting him at parties, in clubs, on committees. But during all those years I think I spent only one half-hour alone with him, and that was a prolonged casual encounter in a club when we both had a little time to kill. We were probably like a cat and dog accidentally sharing the same hearth rug. The point I am making is that we were never friends, although we were both members of the First War generation and had fought in that war, came along as writers at the same time, moved in largely the same world.

He always gave me the impression—at least, during the Thirties—that he was sharply conscious of the fact that I was a popular writer, one whose name was known in the streets. It was as if a very successful music-hall comic and an old-fashioned Shakespearean actor were meeting. He was, I fancy, always too conscious of audiences, their size, quality, status. I remember, during that pink-gin half-hour, he told me gravely that some pieces I was writing for a newspaper then were a mistake. I said I was saying in them things I wanted to say, so why were they a mistake? He then explained that he was thinking in terms of my literary career, of 'being buried in Westminster Abbey', he added lightly. I said that I didn't give a damn where I was buried. He then turned the talk to Women, as if we were two minor characters in a drawing-room comedy of the Nineties, hoping between us to hatch out an epigram.

I am not given to thinking about contemporary writers in terms of literary careers. We seem to me to live in the wrong age for such thinking. If and when the world stops looking like a madhouse crammed with explosives, there will be time to consider whether Smith is Out and Jones is In, whether Brown is Going Up and Robinson Going Down. But there can be no doubt that Morgan cared a great deal about this kind of thing—he was very much the Writer, to be photographed at his desk in his study—and it is ironical that his career and reputation should seem to most of us so ambiguous, so puzzling.

For example; why no title, no honour? He was no enemy of these things. He had a handsome presence, and in full evening dress he would have done credit to any ribbon that the Crown would have graciously allowed him to wear. At a time when so many decorations were lavished upon actors and actresses that the Haymarket Theatre began to seem like an annex of Buckingham Palace, why didn't this name appear one morning high in the Honours List? He was an Establishment Author; he was for years the President of the International PEN; his works, as Macmillans tell us, have been translated into seventeen languages. Why not Sir Charles then—or even Lord Sparkenbroke? And let nobody imagine that these are jeering rhetorical questions. I am genuinely puzzled.

Then, what about his astonishing reputation among the French? Not only did they buy him, read him, discuss him, they organized societies of his friends. It is doubtful if any English novelist since Dickens has had such a following over there. And remember these are people who live on a cultural Saint Helena, who never mentioned Bernard Shaw until everybody else was tired of hearing about him. I can understand the French enjoying a much better English novelist, for sound literary reasons, or a much worse one, just for the hell of it; but why Morgan?

Then why, I ask myself, did I find, let us say, *Sparkenbroke* such an embarrassing novel, or the play *The Flashing Stream*, to which Agate devoted *two* enthusiastic notices, such an embarrassing evening in the theatre? This is the work of a reasonably intelligent, not insensitive, very conscientious writer, of a careful planner and experienced craftsman. Worse men, I truly believe, have been applauded by highbrow critics. Yet here is this embarrassment. It is as if some fatal element, not present in the planning of the work but released by the author as he carries out his plan, begins to poison our minds. Over the work, which may not be ignobly conceived, there is a moonglimmer of silliness. It has a humourless and gravely self-approving tone; a faint but fatal suggestion of Malvolio communing with himself under the stars.

Let us see if his collected essays and addresses yield any evidence of this flaw. In the first of them, he wants to discuss the point made to him by a terribly burned fighter pilot (probably Richard Hillary) that we are all potentially either Nazis or Communists. And this is how the discussion of it is introduced.

... He came to dine at my house in London. Through all the bombardment, I had tried to preserve one amenity

[71]

there: we dined by candlelight and an open fire; and I remember that, after dinner, we went upstairs, I with the decanter and he with the candelabra. I remember it because it was in the upstairs room, just after we had entered it, that he, standing in mid-floor with a candelabrum in each hand, said: 'Nowadays, wherever I go, I ask myself that question about everybody. At dinner, I was asking it about you.' For the moment I had lost his drift . . .

And we cannot help suspecting that his drift had been lost because our author, both at that moment and later when he came to write this address, was seeing himself, and enjoying this picture of himself, as the host who, even through the bombardments, dined by candlelight and an open fire.

Here is a typical passage from another piece:

In popular speech the word *academic* has become, or is fast becoming, opprobrious. An 'academic discussion' is ordinarily thought of as being a discussion which not only arrives at no conclusion but is to be condemned for that reason; it does not occur to the untrained mind that an inconclusive discussion may be in itself valuable. The arrogance of the half-educated can, in the conditions of the modern world, be abruptly overbearing, and it is in the nature of this arrogance to refuse to acknowledge that there are unanswerable questions which are nevertheless worth asking. To ask such questions, to discuss them, to observe how many other questions are implicit in all the answers, or seeming answers, that thought may supply, and to be led by this process into an understanding that knowledge can lead us only into the foothills of wisdom, is to be in the strictest sense—that is to say, in the Socratic sense—'academic'. The modern, popular mind will have none of this; it is, in Meredith's phrase, 'hot for certainties', and feels that any discussion which does not attain to certainty is a waste of time, 'unpractical', 'academic' . . .

The reference to Meredith is a mistake, for now we remember Sir Willoughby Patterne, who could perform in this vein. It is impossible to escape the feeling that Morgan, in this and similar papers here, is performing—acting, and indeed over-acting, the part of the dedicated thinker high above the untrained, the popular, the half-educated.

Let us look at another page:

I remember well, and always with pleasure, the opportunities that I myself have had to see the little drama of my own life suddenly transferred to a new stage with a new cast.

In the year 1913, I was a very young naval officer in the China Seas. Wishing to be a writer, I applied for permission to leave the Navy, which was granted. I travelled home across Siberia, and found myself in England as a civilian. This in itself was an adventure, for I had worn uniform and lived under a strict discipline since I was twelve. Soon afterwards, I went into deep country, lodged with an old tutor in a farm, and set about learning enough Latin and Greek to enable me to go to Oxford. To others this may sound commonplace enough; to me, because my life's point of view had been changed, it was the bravest of new worlds. Scholarship was a dream; I pursued it with passionate ardour . . .

But he had to wait. No sooner had he gained admittance to Oxford than the war broke out, and no sooner was he in action, with the Naval Brigade, than he was a prisoner in Holland, as we know from his novel *The Fountain*.

Finally he came down from Oxford in 1921, and before that year was out he had joined the editorial staff of *The Times*. From 1926 to 1939 he was its principal dramatic critic. We have had better dramatic critics than Morgan, but many much worse: at his best he wrote well, better than he did elsewhere; he was not without insight into and feeling for the theatre; but his standards were never steady nor his temper certain. Writing now as a dramatist, I must add that I never found his criticism much help.

The early naval training, the long internment in wartime Holland, then Oxford and *The Times*, these help to explain him. But to my mind they do not account for the curious histrionic strain in him, his highly self-conscious performances as Dramatic Critic (with a cloak too), Philosophical Novelist, Aristocratic Man of Letters, Lofty Detached Thinker. He was a man with a mirror. One of his best novels, perhaps his very best, is *Portrait in a Mirror*. He collected two series of essays under the title *Reflections in a Mirror*.

He had at his service some fine qualities and gifts; he aimed high, he toiled to deliver the best of himself; probably from the hour that he left the China Seas he followed some shining vision of authorship; but for many of us—and now it seems a melancholy conclusion—all this was defeated by that moonglimmer, by the ghost of a mocking grin, by a mere echo of solemn egoists elsewhere. His was a splendid mirror, and he would have cut a splendid figure

in it if there had not been a little flaw in the glass
—just an inch or two suggesting those comic mirrors
in fun palaces, where the popular, the untrained, the
half-educated, stare at their distorted reflections and
roar with laughter.

Close-up of Chandler

RAYMOND CHANDLER SPEAKING offers us various unpublished pieces, including several chapters from the novel he left unfinished at his death, and a large number of letters written to his publishers, agents, fellow writers and various friends. It is a rather more solid book than it would first appear to be, and Chandler's many admirers will find it good value. Young writers chiefly concerned with the novel of action and violence should not miss it, for Chandler, at his best a master of this kind of fiction, has much to say that deserves their attention.

Though I make no appearance in these pages, I was in fact among the first over here to praise him in print. (Like many good American writers, he was properly appreciated here before he was given any serious consideration in his own country, as he himself points out.) After exchanging several letters with him, I accepted an invitation, early in 1951, to break my journey from Mexico to Santa Monica and spend a few days with him at La Jolla, a small seaside town not far from San Diego. It is the setting of his last completed novel, *Playback*.

He met me at the airport in Tiajuana, and as he drove me up to La Jolla he explained that as his wife was ill he was putting me up in an hotel.(It was a pleasant hotel though I seemed to be the only guest there under 80.) But we had some talk, among other places, in his library, filled with good books that were not there for show. He was in fact extremely well-read, though he was capable of pretending not to be. He was even less like his Philip Marlowe, or any other tough, brash private eye, than I am; and seemed rather shy, ruminative and mumbling round his pipe, more English in manner than American, not unlike a boffin character in an Ealing film.

Later when he brought his wife to London, I entertained them, and thought she was an invalidish and somewhat affected 60, only learning much later that she was really a very gallant 80. She was in fact 17 years older than he was. They were married in 1924, shortly after the death of his mother, with whom he had returned to California in 1919, when he had been demobilized in England. Before anybody sends for Dr. Freud, however, a few more facts might help.

Chandler was born in Chicago in 1888. His father was American, his mother Irish; she divorced her husband in 1896 and took Raymond, her only child, to London. He was educated at Dulwich College, left at 17 to spend a year in France and Germany, passed a civil service exam and had six months at the Admiralty. Before going back to America, in 1912, he lived as a highbrow free-lance in Bloomsbury, writing for the *Academy*, the *Westminster Gazette*, the *Spectator*. In 1914 he enlisted in the Canadian Gordon Highlanders and went to France with the Canadian First Division, no provider of pleasant sight-seeing and picnics, and only left it to join the Royal Flying Corps in 1918. Anybody who thinks Chandler merely pretended to know how rough and tough life could be had better read a few first-hand accounts of the western front, then think again.

Between 1919 and 1932 he tried a variety of jobs in Southern California, finally helping to run a number of small oil companies but not, as an executive, surviving the depression. Then he began writing for the detective story 'pulps', especially *Black Mask*. There is a photograph in this book of a dinner group of *Black Mask* writers, in which we see Chandler, still looking thin-faced, scholarly and a refugee from the *Academy* and the *Westminster Gazette*, standing in a line that has at the end of it the towering though rather ghostly figure of Dashiell Hammett. (It was the only time they met.) How good Hammett had been as a private eye, we do not know, but what is certain is that in American fiction he was a powerful originator to whom full justice has not been done. It is a mistake, in my opinion, to think of him in terms of the films made out of his *Maltese Falcon* and *Thin Man*. He is strongest and most original in *The Glass Key*, not simply another 'mystery story' but a genuine novel of violence and city politics in the gangster era.

Chandler, whose first full-length story, *The Big Sleep*, came out in 1939, owed something to Hammett but not very much. His qualities and his whole approach were quite different. Hammett, arriving by way of Pinkerton's, wanted the reader to share a kind of experience he himself had known; his flat, hard style (his own, not borrowed from Hemingway) and laconic manner of narration drove at realism. 'This is how it was,' he is saying. But Chandler, altogether more self-conscious, really a literary man and not a story-teller shaped and hardened by experience, approached the novel of action and violence from the other end. Deliberately he developed and experimented with it as a literary form. If there should be any doubt about this, a glance at these letters will immediately remove it.

As he freely confesses, Chandler was not a natural story-teller, a fertile plotter. This is proved by his habit, astonishing to me, of making use in his full-length novels of earlier short stories. Moreover, he has not the forward movement, the natural follow-through, of the born story-teller. The novels in the new *Second Chandler Omnibus*—*The Little Sister*, *The Long Goodbye* and *Playback*—seem to me badly constructed, weak narratives on the 'murder-mystery' level. Nevertheless, though generally inferior to the novels in the *First Omnibus*, they can be read and, after an interval, re-read with pleasure if you have, as I have, a taste for this writer's sharp flavour.

Consider, for example, *The Little Sister*, which Chandler himself, as we learn from these letters, did not like too well. The underlying story pattern seems to me a complete failure. It leaves one neither knowing nor caring. But many of its episodes, as scenes, are astonishingly good. And what are perhaps the best—those in the film agent's office and in the studio —add little or nothing to the story line. They exist in their own right. Here is the key to Chandler, who was not really writing 'murder mysteries' at all. He accepted a mediocre form—it is his own phrase—and made something like literature out of it.

He put together mosaics of brilliant scenes. He

took that Black Mask and worked over it in bright enamels. He turned the American 'mystery story' into a kind of private theatre, almost as artificial in its way as Restoration Comedy. He was a highly self-conscious novelist who would not venture on a novel. (This explains the uneasiness and touchiness displayed in these letters; when we are sharp with everybody we are criticizing ourselves.) In a sense he was like those dons who dare not come out into the open as novelists and so write elaborate detective-puzzles under false names. He did not write that kind of story —and his *Simple Art of Murder* contains a devastating criticism of it—but he did cling to the murder-and-detection rigging when he could have done without it, as some of us told him. He had to have, like a frame for the mosaic, the gunmen and the menacing whispers over the telephone, the night-club gambling, the grilling by the cops, the ice-cold whisky and the hot-tongued blondes.

Because such material is cheap and easy we must not imagine that what he made out of it is cheap and easy too. To any reader with an eye and an ear Chandler's scores of imitators have never come near the edge and brilliance of his scenes. Behind this talent of his for writing dialogue, description (sometimes overdone), social comment, was an odd character with an odd mixture of experience. He was an American educated in England. He began writing in the London of Saki and the *Westminster*. He was a man with a literary temperament and training who, when he started writing again, hammered out tough tales for the 'pulps'. Rather late in life he acquired the persona of a sardonic professional storyteller, ready to take Hollywood and the big money in his stride, but he remained at heart—in the better sense of this term—an amateur of letters. There are two photographs in his book, one taken in 1958 (all persona), the other perhaps 35 years earlier; it is hard to believe they are of the same man.

He did not go to Southern California to write but to earn any kind of living, all the way from picking apricots to running oil companies. An immense variety of experience went into his fiction. This explains why to some of us, not unacquainted with the region, he is not simply the wittiest of the 'murder-mystery' writers but the man who comes nearest yet to being the novelist of Southern California. Its scene is being dazzlingly illuminated by the searchlight flashes of his scenes. And this is no Deep South, a lingering survival, alien to most of us. Here in Southern California is a much-admired, widely-imitated section of our western society, the filmgoer's dreamland, the teenager's Mecca. Its antics and values today will be our antics and values tomorrow. And it is here that Chandler, while shaping and colouring his mosaics for our entertainment, points his torch and makes his comment.

There are so many sharp comments here in his letters that I have marked too many passages and now, when I have space for only a few, may miss the best. But here are some for us writers:

> I know you publishers. You send the proofs off by air express and I sit up all night correcting them and send them back the same way. And the next thing anybody

hears about you, you're sound asleep on somebody's private beach in Bermuda. But when anybody else has to do something, it's rush, rush, rush . . .

The publisher could justify himself perhaps, but he won't give any figures out. He won't tell you what his books cost him, he won't tell you what his overhead charge is, he won't tell you anything. The minute you try to talk business with him he takes the attitude that he is a gentleman and a scholar, and the moment you try to approach him on the level of his moral integrity he starts to talk business . . .

. . . The very nicest thing Hollywood can possibly think of to say to a writer is that he is too good to be only a writer . . .

. . . I have done everything from giving would-be writers money to live on to plotting and re-writing their stories for them, and so far I have found it to be all waste. The people whom God or nature intended to be writers find their own answers, and those who have to ask are impossible to help . . .

. . . It is not enough for a critic to be right, since he will occasionally be wrong. It is not enough for him to give colorable reasons. He must create a reasonable world into which his reader may enter blindfold and feel his way to the chair by the fire without barking his shins on the unexpected dust mop. The barbed phrase, the sedulously rare word, the highbrow affectation of style—these are amusing but useless. They place nothing and reveal not the temper of the times. The great critics, of whom there are piteously few, build a home for the truth . . .

After comparing two kinds of novelists, the solid practitioners and the rare artists, he goes on:

Not that I class myself with any of these people. I really don't class myself at all, nor greatly care about it. I'm still an amateur, still, psychologically speaking, perfectly capable of chucking writing altogether and taking up the study of law or comparative philology . . .

He wrote that in 1949, when he had already entered his sixties, and it is the truth about one side of him. Like most good writers he was very much a divided man. The opposites in him can be found generously displayed.

The Happy Introvert

OUR CIVILIZATION IS monstrously lop-sided, so over-extroverted and so ignorant or contemptuous of man's inner world, that it is now in danger of destroying itself. Across the road we have been travelling for the last hundred years or so, turning it into a dead end, is the H-bomb. This progress towards a time of terror was foreseen by Dostoievsky and Nietzsche. The age being so one-sided, it is not surprising then that the arts, attempting to restore a balance, are more deeply introverted than they were in earlier ages. What is regarded as 'serious modern literature'—not unreasonably, even though many leaders of literary opinion have been themselves not well-balanced—has been the creation of introverted writers, often almost lost in their inner worlds. Nor is it surprising that so many of these writers should have been hysterically defiant, despairing, wretchedly unhappy. Artists want to go their own way but they also want to be widely understood and appreciated, not misunderstood and rejected by their own age. The unhappy introvert in modern literature, his work often darkened and distorted by his feeling of frustration and his bitterness, is to be expected. What is unexpected and so really surprising is a writer of power, as deeply introverted as the others, who seems as happy as the rest seem unhappy. John Cowper Powys is an original, perhaps in this sense a unique figure in modern writing, because he can be fairly described as a happy introvert.

The best evidence leading to this judgement—and he would agree at once with this himself—is to be found in his fiction. But here I am not concerned with his novels, and so would point to various minor works, such as *A Philosophy of Solitude* and *In Spite Of*, and above all to what is a major work, his astonishing *Autobiography*. The story it tells, ending in the early 1930's (it was published in 1934, probably a year or so after it was finished) and bringing him into his sixties, is no record of fortune's smiles and gifts. He was for ever suffering from stomach ulcers, which landed him in hospital on many occasions. Both in England and America, too often he went from one lecture engagement to the next wrestling with pain, nausea, vomiting, sustained somehow by mournful diets of bread-and-milk and the like. For thirty years he lectured for a living, chiefly in America, spending days and nights in trains, sometimes on his way to familiar audiences that knew and loved him, at other times arriving in women's clubs, packed with ladies searching for 'the finer things' who probably regarded him with bewildered suspicion and hostility. Manfully he paid his way, facing squarely his family responsibilities, but it must have been almost always a near thing. And what was worse was that time was running out; he was the eldest and the genius of the gifted Powys family; both Theodore and Llewelyn were enjoying literary reputations when he was still unknown, except to some scattered and dazed lecture audiences; and he was well into his fifties before he

[85]

could begin writing in earnest. Moreover, from first to last he was carrying a load of neurotic obsessions that would have sent most men tottering towards a psycho-analyst's couch. And he was a sensualist—it is his own term—debarred in one way or another from almost everything the average sensual man enjoys most. Yet we can call him the happiest of the deeply introverted moderns.

It is true that in the end everything came right. The books were written, then read, enjoyed, admired, at least by those, not necessarily critics, capable of appreciating originality, genius as distinct from talent. The lifelong semi-invalid entered a vigorous and productive old age. The neurotic load was lightened by will, imagination, humour: no analysts were needed; Powys was his own—and far superior—medicine man and magician. But when he wrote the *Autobiography*—or, for that matter, the earlier and longer novels—this serene and almost cosy ending was not in sight. Then, the way was still hard, the weather dubious, the goal hidden. But we have only to read the *Autobiography* to discover him as the strangely happy introvert. And if I seem to be labouring this point, I would say to the objectors—name me another modern of anything like this size, deeply introverted, taking his stand in his own inner world, who is so free from bitterness and despair, who has such breadth and buoyancy, such ease and prodigality. It is as if from the mouth of some familiar black pit we saw Pegasus come winging out, white and dazzling.

Round about p. 500 in the original English edition of Jung's *Psychological Types*, we can find some account of John Cowper Powys, not of course the man himself, the complex personality or the writer, but as a basic type. He is—with some differences of his own —among the Introverted Sensation Types. These bring sensations of the outer world into the magical depths of their inner world, where all is mythology and—to quote Jung—'men, animals, railways, houses, rivers, and mountains appear partly as benevolent deities and partly as malevolent demons'. Such a one might stare at a flower, a patch of moss, the corner of an old wall, or what might seem to another a commonplace stretch of road, and know strange forebodings and fear or an uprush of ecstasy. What would seem dull to most of us would seem alive and magical to him. But to enjoy his peculiar temperament he would have to demand what so many people now dread—solitude, loneliness. This is not, I suspect, a rare type, though not to be found at most cocktail parties or indeed at meetings of authors. It could easily be discovered among men who despise gregariousness and cheery good citizenship, who often break away to lead what seem to us to be hard and monotonous lives, like some of the leathery oldish men I met years ago in the Arizona desert, where they were 'dry-washing' for gold, earning just enough to keep them in bacon, canned beans and tobacco. The type seems uncommon because such men do odd unsocial jobs, live in out-of-the-way places, and when encountered, though not unfriendly, are tongue-tied or close-mouthed after much solitude. But it really is uncommon, a rare odd fish indeed, when it has at its command a wide culture and astonishing gifts of

[87]

expression. And now we arrive at John Cowper Powys.

Let us dip into the *Autobiography*, quoting one out of scores of similar passages:

How can I find the right expression for the feelings that came to me in those days when the wind blew in a certain way as I followed some muddy grass-track along the edge of the Ely Road or the London Road? How can I describe the feeling I got, as if all the scarce-noticed sensations that had come lightly and incidentally to long generations of my ancestors, when they met the rain, or felt the sun, or heard the calling of rooks or the twittering of sparrows, or saw the smoke rising from human hearths, were rushing over me, in a hardly bearable flood of ecstatic happiness, simply because, on that undistinguished road to the railway station, I heard some patient shop assistant mowing his scrap of grass behind a privet-hedge?

I know perfectly well that everybody born into the world has the feelings I am describing, is visited by these indescribable and apparently causeless transports. I am not in the least suggesting that I am peculiar in this. But why, in the Devil's name, then, do we go on making a cult of everything else except these? Why must politics, religion, philosophy, ambition, revolution, reaction, business, pleasure—all be considered intensely important, and these rare magical feelings not be considered at all?

And then we can add to this passage another, again one of many that might be quoted, from *A Philosophy of Solitude*:

The hour is at hand when an immense number of men and women in all countries of the world will revolt—

secretly, passionately, obstinately—against the crowd-opinions that have turned man's heart away from its rightful world and made it a slave of the unessential. The hour is at hand when thousands and thousands of men and women will recognise that the utmost all the Governments, all the Revolutions and Reactions, all the economic upheavals and improvements can do, is to supply them with a minimum of livelihood, a minimum of security and peace, a minimum of labour and its reward.

Let the revolutionaries and reactionaries, let science and machinery give us our bare living, and bare security against famine, our bare peace of mind, and they have done enough. Their States and their State-Upheavals, their Politics and Economics, their Inventions and Industries, are but means whereby men and women can enjoy the few years of harmless happiness that intervene between the two great Silences, between the eternal Un-born and the eternal Dead.

It is a strange madness to lay the life-stress upon anything less significant, less mysterious than life itself. By all means let the whole world be organised into one great Productive Machine, into one great Productive Economic State. By all means let us each labour, like obedient slaves, for this World-Organisation, for four or five hours every day, and receive, as our return, food, shelter and freedom from panic. But for the rest, the important thing is not external at all, not social or gregarious at all, not necessarily human even. The important thing is how, as individual solitary spirits, who might have been born on Uranus or Saturn rather than upon the earth, we are going to strengthen, deepen, intensify our ecstatic happiness in life and our philosophic acceptance of death. . . .

Now to innumerable introverted sensation types, indeed to all deeply introverted types, people who may have never read a word of his and feel baffled and frustrated and in despair as the man-made world closes in on them, Powys offers a way out, a new and more satisfying kind of life. And they should certainly read *In Spite Of*, which Powys, writing in his eightieth year, boldly described in its sub-title *A Philosophy For Everyman*. But Everyman may well be a gregarious extrovert. There is a certain innocence in Powys's assumption that behind all our various disguises and antics we are really at heart so many introverts of his own sort, to be saved by long solitary walks. And he had not looked hard at the political scene, even in the earlier 1930's when he wrote the passage I quoted above, if he could imagine that modern men can be safely indifferent to 'all the Governments, all the Revolutions and Reactions, all the economic upheavals and improvements'. The Nazis would not have left him in peace among the Welsh hills. Communists might not allow him to publish anything at all. A World-Organization, regarding cheerful anarchy as treason, demanding absolute loyalty to itself, might order him to be brain-washed. And a nuclear war might leave nothing to enjoy and nobody to enjoy it. We can no longer afford to ignore the politicians; they are not simply arguing a long way off; they are busy trying to mould, shape and colour our lives; therefore we had better discover which of them would do us the least harm.

Objections of this kind, however, are really out of place. It is as if we interrupted an orator to ask him to define a term or to point out that he is not being entirely consistent. Readers of the *Autobiography* will remember that not long after he had left Cambridge, when he was earning a very modest living as a weekly lecturer at various girls' schools along the South Coast, Powys decided, as he told his brother Littleton, that he had invented a new art, the art of *Dithyrambic Analysis*. This is the sort of thing high-and-mighty young men tell one another, and Powys, in the middle of describing his youthful fears, follies and obsessions, is humorous about it. But in fact he must have come near the truth. He brought out of those years of lecturing in America, where he was immensely impressive on the platform, a famous 'spellbinder', something that might fairly be described as being dithyrambic and analytical. It is writing that is oratorical; not words arranged to catch the eye but an eager voice in print; yet a voice that while it seems to be eloquently improvising—and we are told he could do this for a couple of hours on the platform—serves a mind that can be most delicately perceptive and aware of the finest shades. He might be said to address us from two very different levels. On one, where he is a figure larger than life in a rather theatrical fashion, a Henry Irving of prose, he performs gigantically, in modes tragical, comical, philosophical, grotesque and fantastic. On the other level, far from the limelight, on the dusky edge of the unconscious, where he is a poet not a performer, he can catch and illuminate a look, a tone, a mood, a memory, that would escape most writers of our time. Readers who have dipped into Powys and do not like him have usually not given themselves the chance of enjoying him on this second level, having been antagonized by the antics and dithyrambs, the drums and trumpets, on the stage above. Such readers should try again. For my part, though at times feeling exasperated (and it is major writers in their large and loose fashion, without the tact of little masters, who *do* exasperate us), I can enjoy almost everything on both levels.

Llewelyn Powys, who came close to worshipping his eldest brother, thought the major part of the *Autobiography*, describing John's first forty years, a marvel of truthful narration and self-analysis; but he disliked the final chapters, covering their author's next twenty years, because in them narrative and analysis give way to dazzling performances in an intellectual three-ring-circus. This is severe family criticism, and there is no reason why we readers should echo it. Indeed, there are as many good things in these final chapters as there are earlier in the book. One of them is my favourite quotation from Powys, who, after describing an old friend, goes on to say: 'He combined scepticism of everything with credulity about everything; and I am convinced this is the true Shakespearean way where-with to take life.' (People who do not understand this observation at once should forget about it; it is not for them.) There are too passages here about America that seem to me beyond the range of any other English visitor there. We have all been compelled to read and to listen to an immense amount of claptrap about Anglo-American understanding; here in the *Autobiography* we can discover a real understanding being created out of experience and perception, poetry and

philosophy. He admires and lovingly describes much
that the visitor in a hurry, trapped in the cities, never
discovers in America; yet he is equally eloquent, in a
manner not without grotesque humour, about what
he calls the 'phantasmagoric horror' of America:

> The horror can be very big. But it can also be very small.
> Most things of this sort can be detected by their smell;
> and I think this particular horror is usually found—like
> the inside of an American coffin after the embalming
> process has run its course—to smell of a desolate varnish
> and unspeakable decomposition. The curious thing about
> it is that it is a horror that can only be felt by imaginative
> people. It is more than a mere negation of all that is
> mellow, lovely, harmonious, peaceful, organic, satis-
> fying. It is not a negation at all. It is a terrifying positive.
> I think at its heart lies a sort of lemur-like violence of
> gruesome vulgarity. It certainly loves to dance a sort of
> 'danse macabre' of frantic self-assertion. It has some-
> thing that is antagonistic to the very essence of what the
> old cultures have been training us to for ten thousand
> years.

In the *Autobiography* as a whole, as he remembers
himself in this place or at that time, recapturing the
finest shades of feeling and yet, so to speak, creating
out of himself a huge half-comic character, he is a better
advocate of his basic type and the life of introverted
sensation than he is in the books devoted to this subject. We are shown directly how obvious disadvan-
tages—ill-health, lack of money and position, neurotic
obsessions—were more than cancelled out by advantages belonging entirely to temperament and outlook. Always, except of course when deliberately
remembering, he lived in the present, making the

[93]

most of whatever it offered him. He lived without ambition, that great destroyer of sensuous satisfaction
and easy contemplation, forbidding that inheritance of
the earth which rightly belongs to the meek. In this
sense, though obstinately, toweringly, his own man,
Powys here is one of the meek. And his astonishing
frankness, which to my mind never becomes embarrassing as some other men's confessions do, has
behind it this genuine humility, not towards other
people but towards life itself, together with what I
have already suggested as a humorous enlarging,
heightening, caricaturing of himself. So we have here
the life-story of a Comic Character in a book that is
deeply serious, often profound, at times entrancing
in its beauty. It is magical because it is the work of a
man who believes, as he has told us more than once,
that by living intensely between our outer and inner
worlds, bringing sensation to our depths, we can
indeed work magic. It is a masterpiece revealing the
happiest of our modern introverts.

Lost Lather

WHO WANTS TO know what I feel about my shaving cream? Not six people on earth. But have patience, the rest of you, because soon we shall be doing a lathery slide towards matters of wider interest and greater weight. And, after all, I must begin somewhere.

I have been using this particular brand of shaving cream for many years now. During all those years except two, the last, I was a fond and even proud customer, ready to boast of it in any company. It had two unusual qualities. First, there was something in it that made it seem admirably cool and refreshing. Secondly, a little of it went a long way, so that it was actually more economical than other and inferior shaving creams. So for years and years we spent a pleasant minute or two together every morning.

Now I still buy a shaving cream offered to me under the same label. But the stuff itself is different. It has lost that cool and refreshing quality, and it does not last half as long as it did. If I were not both too indolent and too despondent, I should buy no more of this bogus stuff but experiment with other shaving soaps. Using the same label, it is a fraud. I really must make an effort, so that no more of my money encourages this swindle.

My guess is that the firm originally responsible for the fine shaving cream, probably a comparatively small concern, was taken over by some giant combine, which proceeded at once to manufacture a cheaper

[95]

soap-cream, to pass under the old aristocratic label. This suspicion seems to be confirmed by the fact that with this cream now is an advertisement of something special for the family. The original manufacturers, I am certain, were not in this family market at all. They were not out to capture Mum; they were busy putting on the market a first-class shaving cream, now gone for ever.

We read and hear a great deal about how much money people should have, but very little, it seems to me, about something equally important—indeed, more important—what in fact the money can buy. I feel that not only should many prices be forced down but that also a tough effort, standing no nonsense from anybody, should be made to ensure that the public is not being swindled. Short weight, dwindling numbers, inferior quality, the prostitution of decent old trade names; the racket is in full swing. And if I, a man, feel this, what must many women be feeling?

If half the things I buy are worse than they used to be, not meant to do their job properly and be enjoyed but to make some quick money, I am no better off if the firms concerned have to pay a profits tax. This merely makes the Treasury and the government richer, encouraging them to invest more in super-fast aircraft that nobody in his senses wants, to spend more than ever bolstering up strategic policies devised by Lord Palmerston. What is needed is not a tax on the swindle but an end to the swindle. If one man cheats another, he may be hauled into the dock; but if a board of directors cheats the whole country—for example, by offering a cheap new product under the name of a good old one—they are regarded as sound substantial fellows, not as rogues heading for gaol. So work a confidence trick on the largest possible scale—and you are made.

The truth is, of course, that we in Britain are now over our heads in Admass, which we borrowed from America. I remember how, during the 1930s when I spent periods of several months in America, I would jeer at the poor quality and workmanship of the many odds and ends I had to buy there. But now it is the same here. This is not because the English have themselves deteriorated, but really because, wanting to go ahead and be affluent, we are now in Admass, all getting more money but needing more money still because it seems to buy less and less. Being Admassians, we are all now busy swindling one another.

You can see how it works. If the quality of a product is deliberately debased, and the people concerned can get away with it, perhaps by way of increased and bolder advertising, then profits, salaries, wages can rise. Yes, a lot of people will have more money to spend. But they will spend most of it on products of equally inferior quality. Again, a foreman and his workmen who want more money for turning out a poor job will find themselves buying things that are other foremen's and workmen's poor jobs. The hammers break, the screws bend, the knives will not cut; the patent medicines do not fulfil their claims; the doors and windows of the wonderful new car will not close properly; the shoes wear out and the clothes fray; and the fabulous new foodstuffs will not feed anybody. And everybody is exasperated, and because

the only Admass answer is more money, then there
will have to be more money. Then the job is worse,
the quality lower, and so it goes on. We go round a
mulberry bush that has not borne honest fruit for
years.

Now, picking up the shaving cream again, we can
turn to another aspect of this matter. The loss of
quality in something I use every morning has dimin-
ished and impoverished my world a little. (Give me
time and I will try some other stuff—or grow a
beard.) And it must have hit some other men much
harder. After all, some chemists, years ago, must have
enjoyed improving that shaving cream, giving it its
pleasantly cool and lasting quality, until it was the
best on the market. But depriving it of this quality,
simply making it cheaper and easier to manufacture,
cannot have been a very enjoyable task. It must have
been a mean job. A man could not feel better after
lending his skill to this fraud on the consumer. And
there must be an enormous number of such men now,
men who go to work shrugging their shoulders, wondering what the next mean little job will be. Once
there was pride in the work, a sense of honour about
it. Now—to adapt Fitzgerald—I wonder often what
the cheaters buy/One half so precious as the Pride
they sell.

Now if we could only add up what the customers
feel and what some of the producers must long have
felt, we should arrive at an appalling total of distaste
and dissatisfaction. But it is only figures that can be
added up, not feelings. And Admass is wonderful with
figures. They are on its side. They can prove that

[98]

everything is getting bigger and bigger and better and better. The statistics and graphs really know, unlike people, stupid and mumbling people, who do not seem to be sure about anything; though often out of politeness, when nice young men and women are sent round to ask them questions, they will give the answers they feel they are expected to give. Nevertheless, somewhere behind the figures and statistics and graphs and votes of thanks to the directors, piling and piling up, thickening and thickening, is this sum total of distaste and dissatisfaction and a general feeling that somehow life as we know it is a fraud. I suppose I add a little to that vast, smouldering, reeking heap every morning as I lather my cheeks.

Though communism has its virtues and is far from being the devil's brew it becomes in western propaganda, I do not want it. I do not want party managers to do all my thinking and to decide my tastes for me. I dislike its smug pedantry, the curiously grey atmosphere it always seems to create, its bureaucratic planning that overlooks so much, so that just when heavy industry is going right, there are no bedroom slippers, shampoo sets, or reeds for oboes. But the West will really have to find a better alternative to it than Admass, production for quantity without regard to quality, the profit-at-any-human-cost motive, the legalized public swindling, the destruction of decent men's pride and honour, the idea that nothing is more important than money (even though it buys less and less of what is really worth having), its increasingly obvious failure to provide a good life based not on figures but on feelings. And it is no use anybody pointing to America. Every intelligent and sensitive American I know—and I have a wide acquaintance there—has detested Admass for years. We take the wrong advice.

Which reminds me. Could anybody recommend a shaving cream that has a certain cool and refreshing quality and that lathers well with only about half an inch of it on the brush? Or isn't there one any more?

Eroticism, Sex and Love

OUR SOCIETY WOULD be healthier and happier, I
believe, if we were not so dangerously confused about
eroticism and *sex* and *love*. If we could begin to agree
about what *eroticism* and *sex* and *love* stand for, we
might stop writing and talking angrily at cross-
purposes and begin getting our values right. This is
particularly important for young people and it is
chiefly for their sake I am writing this piece.

Now for various reasons, some of them obviously
commercial, eroticism flourishes in our society on a
scale never known before, not even during the deca-
dence of Imperial Rome. One reason for this is that
eroticism is a short cut to masculine interest and
curiosity; it is a safe and easy card to play. Let us say
you are publishing a cheap paperback edition of a
classical novel. The novel may contain no scene in
which a blonde is having the clothes torn from her
back, but to play safe, commercially, you display a
half-ravished blonde on the jacket. The appeal here is
not to sex, as too many people imagine—and it is
certainly not to love—it is entirely to the eroticism so
characteristic of our time.

Eroticism, unlike sex and love, apparently offers
something for nothing. It is sexual pleasure without
sexual responsibility. It is having your cake and eating it. Unlike sex, it is not completely natural, and it
is at the furthest possible remove from love, which is
supremely personal. Eroticism is impersonal, which

explains why women may lend themselves to it but never believe in it, and it is artificial, man-made, belonging to a technically advanced but dangerously confused civilization.

Eroticism, we might say, is the twanging of a single nerve, concentrating upon a certain kind of excitement and pleasure to the exclusion of everything else. It is solitary and self-regarding, other persons involved in it being treated as instruments, things. Nothing worth calling a relationship can be created by it. One sex cannot do the other sex any good in eroticism. The opposite sex is not really *there*, so to speak, in its true complementary character. We are told that Oriental soldiers and sailors, at one time, took with them life-sized dummy figures of women with which they pretended to have intercourse. That was eroticism.

But in our society we have not even the excuse of those soldiers and sailors, who may have spent long periods with not a real woman in sight. We have deliberately perverted ourselves, transforming honest sex into this nasty auto-erotic stuff. For eroticism makes use of the broad sexual urge, which might lead to love, and narrows it and directs it into a blind alley, turning something that might be fruitful into what is solitary, barren, and for ever unrewarding. And we are doing this on a huge and ever-increasing scale.

Let me give you an English example. In England now we have more and more so-called clubs entirely devoted to eroticism, displaying not only strip-tease but also obscene acts of sexual sadism and masochism. If such

[102]

clubs were patronized only by teen-age lads, naturally curious, it would not be so bad, but in fact their
chief patrons, especially in London's Soho, are middle-
aged prosperous men. And when middle-aged business men, perhaps entertaining their customers, have
to spend their afternoons and their money gaping at
such displays, then there is something wrong with
our society.

It is a mistake to imagine that Western Man is
more highly-sexed than he was or more capable of
love. He is merely trapped by eroticism, that twanging of a single nerve in the dark. More and more men
are crowding into this blind alley, not demanding
more life, richer relationships, but only a barren tit-
tillation. The encouragement and exploitation of
eroticism, sometimes out of hatred of Woman, fear of
real sex and love; but mostly for commercial gain, is
now one of the worst features of our Western civilization. We are busy corrupting ourselves.

It is only fair to add, however, that the publishers of
paperbacks do not seem as busy with eroticism as they
were a few years ago. I have done no close checking
but I do get the impression there are now rather fewer
half-ravished blondes and strangled brunettes selling
the newer paperbacks. But there are still far too many.
I have a weakness for tough 'private eye' tales, in the
tradition that began with Dashiell Hammett and to
which my friend Raymond Chandler, a superb nar-
rator, made a notable contribution. I enjoy these tales
not because they are full of violence but because the
best of them are told with uncommon skill, suggest
character and background with an economy the ordi-

nary novelist rarely achieves, and keep alive my interest and curiosity. But even in the best of them there is too much suggestion of sadistic eroticism, and on the lower levels there is a deliberate pandering to the worst feelings of the sex-starved and woman-fearing or woman-hating male. The mutilated corpses of voluptuous blondes that turn up so regularly in these stories are not there by accident. They are there to please the customers, men ready to hate what they cannot possess.

Moreover, it is not only on the 'private eye' level of fiction that eroticism is offered as a bait. There is plenty of it, spiced with sadism and masochism, in a large proportion of best-selling novels. Some of these are really the old-fashioned novels of American small-town life, with the same background and cast of characters (e.g. the wild girl, the puzzled young man, the envious spinster, the good old doc), with one important difference, that now the people are caught with their pants down, and what was once referred to very vaguely—rape, for instance—is now described in detail. Take the eroticism out of many of these novels, and their sales could be divided by a hundred. They are using the same bait as the gaudiest of the paperbacks.

The movies of course have dealt in eroticism for many years now. But the appeal is more blatant than it used to be. For example, although Garbo was a symbolic figure of mysterious exotic sex (the best instance I know of what Jung called 'the *anima* archetype'), quite apart from being a superb actress she was not really a figure of obvious eroticism, simply a lascivious dream creature. She suggested Woman herself, not a mere sensual toy, a thing for secret appetites. But when we arrive at Bardot and the like, we are at once entangled in deliberate eroticism. The movies have gone into the strip-tease business.

I never knew Marilyn Monroe but I enjoyed her film performances, not because she was a superb 'dish'—I never think of women as dishes, and if I did then Monroe would not have been my first choice from the menu—but simply because the attack, the humour, the sparkling vivacity, of the 'dumb blondes' she played were enchanting. In short, I enjoyed her as an actress. Within her limits she was an exceptionally fine performer. Her tragedy, it seems to me, was that feeling basically insecure, because of her early background, she wanted to be appreciated as an actress and to be recognized and understood *as a person*. But she found herself, in and out of the studios, clamped into the role of a symbolic figure, perhaps the supreme symbolic figure in our time, of eroticism. She was offered not as a woman but as a thing to twang that male erotic nerve. And it is my belief that she was so deeply conscious of this humiliating role, so profoundly disturbed by the idea that her huge mass audience never accepted her as a woman, a real person, that she felt herself being destroyed and did nothing to resist that destruction. So she was, as many people realize now, one of the tragic figures of our time. We wonder at the callousness and cruelty of the crowds at the Roman games and circuses, people who could watch men and woman being butchered or torn to pieces by wild animals in the blood-stained arena. But we have our own callousness and cruelty, our own blood-stained arenas.

Now to my mind it is a great mistake to condemn all this eroticism as 'sex'. I disagree entirely with all those moralists who are always telling us there is 'too much sex' in movies, stage shows, fiction. They are confusing two very different things. And it is this confusion that has in fact encouraged eroticism. In other words, eroticism has got away with it just because so many moralists and social reformers have mistakenly condemned it simply as sex. Ordinary people very sensibly feel that there cannot be all that wrong with sex, that while there may be a lot of sex in movies, shows, fiction, after all there is just as much sex, if not more, down the nearest street. And of course they are right.

Sex is not something wickedly thought up since grandma was a girl and the preacher was at college. It is a natural hunger and need, built into us from the beginning and consciously felt as an urge from the age of puberty onwards. Of course we can fight it and starve it, just as we can turn ourselves into living skeletons by eating the merest scraps of food, or dangerously dehydrate ourselves by drinking the barest minimum of fluids. But it is as natural for young people to be deeply concerned with sex as it is for them to use their lungs, arms and legs. To blame them for it is idiotic. They would not have come into existence if it had not been for sex.

I am not going to pretend that there is no difference in our civilization between eating, drinking, and making love. We have inherited some very complicated feelings about sex, including some that suggest a strange sort of guilt. As if we ought to know some other and nicer way of producing children! The truth is, the roots of our civilization—together with all these feelings we have inherited—go back about 2,500 years to a time of transition from matriarchal to patriarchal religious and social systems, when men came to believe that Woman was the enemy of Man's conscious development, that unchecked sexual indulgence robbed men of the energy, will, purpose, necessary for civilization. To this day, I believe, it is largely men not women who feel guilty about sex. And there have been many peoples, not necessarily savages but outside our particular civilization, who have never known these feelings of guilt.

Each sex wants and needs something from the other sex. (I have already shown that this is not true of eroticism, which is entirely self-regarding and does not go out to the other sex.) But it is a mistake, made far more often by men than women, to imagine there is nothing but physical desire here. Indeed, the older I get the more I am convinced that sexual intercourse itself is far more a *psychological* than a physical act, and that this—really the psychological relationship—explains the seemingly mysterious sexual successes or failures. We are not bulls and cows, so there are innumerable decent couples who are simply not right for each other and do not discover this until they have been married for some time. This is why divorce should be by mutual consent, without any faking of bogus evidence about adultery or cruelty. In Britain you have to make up a dirty story to convince the judge he should grant you a divorce, and then all too often he abuses you as a dirty low fellow because he believes this story, forgetting that he asked for it.

Now men often persuade themselves that they 'want a woman' as they might want a meal or a smoke, but nearly always this is so much cynical self-deception. In fact they need a great deal more than that—unless they have been completely perverted by eroticism—and what they really need is the psychological relationship with Woman herself, the other and complementary sex. Even the sailor hurrying to the nearest brothel is unconsciously in search of this relationship, though he may imagine that all he wants is perfunctory and brutal copulation. But it must be clearly understood that on this level we are discussing, there is no relationship of *persons* but simply a relationship between the sexes as sexes, not this man and that woman but Man and Woman. When we come to persons, we arrive at love.

Eroticism, closing in on itself, wanting a sensation and not another person, bars love out. Indeed, too much eroticism probably makes real sexual love impossible. Not that this love is easy and entirely effortless, as ten thousand pieces of sentimental claptrap assure us it is. Here it is worth pointing out that as our own age has become more and more insecure, less and less certain of itself, as more and more people have felt bewildered and fearful, there has been an increasing emphasis, not only in fiction and drama and the movies but also even in advertising, upon the value and joy, the magical saving grace, of sexual love. This is not necessarily wrong, but it can be argued that we may now be asking sexual love to shoulder too many burdens, overloading it to the breaking point. It is being offered to us too often as an effortless rescue operation, in a kind of fairy-tale atmosphere in which everybody can 'live happily ever after'.

But we never get something worth having for nothing. This is the mistake, as we have already seen, of the men who prefer eroticism to love. They dodge responsibility, so pay nothing in human terms, but then they do not get anything worth having. The true lover is ready to pay everything, all that is of value in his life. But we must not confuse love with the state of *being in love*. It takes two people, in a consciously creative partnership, to love, only one to be in love. A boy or girl, man or woman, can easily fall in love with somebody who is not really there at all—in other words, with a magical image projected from the unconscious on to somebody whose real self may bear no resemblance to that image. All uncontrollable infatuations—and these are possible at any age—are in fact self-produced, and outside true relationships. The infatuated man is being bewitched by the magic of his own unconscious depths.

There is probably some truth in the idea that deep enduring sexual love is only possible between certain types of men and women. Types that are wrong for each other cannot mate successfully because they are psychologically ill-matched and therefore cannot even be physically aware of each other in a satisfying way. (This accounts for the break-up, often puzzling to relatives and friends, of many marriages.) All this may have something to do with the fact that most of us have an element, to a differing degree, of the opposite sex in us. Perhaps the 100 per cent male, an insufferable fellow, can only be happy with the 100 per cent female, almost a talking cat. Perhaps a man who is 80 per cent male and 20 per cent female is happiest with a woman who is 80 per cent female, 20 per cent male. But this is idle conjecture, if only because we do not know what these percentages are.

I am myself suspicious of sexual love that appears to rest on no foundation of respect, admiration and *genuine liking*. This may seem odd because love is greater than these. Yet I have known a good many married couples who would have been indignant if they had been told they did not love each other, who would have declared at once and in all sincerity that they did, and yet obviously *did not like each other*. And though sexual love, in all its delight, tenderness and trust, is more than liking, I feel it ought to contain an immense amount of liking. We ought to be married to the kind of person we like enormously—a wonderful magical man—a glowing gem of a woman, a sweetheart and a honey. And if we are, then we can go down the years, not just feeling or accepting love, but consciously creating it, turning a relationship into a glorious work of art. We may have first entered into this relationship, and all the treasures of living it can bestow upon us, by way of an honest sexual attraction. But what is certain is that we shall never find it, or anything else worth having, in the blind alley and dead end of eroticism. Youth, please note!

Gay with the Arts?

TWO POINTS I make at once. At all times and in all circumstances Miss Jennie Lee has always seemed to me a most appealing and gallant figure, and whether she succeeds or fails with her present task I shall be ready to doff my bonnet or wave it, just as she pleases. So no criticism of her is intended here. The second point is that, though fiercely radical politically and socially, culturally I am conservative, like many a better man before me (Lenin, for one). It is true that in my time I have risked a few experiments, especially on the stage, but in contemporary terms I may be truthfully described as a not-with-it Square. And this, together with my respect and affection for Miss Jennie Lee, must be borne in mind.

Now I am all in favour of Britain going gay. I still applaud, though hardly anybody else does, the best attempt at public gaiety in my time—the 1951 Exhibition, which the Tory press attacked when it was there and has sneered at ever since. I also realize that the hardest thing to achieve in this country is the kind of innocent gaiety that is so often found abroad. There is a twist in the British character that either refuses to attempt gaiety or quickly transforms it into something rather unsavoury and sinister. Indeed, the very term 'going gay' used to refer to a particularly brutal and cynical type of prostitution, turning pretty girls into hard-mouthed and steely-eyed drabs and sluts. I do not know what night life in London is like now, because I

[111]

never sample it, but I can understand why some foreigners tell us that London is the wickedest city in the
world. We have to go home, lock the door and draw
the curtains, to be gay—that is, if there is any gaiety
in us. Many people of course allow television to be
gay for them, but all too often this has been a Frost.

But if Britain can at last go gay with the arts, as
Miss Lee has suggested, then well and good. I will
try to be around to shout hurrah. But if, as I imagine,
the people are to be offered the choicest contemporary
creations of our arts, whatever is representative, significant and most 'with-it', then some fine talents will
be sent on the road, but the gaiety may be missing.

Let us say that we are among the steel-workers in
Puddleton. The town has been promised a show of
pictures by one of the most original and highly-
praised painters this country has. Ignoring for once
their clubs and singing rooms, the steelworkers have
a good wash and brush-up, collect their wives and
daughters, and hurry off to the Puddleton Art Centre.
There they find themselves surrounded by disinte-
grating tycoons and screaming popes, the painter
selected to delight them being Mr Francis Bacon. His
work will deserve every adjective sent out by the Arts
Council to accompany it. But I doubt if Puddleton,
not a cheerful place at any time, will go gay after con-
templating Francis Bacon's grim despair.

Again, the textile workers in the West Riding
believe they can enjoy good music. They appreciate
splendid sound, sonorous and a bit lush (my own
taste exactly). So they pack the Town Hall when they
are offered what three men in London believe to be

the pick of recent compositions. These are works of great skill and unblemished integrity, but they disdain any suggestion of splendid sound, being intensely cerebral experiments in atonality and contrapuntal austerity. 'Nay, Ah couldn't make head nor tail of it,' they will tell one another in Bradford, Halifax, Huddersfield, 'all of 'em scrapin' an' scrapin' away!' Any gaiety? I doubt it.

But there is still the theatre, that stronghold of popular art, able any night to transform a thousand people of all kinds into one collective sensitive being, wondering, laughing, crying. Well, here we ought to be all right because we have recently enjoyed a renaissance. For my part I consider this an over-statement, but I do think there really is a lot of good youngish playwriting talent in the country, and if its works are more often praised than performed, that is largely the fault of our theatre organization.

And perhaps the most formidable figure here is Mr Harold Pinter, whose originality and great technical skill we should all admire. So let Mr Pinter be cajoled, flattered, bribed handsomely, to entertain Coketown, which has been in need of cheering up for the past century. But though I think the experiment should be made, I can't see the surly folk of Coketown going gay with Mr Pinter. He may easily confirm all their suspicions. For generally with Mr Pinter, menace is on its way, messages are mysteriously seeping through but they always contain bad news, never good news (though Mr Pinter must have had far more good news than bad news himself) and things begin to look rather black. And this may be telling Coketown what it has known too long already, and what it may be most in need of now is a piece or two of good news, with some things, black hitherto, suddenly turning apple-green and pink.

Leaving Mr Pinter now for the avant-garde in general, I must confess I find myself baffled by what I take to be its three main themes—uncertainty of identity, difficulty or impossibility of human communication, the total absurdity of life. I can imagine a man being haunted by these ideas, but he would be some wretched solitary wondering whether to end it all, and I simply cannot see him *as a writer*. To begin with, a writer is sufficiently certain of his identity to insist upon having his name clearly printed on title pages and play-bills. Again, if he genuinely believes communication to be impossible, then why is he writing and how can he communicate his belief that communication is impossible? Finally, if life is totally Absurd, then how does he come to depend upon publishing and play-producing, which demand some degree of order and responsibility in human affairs? How can life be Absurd except where it involves publishers, printers, binders, booksellers, theatre managers, actors, scene-painters, box offices, and the banks into which the royalties go? Am I to believe that these laureates of the Absurd would show no surprise if, after having bought a railway ticket, they were conducted to a balloon, or found on a restaurant table, in place of the dinner they ordered, half a pig and eight pounds of chocolate and a gallon of buttermilk?

I have suddenly remembered attending the opening of the first surrealist exhibition in London, and finding

[114]

one of its organizers angrily denouncing the gallery attendant who had mixed up some of the numbers. But why, as I said at the time, shouldn't there be surrealist gallery attendants? Or surrealist patrons who bought pictures to jump on them and signed their cheques Hereward the Wake or Diane de Poitiers? Why should the artists have all the fun?

Very well, I am exaggerating. Nevertheless, I am suspicious of beliefs that refuse the test of ordinary living. There is a good deal of mere 'with-it', not far removed from the 'In' and 'Out' nonsense in fashion magazines, among the avant-garde writers and the people who publish their books and produce their plays. What is probably most genuine here is a kind of vague pessimism that shrinks from attempting to improve the human lot and so declares it cannot be improved. (Many critics overpraise these writers because they themselves share this pessimism but dare not proclaim it.) And perhaps it all began when the Gestapo took over the Left Bank.

With Miss Jennie Lee I shall now associate Mr Arnold Wesker (who has a kind of noble simplicity like one of Tolstoy's virtuous characters) for he too wishes to take our contemporary arts to the people, gaily too if possible. Dear friends, I hope you will succeed. But do not try to ignore that horrible great gap, which has been widening ever since the end of the First War, between what is held to be truly representative contemporary art and what most people, not necessarily stupid and insensitive, are ready to understand and appreciate. The truth is, we seem to be desperately short of what Van Wyck Brooks used to

call 'primary' writers or composers or painters or
sculptors, born bridgers of gaps. (Shakespeare is the
master of them all—or was, before the boys rammed
him into the Theatre of the Absurd and the Cruel.)
As a mass culture develops and hardens, then scornful
young artists react violently against it, determined
that its white shall be their black, its black their white.
If it is easy, then they must be difficult; if it insists
upon optimism, they insist upon pessimism; if it
allows only happy endings, they will have none of
them. The gap can be bridged—look at Chaplin, who
refused even to admit it was there—but for some time
yet the going will be hard, and not, I am afraid, very
gay.

Buzz-and-Bruit

ONE OF MY troubles—I have lots—is that I was born a Victorian and am now too old to accept Buzz-and-Bruit and the Mish-Mash in the Middle. What these are, I will explain shortly; my subject now is me. I grew up during the years just before the First War, and among people who respected and admired talent, once they had taken a long hard look at it and it still stayed there. This applied to all kinds of talent, from Shaw and Wells to Little Tich and George Robey. These people understood that there are many different kinds of talent, easily distinguished from one another. They did not confuse Shaw with Robey, Wells with Little Tich. They were not easy to please, but once they knew the talent was there, they were loyal and even affectionate.

In this respect, to quote a song of the time, I have long 'been following in father's footsteps, following my dear old dad'. I love talent. It does much to redeem our species, which could take lessons in decent conduct from gorillas. At the sight or sound of it, I want to clap my hands and cry out. (Time after time I switched on *Not So Much A Programme* in the hope that Eleanor Bron would be shining above its murky confusion.) The thought that I may have failed to recognize and appreciate genuine talent, any kind, loads me with more guilt than any of my sins of the flesh. But what about genius? Forget about genius. There is very very little of it, and time must pass before it burns clearly in its appointed place. I have said it before and now say it again: there is too much genius, these days, and not enough talent.

What has now taken place of the presentation, recognition, appreciation of talent—and what I am too old to come to terms with—is Buzz-and-Bruit and the Mish-Mash in the Middle. Although talent may be involved here, usually to its ruin, it is certainly not essential, and some of those who are the most loudly buzzed and bruited cannot show a glimmer of talent. Many of the spotlighted splashers in the Mish-Mash are people who are well-known for being well-known. Possibly, like the haughty young men and girls in the advertisements, they are setters of trend and pace, something I am too old and stupid to understand. What is certain is that for the time being they are 'In'. I used to wonder what they were in, but now I know. They are in the Mish-Mash in the Middle.

It is in the middle, of course, so that it can be given the maximum attention. It is ringed round with cameras and microphones and lights. It is where thousands of youngsters ache to be, and where millions of innocent chumps, humbly admiring, know they could never be. It is both served and manipulated by some dailies, the Sundays and the smart mags, TV and radio. Everything in it is 'exciting'. And it obliterates the difference between great talent, little talent and no talent. It is in fact a notable transformer and leveller. Bishops, philosophers, senior politicians, soon lose their individuality, together with their dignity, and find a sort of agency-and-show-biz common ground. Its values are those of variety agents and admen. This is the Mish-Mash in the Middle, and it is doing the country about as much good as a daily addition of viruses to the public water supply.

Some exaggeration there, no doubt. Nevertheless, we are in a pickle. One reason why I pay 16 times as much for my pipe-tobacco as I did when I began smoking is that we are spending so much on education. But as fast as we educate youngsters we turn on Buzz-and-Bruit to make them uneducated again. The values and standards they may have brought out of school or college are too often swept away by the mass media. The brightest lights are illuminating the Mish Mash. The youngsters are shown a society in which James Bond is fiction's greatest achievement, pop singers are more important than fine musicians, TV personalities are in the centre and artists, philosophers, scientists are in the dark outside, and one starlet or model is worth a thousand teachers or nurses or probation officers. This is not a healthy society, and I like to think it is the result of a long Tory rule. But unless Labour can soon change it radically—and this means improving the street as well as enlarging the school—we may find ourselves in a community incapable of making the effort to save itself from decline and ruin.

Talent, as I suggested earlier, is precious. If we can, we must prevent its self-destruction. And Buzz-and-Bruit, the first stage, and the Mish-Mash, the second stage, are not the friends but the enemies of talent, partly because the people busiest in them, doing the 'In' publicity and arranging the TV and radio programmes, are often themselves without genuine talent. They do not love it; they feed on it. And secretly, I suspect, they want to bring its possessors down as early as possible to this agency-and-show-biz common ground, where all are 'personalities in the news'.

Then there is something else, even more important. Gifted young men and women, preciously endowed with talent, often have temperaments that leave them wide open to the appeal of Buzz-and-Bruit, to the attractions of change and excitement, noise and glitter and what the little girl I knew called 'being in the importance'. After all, it can be dull sitting at home nursing a talent. It is hard to live quietly if you have been invited to attend and perform in a three-ring circus just down the road. But though it may be death, as Milton tells us, to hide talent, I say it is equally deadly to rush talent under the lights of the circus.

After more than 40 years of professional authorship, I ought to know something about what happens to writers. And I say that unless they are exceptional indeed, they cannot sustain and fully employ their talent unless they are prepared to lead what may appear a rather humdrum existence. The worst thing for a successful writer is for him to begin playing in the full glare of publicity the part of a successful writer. Instead of getting on with their work, at a time when their creative energy should be at its peak, too many writers, after a quick success, have wasted themselves and their talent on the demands of Buzz-and-Bruit and on splashing around in the Mish-Mash. And the temptation to do this is far more pressing now than it used to be, before the mass media were so powerful. There may be money in it of course; we were told that Mr Norman Mailer made £170,000 out of his last novel before publication, when it was looking its best; and he is a Buzz-and-Bruit figure if there ever was one. But though he was received here like a conquering hero—which was B-and-B claiming its own—he stays in my book as one of the victims.

Not only do creative artists of all kinds need to keep out of Mish-Mash, to live quietly with their talents, but so do performers. Actors who have any respect for their audiences should take time to brood over their parts and should save most of their nervous energy for their performances. Bouncing around in the Mish-Mash will get them into the news and film contracts, but it will play the devil with their talents. Gifted young players are now forced on like rhubarb; they are buzzed and bruited into stardom while they are still in their twenties; they are paid hundreds a week perhaps only two years after doing weekly Rep and living in a basement on baked beans; and no wonder some of them go racketing and clowning around, never nursing their talents. They think they are dancing on top of the world when actually they are so much mass-media fodder. Hardly anybody with them in the Mish-Mash cares a damn what will be happening to them in 10 years. No long views and loyalty there.

We are creating an atmosphere that is bad for almost everything worth having. It is bad for the arts and talent, as we have seen. It is bad for people's values and standards. It encourages the young to waste time and attention on the wrong things. Already it is influencing politics, in which principles and ideas play a smaller and smaller part, and Buzz-and-Bruit is at work changing elections into cup-ties and political leaders into Mish-Mash 'personalities' ready to do anything in front of a TV camera. I am not in favour of bringing a humourless priggishness into our public life, as the communist countries do. Indeed, we could do with more real humour and far less sneering and sniggering. The genuine humorist is a serious person. He knows that the essential life of a community is deeply serious, depending on all manner of sensible values and standards. It is not made out of trend-setting, who's in and who's out, show-biz attitudes, people well-known for being well-known, mass media that discover geniuses in May and forget them by September, and public life as a three-ring circus. If, as we are told, the world no longer takes us seriously, that may be because we no longer take ourselves seriously. We may on occasion take ourselves solemnly, a very different thing. And for the rest— too much Buzz-and-Bruit and Mish-Mash.

Writer at Work

I HAVE JUST finished dictating replies to letters (but not from friends) and they have taken rather longer than usual, for it is now 11 o'clock and I ought to have been working for the past half-hour. Please note that I don't count dictating letters as work, though I have a suspicion that many businessmen would regard what I have been doing for the last 80 minutes or so as a goodish morning's work. (But do I really know anything about businessmen in their offices? No, I don't.) Among the letters I have just answered is one from an American graduate engaged in research into the Creative Process. Clearly he would like to have a lovely long chat about my Creative Processes, which he will then be able to compare with other people's Creative Processes. My reply to him, so polite but so evasive, was not untouched by the Creative Process. And perhaps this piece might help him.

Left to myself, to get down at last to some work, I notice on my desk the sheets of an article lying loose. They ought to be fastened with a paper-clip. So now I look around for any paper-clips I have removed from letters. I have on my desk a battered and discoloured little tin box—its label, *Paperfasteners Price 6d.* now hard to read—that I must have had for well over 40 years. It still contains some paper-clips but I leave them undisturbed if I can find any others. The truth is that in these matters I am mean as hell, a kind of miser in the stationery department. And the elaborate and expensive arrangements common in offices, especially those of large organizations, I always regard with a curious mixture of awe and contempt. What reckless-ness! What mad spending!

Having found a paper-clip and fastened the sheets of the finished piece, I prepare to do a new one. Slowly, very carefully, as if about to perform a diffi-cult operation, I put a sheet of what is, I hope, the cheapest typing paper on the market into my machine. (How many times have I done this? The figure must be astronomical.) Facing and rather daunted by its blank white stare, I re-light my pipe. My wandering eye is now caught by a number of pipes that I keep in a wooden bowl. I notice a certain gleam of highly polished briar. I fish out this particular pipe, which I haven't smoked for some time, and discover there is too much hardened dottle and carbon inside it. I must take a knife to it.

But for once I have left my beautiful silver pipe knife (present from a daughter) somewhere upstairs, and I am too lazy to go up and find it. (Besides, I am working.) However, I remember that in the top drawer of my desk I have one of those red Swiss knives that offer implements for everything. I buy them—and I use the plural because I keep losing them —at airports when I am feeling bored between planes, chiefly in the hope of impressing my grandsons, immature technological types. So I find the knife but also find that I cannot pull out the blade I want. And for once I know why.

On a flight from Nova Scotia to Boston, last August, a tin of liver salts somehow burst open in my bag. It was not a large tin. In point of fact I rarely take liver salts, but when I am packing for a journey I tend to behave as if I were preparing for an expedition to the Antarctic or the Amazon. In some mysterious manner the salts in this small tin multiplied like the loaves and fishes, so that everything in the bag had its share of them. This included the Swiss knife. So I cannot pull out the blade because it is sticky with liver salts.

I now remember that in this same top drawer there is somewhere a pointed pipe-scraper that I have used before to prise open tins of tobacco. It is not easy to find. The drawer is crammed with broken ballpens, old pocket diaries, cottonwool (I stuff it into my ears when I am typing), pipe cleaners, bottles of type-writer oil, picture wire, lighters that no longer work, railway timetables long out of date, letters and bank statements I meant to put somewhere else, and very handsome cases for fountain pens that I feel vaguely I ought not to throw away. (Probably because I forget there are no longer young children about the house; they will gladly accept and use *anything*—at least for 10 minutes.) And after poking about in all this stuff, I find the pointed pipe-scraper, and, not without some difficulty, I am able at last to lever out the blade of the Swiss knife.

Now the bottom of the pipe bowl has been cleared and I have run a pipe cleaner through the stem. The pipe is ready for smoking, but I don't do anything with it because I am still smoking the pipe I re-lit. I am also still working, though as yet not a single word has been typed on that blank waiting sheet. Now I tear off a page of the calendar on my desk, to bring myself

[125]

into the right month. The Creative Process probably keeps its eye on this sort of thing. And now I look around for something else to do, a touch here, a touch there, that would improve the look of my desk. And if all this leads you to condemn me as one of those neurotic tidying-up fusspots, you are going out of your mind. I can exist cheerfully in a huge clutter. All I am doing now is delaying the moment when I shall have to begin writing. For 55 years I have been writing—and for print too—and I still hate starting. Indeed, I think I grow more and more reluctant to begin.

Writers can be divided roughly into two kinds. There are those who do not know what they want to write until they have written something. So they dash away but then fill the waste-paper basket with one rejected draft after another. And I could never be one of these people, if only because I am very mean about paper and waste on this scale would appal me. I belong to the other group, the writers who set down what is in their heads and, apart from an occasional doubtful scene or clumsy passage, do no re-writing. Once we start we go steadily on and on. But this means we are always reluctant to start. We feel there is something inevitable, leading to triumph or disaster, about the way in which we begin. So we are afraid of beginning.

This dithering about for half-an-hour is merely to delay starting a short piece. When faced with a long and fairly ambitious work, I can dither for weeks. I make notes I am never going to look at again: I browse around in reference books, pretending there is something I may need in them; I order another kind

[126]

of typewriter ribbon; I ring up people I don't really want to talk to; I answer letters that have been lying around for a week or so; I am willing to do all manner of little jobs that I try to dodge at any other time. Anything, anything, rather than commit myself to that first page. I am like a man at the heart of a maze, wondering which of a dozen exits he should choose. And this is closer to my situation than it might first appear to be, because even before I have actually started I am longing to get out and be free, to walk easy and clear, free from the weight and pressure of this work I have condemned myself to do. The real Creative Process (American graduate, please note) has been going on for some time, hardly ever leaving me alone, and too often robbing my outer life of much of its colour, tone, flavour, like an endless honeymoon with a succubus. And through all this delaying and dithering—and I am at it still, now trying to find a notebook I don't really need—the Creative Process is at work, is indeed rapidly increasing the pressure until I am compelled to find some words.

Hundreds of people have told me what a wonderful life I must have. Whatever smirking reply I may have given them, I have always known they were quite wrong. Most writers enjoy only two brief periods of happiness: first, when what seems a glorious idea comes flashing into the mind; secondly, when a last page has been written and you have not yet had time to consider how much better it all ought to have been. Much of the rest might be described as mental pregnancy with successive deliveries, and all without any smiles and blessings from Mother Nature, for we are no use to *her*. Have you ever met a really happy writer, a Corot or Renoir of paper and print? I never have. Now I come to think of it, the happiest men I have ever met—belonging to several different countries—all ran marionette or puppet theatres. O-ho, o-ho! Isn't there *something*, at least the ghost of an idea, somewhere there? But what did I jot down, years ago, in that old black notebook? And where *is* that notebook?

Doubts About Dynamism

THE LEADERS OF our three political parties, together with the public men who support them, all seem to share one assumption. And as far as I am concerned, what they assume is quite wrong. I don't wish to live, as they appear to think, just off Madison Avenue, New York City. Yet this is what they seem to offer us as a target, a goal, a reward. We have only to try a little harder and we can get there. And they are so confident that this is what we want that all the leading politicians bring it into their perorations. We have only to follow them to find ourselves living in a dynamic society. This sounds fine but every time I think about it I see that I don't want to live in a dynamic society. I want to live in a sensible, pleasant and civilized society, with Madison Avenue well out of sight.

I have dragged in Madison Avenue because all this talk about dynamism and growth and how wonderful our life might be in 1970 is based on its values. Everybody will have a car and drive home in it to watch colour television and eat frozen scampi and artificially-flavoured peas. We shall be living in an adman's dream. But is this what we really want? No doubt we must pay our way but do we have to keep on paying a bigger and bigger way so that everybody can have an electric toothbrush? Before we listen to any more appeals to hurry up and go and get there, we ought to ask ourselves where the hell we think we are going.

Take an obvious example. We are told we could soon double the number of cars in private ownership. But this would be a nightmare. In order to cope with all these cars, the whole face of the country would have to be changed, all cities and larger towns re-planned and rebuilt, billions of pounds spent—and for what? Society does not exist simply to provide motor transport. Except to half-dotty teenage lads—and of course people in the automobile trades—there are more important things in life than owning a car. I suspect that half the people who own cars now would be better off without them.

One reason why owning a car appeals to so many people is that they are becoming more and more restless. They don't know where they want to go but they want to go somewhere. Life might be better there; it isn't satisfying here. Our whole society is restless, dissatisfied, longing for somewhere else, something else. Hence all this go-go, git up an' git. Nobody has enough money, not even Mr Clore. Pay may go up but then so do prices. And there is always something you long to buy that you just can't afford—or can you? Every night, after the admen have done with them, millions of couples are arguing, trying to plan, suddenly deciding to spend more than they can afford. Is this the good life? It is not.

The possibility of doing good work, on any level, begins to recede or vanishes altogether when the community seems to look like a kaleidoscope. Standards of all kinds disappear. Fashion always seemed so restless that it was absurd to any sensible mind, but now fashion has taken over everything. The newest periodicals exist to tell us what is up-to-the-minute in all sections of human activity—who and what are 'in touch', who and what are out. We are all—not only manufacturers, shopkeepers, restaurateurs, but politicians, artists, philosophers, scientists—in a huge dress show, modelling hard. And clearly a society behaving like this is well on its way towards intellectual and moral bankruptcy and final idiocy. So how will being dynamic help? We don't need an accelerated pace but a change of direction.

I shall be told that I am an elderly man, surfeited with change, afraid of the future (I am, too). But when I condemn society I am thinking about people much younger than myself, and all the evidence, from chaos in the arts to vandalism and violence in the streets, suggests that it is the young who are restless, dissatisfied, longing for something they cannot find. And I do not believe that what they long for is our society plus a giant dynamo, to speed up everything. This explains their sceptical attitude towards the politicians and their perorations, because what they are promised is more and more of the same kind of thing we have now, coming at a faster rate. They grow beards and throw away their neckties to demonstrate that they are not with it. What they are not with is the Madison Avenue idea of life, which we are told we can fulfil if we are sufficiently dynamic. It is as if we were all asked to run as hard as we can go to catch sight of a new advertisement of a detergent.

Many moralists of my generation condemn our society, especially in its more American aspects, for being too 'materialistic'. They seem to me to have missed the point. 1965 is in fact less materialistic than 1900 or 1865. And America is less materialistic than Europe. What is wrong with the American style of life we are so busy reproducing is that it starves both the soul and the senses. It chiefly exists in a sterile realm of figures, diagrams, abstractions, in which flesh and blood and the taste and touch and solidity of material things are just a nuisance. (It is entirely masculine: women instinctively hate it and are only kept from revolt by being blinded by science and technology, Cold War propaganda, the H-bomb.) This realm has a dehumanising process that is beginning to make all cities look alike and all food taste the same, and is already making plans to replace any organ of the body that gives trouble with something made of plastics. It would like everything to be made of plastics. It makes the world seem more and more monotonous, boring, anaesthetising to everybody except its own experts, practitioners, power men. But it is not materialistic; it is bloodlessly immaterialistic, which is worse, and it is about as close to the good life as *Time* magazine to Keats's poetry.

Apart from the lowest social level, on which even the very elements of decent living are still lacking, it seems to me that we should now concentrate on quality and not on quantity. We need fewer things but better things. Too much time, energy and money are spent now in the manufacturing and advertising and marketing of junk. Too many men and women put themselves in pawn because they have acquired things they never really wanted in the first place. And the quality of so much that is readily sold and bought has gone down and down. Bad workmanship is taken for granted now; if we want something properly made, of a quality that our grandfathers assumed to be there at any price, we have to pay four or five times as much. We can buy, let us say, a boojum-teaser for 17s. 6d., but if we want something that can be depended upon to tease boojums for a few years, then nothing less than the special £3 10s. article will do. There are of course honourable exceptions, but too many people are in this Admass racket, which, as I have suggested before, is idiotic because the men who are cheating the customers to make more money do not remember that when they come to spend that money, then they will be cheated too. And, as I have also suggested before, there is an atmosphere here that begins to corrupt everybody who has to exist in it.

However, this does not mean I have nothing to suggest that I have not suggested before. I have— and it is this. We should not be asked to go blinding on, demanding more and more of what we have now, devoting ourselves to lines on a chart. A bad pattern is not improved by being enlarged. If we are already going wrong, then by hurrying we shall go even wronger. And I believe that an enormous number of people, doing all manner of jobs, feel this instinctively. That is why they don't respond to these eloquent appeals for new and more dynamic drives. If they don't particularly like what they have, they don't want more and more of the same, they want something different.

Many of them long for a little peace of mind. They

would like to be members of a society not so obviously restless, dissatisfied, close to violence, rushing God knows where. At heart they do not want to earn another £10 a week, to begin paying for a car, colour television, a larger washing-machine. They may want some radical reforms—as I do—but on the other side of those reforms they would like to see a society that would not be always using a stopwatch and taking its temperature, a society that had some better standards than those of a fashion parade, a society in which a man could consider, without fear and panic, his own position in it and the future of his family. Such people, who have all my sympathy, don't want to hurry along but to settle down, if only for a change. They would welcome a chance to escape from this endless worrying and nagging about production, prices and wages, from all the Admass devices to tempt somebody in the family to try more hire purchase, perhaps for an opportunity at last to feel something deeply, to think a bit, or to enjoy that little peace of mind. And these, please note, don't cost money; you haven't to work overtime to acquire them; and of course because they don't swell anybody's profits, no campaigns are being planned to recommend them.

So this is far from being a Tory argument. It is the Tories, as we know after 13 years of them, who are happy with Admass. It could be a Labour argument, but only, I feel, if Labour begins to correct and develop its thinking, which so far, perhaps of necessity, has been too narrowly concerned with figures and charts. The great question, like a vast curve of fire in the night, still remains—What kind of lives are people living? If they are so fortunate to be living now, as they are so often told, then why does the crime rate go up and up, why is there so much vandalism and violence, so much cynicism or apathy, so little sense of a common purpose, so small and feeble an identification with the community, with that very society which they are told has done so much for them? Drive and dynamism are all very well, but they may be dangerous if the driver doesn't know where he is going and the dynamo has been installed to produce only more trash and folly.

Student Mobs

BEING A FAIR-MINDED man, I begin this piece by admitting that I may have some slight prejudice against students. This is stronger on the negative than on the positive side. It is not that I dislike students as such; it is more that, unlike so many people, remembering their youth, I don't regard student antics through a nostalgic haze. True, I was a student myself once, but then by the time I went up to Cambridge, in the Michaelmas Term of 1919, I was a man not an overgrown boy, already in my twenty-sixth year and a battered old soldier. I wanted to get on with my life and not clown around with lads newly released from school and given their first cheque-books.

I didn't see then—and have never seen since—why young men in universities, turning themselves into mischievous and sometimes dangerous mobs, should be treated indulgently, as if they were quite different from mobs of garage hands, apprentice fitters, bus-drivers. Indeed, there is a case for more severity. Students are not supposed to be ignorant and stupid. If they are, then they should be sent home and not receive higher education at public expense. They are wasting not only their own but also other people's time, energy and money. There must be countries now in which peasants are going without substantial meals and some decent clothes so that a lot of lads can spend several years in universities. Such lads should begin to develop a sense of responsibility. They should be the last and not the first to create howling destructive mobs. They should be reading books, not burning them.

It is not the occasional 'rags' that get out of hand I am thinking about now; it is the so-called 'demonstrations' that seem to make an appearance every few nights on the TV news. I do not care whose side they are supposed to be on, I am more and more depressed and revolted by these idiot processions, with their banners and slogans and mindless grinning faces, on their way to break windows, smash cars, burn furniture and books, terrify women and children, and to reduce international law, custom and sensible usages to chaos. In many instances, of course, these 'demonstrations' are anything but student improvisations, having been organized by governments on a secret rent-a-mob basis. Even where governments have apologized, it is hard to believe that the student mobs could not have been checked and dispersed before any real damage was done. And this is all part of the darkening picture.

We live in a curious age. We are offered glimpses of a genuine world civilization slowly emerging—the UN special agencies, organizations like Oxfam, and here and there, as I have seen for myself, remote enterprises, dedicated to healing or education, with international staffs of selfless enthusiasts. And such glimpses warm the heart and brighten hope. But along with these are sights and sounds that suggest that the whole fabric of civilization, the work of centuries, is rapidly being torn apart. Two official policies clash, and instantly embassies, consulates, centres of information services, are surrounded and then attacked by howling mobs of students, at once defying law, custom, usage. And that this may not be merely so many hot-headed lads escaping all control, that it may itself be part of government policy, mob antics as additional propaganda to deceive world opinion, makes our situation even worse. It is as if we were all compelled to exist now in a sinister circus. No doubt governments have always been dishonest and hypocritical, but now it is beginning to look as if power-mania is ready to destroy those long-accepted forms and civilities that make international relations possible. The time may soon come when ambassadors will have to move around in tanks, and embassies and consulates will have to be fortified or abandoned. And perhaps students on admittance will be given machine-guns and flame-throwers.

There is something else, just as bad, perhaps even worse, and evidence of it is amply supplied to us by TV cameras and mikes. What we see in these student faces illuminated by burning cars and bonfires of books is not the glow of political enthusiasm but a frenzied delight in destruction. Whatever country or party they may be demonstrating for or against, what really inspires them is an urge towards violent demolition. They don't know—and may never know —how to make anything worth having, but they need no courses on wrecking and destroying. If degrees were given in window-smashing, car-overturning furniture-firing, they would all have them with honours. They may still be weak in sciences and the arts, medicine and the law, but they already have Firsts in Hooliganism. I doubt if some of them even know which side they are shouting for, their minds having abandoned the intricate and tedious arguments of politics as they joyfully contemplate the destruction of other people's property. What sort of doctors and lawyers and chemists and teachers of languages they will make, we cannot tell; but there should be no shortage of recruits with degrees for demolition squads and wrecking crews. Soon there may appear on many a campus those huge iron balls with which New York keeps knocking itself down. At a signal from the Ministry of Foreign Affairs, out they will roll, to demolish an embassy or two before it is time for any evening seminars.

In this enthusiasm not for politics but for destruction and violence, these students may be said to be taking their proper place, right up there in the van, giving a lead to youth everywhere. For we live, I repeat, in a curious age, which is trying hard to abolish want and disease but is also abolishing, without trying, any regard and respect for other people's possessions. And it is in the countries where lads are now most carefully and expensively nurtured that they proceed to knock hell out of everything. They may grow up under capitalism or socialism but what they really care about is vandalism. Now that they have sufficient money to take special trains to football matches, they will wreck them on the way back. Well-paid and full-fed youth has already done more damage than all the hungry millions of the Bleak Age. Towns that would not risk a penny rate for the arts are now having to face a bigger bill every year to restore public property that has been idiotically or malevolently destroyed. A woman who had taught in junior schools for forty years told me that the most recent children were far and away the most destructive she had ever known: they just wanted to smash things. It is as if creatures from other planets had arrived, taking the shape of playful kids who put things on the lines in the hope of de-railing expresses.

It was rough in the North when I was a boy there. Boys came to elementary schools in clogs; on Saturday nights there were drunken fights, with much smashing of crockery, in the streets 'back o' t'mill'; and when in my middle teens I played football (sometimes on grounds made out of cinder tips) in a local league, both players and spectators could be very rough indeed. But I don't recall any of this curiously malevolent destructiveness and this violence that mark our present time. If youngsters, together with their parents, were aggressively rough, it was because they knew no better, but I cannot remember any of the deeply disturbing psychopathic element that seems so common today. There might be fights between pugnacious equals but helpless people were not being half-killed merely to round off an evening's amusement. Our destructiveness and violence today do not seem to come from any surplus of energy but from a neurotic or even psychotic heartlessness, a cold disregard of other persons, a hatred of life. And something very much like it, only of course further developed and more subtle, has crept like a huge cold serpent into too much of our fiction and drama. There are people among us who don't seem to belong to the human race. And while I won't join a mob to smash their windows, overturn their cars, burn their furniture and books, I'll be damned if I'll admire 'em.

It is all very odd, bewildering, really rather frightening, for while we can just about deal with it today, what will it be like tomorrow? No sooner do we appear to have made the world safer than a strange half-mad gleam comes into its eyes. The young arrive eager not to create but to destroy. The students never march to build a house but only to knock one down. Like those sinister puffs of steam we notice in New York streets at night, threats of violence, puffing from some hell below, multiply even while we elaborate the techniques and apparatus of a world civilization. And though I am familiar with all the usual explanations— H-bomb, no religion, bad homes and irresponsible parents, dead-end jobs, boring environment, and the rest—I remain puzzled, never entirely convinced, still wondering if there might not be some unknown factor, a vast X in the dark. Meanwhile, I think I could take some newsreel footage showing me students making something instead of breaking something— or even just studying.

Censor and Stage

THIS IS A more complex and difficult subject than it is generally allowed to be. Naturally it seems absurd that a serious dramatist cannot reach the stage without being first inspected by an elderly Court official and his assistants. If the Lord Chamberlain won't have this and objects to that, then we ought to pelt him with old scripts and large blue pencils and drive him out of office. But truth—and not any tenderness for the Lord Chamberlain—compels me to point out that we are over-simplifying the situation here. His lordship's office has two functions. And the second of these, the one almost always overlooked, is not concerned with censoring plays but with giving them a licence to be performed.

Once they are in possession of this licence, the dramatist and his manager and his players, so long as they don't begin changing all the lines and the 'business', are safe from interference. The Coketown Borough Council cannot send somebody on Tuesday to cut the third act. The police cannot march in on Wednesday to close the show and arrest the cast. The magistrates, sitting on Thursday, cannot start bullying and fining everybody. Mrs Grundy and her friends, purple in the face and screaming, cannot hound the company out of town. And what cannot happen here, because of our licensing system and its official protection, has often happened elsewhere, notably in America. To assume it would never happen here, whatever our circumstances, to believe that our city and borough councils, police, magistrates, Mrs Grundies, would never adopt such illiberal and intolerant attitudes is to take up residence in dreamland.

Let us suppose that all this Lord Chamberlain censoring and licensing were abolished next month. What would happen? First, those writers and directors who love shock tactics, who genuinely believe (some of them, anyhow) that it is good for an audience to be unpleasantly surprised, startled, shocked, disgusted, revolted, would rush to the far limit of what actors and actresses would be ready to perform. (And Mr Tynan, who after all is literary adviser to the National Theatre, has announced in public that he for one would allow sexual intercourse to be seen on the stage, if a play demanded it; though I doubt if he has really worked this out—'props' and all.) There would then be hell to pay. Plays would be opening and closing in a blizzard of writs, injunctions, arrests, fines; and play-writing, directing, acting, would become dangerous occupations. The theatre would run into so much trouble that it would soon decide to censor itself. Nursing its wounds, it would probably be far more timid, playing for safety, than the Lord Chamberlain himself. And the Cruel and Absurd boys, the *Take-a-look-at-this, you squares* types, would be worse off than they are now.

People who argue for complete freedom in the theatre always seem to me to ignore certain important factors. One of these is the peculiar state of English society at the present time. Widely accepted standards of taste, conduct, feeling, have almost vanished.

[143]

As directors of TV programmes know only too well, our public now reaches the widest possible extremes, from *Anything Goes* to *Nothing Goes*. The Battersea Girls arrive to face the indestructible Mrs Grundy. In one suburb they will take six teenagers raping an elderly woman; in another a hand on an ankle is disgusting. There may be a lot of people in the middle, many of them just waiting for a pension or death, who don't much care what happens, but towards the extremes the Cavaliers and Roundheads are at it again. And the appearance of a free anything-goes theatre may be the signal for the puritan rearguard to turn and transform itself into another charge of Ironsides. And God (presumed to be on their side) only knows what might be swept away then.

Another important factor, generally ignored, is concerned with the profound difference between what is read and what is actually seen taking place between solid bodies, on the stage. A play in performance is not just another book, as so many opponents of any censorship seem to imagine. What may be read about or even discussed on the stage (and I for one would allow very wide limits here) is very different from what is actually *seen*. Take sex, as the most obvious example. It is deeply subjective, something felt from the inside, and we can best appreciate it by being made to share a lover's thoughts and feelings. But unless we happen to be *voyeurs*—and most of us aren't—we simply don't want to regard sex from the outside, to watch two bodies turning into the beast with two backs. As soon as sexuality is intense, it should be private; the lovers should move into the next room.

And this is not some sort of prudery that ought to be challenged; it is part of our common human nature, which the theatre exists to show us. I have no doubt that people like Mr Tynan are not simply talking for effect but really wish to champion the intelligent and sensitive dramatist who needs complete freedom. But in my view a dramatist who insisted upon showing us sexual intercourse would be neither intelligent nor sensitive. He would be defeating his own ends.

Even now, when there is a Lord Chamberlain with a blue pencil, some of our younger playwrights are defeating themselves by insisting upon certain scenes he was probably reluctant to pass. They seem to me to be lacking here not only experience but imagination: they read their plays without visualizing them in front of an audience. So they introduce scenes of violence that might pass in a tough melodrama, a simple goodies v. baddies affair, but are as much out of place in plays about human relationships as a tank would be in a ballet. The fact that such scenes might occur among these people in real life is beside the point. The playwright, like any other artist, has to be selective; he has to decide what sort of attention, what kind of response, he needs from his audience; and he will go wrong if he mixes powerful broad effects, which make us want to shout for a doctor and the police, with small subtle effects, a remark here, a tone of voice there. If we have just seen somebody carted off, beaten up and bleeding, we are not ready to appreciate the lack of true communication between the characters left on the stage. And if anybody tries to rebut this by mentioning Shakespeare, I can only reply that these playwrights are not Shakespeares and are not in fact writing his kind of drama and that we in the audience are not Elizabethans. I will also add that some of our young directors, not long out of their Kotts, have been busy recently exaggerating Shakespeare's violence, so that when he asks for two eyes to be put out, they try for six.

All too often there is something disingenuous in the claims made on behalf of the cruel and violent drama. The chaps who direct it may be painfully doing a public service, rescuing us from our complacency, and then again they may not: they may be just enjoying themselves in their own way, well aware, as showmen, that shock tactics can lead to some very useful publicity. And there seems to me no truth in their notion that we can be purged of our longing for violence by having our noses rubbed in it at the playhouse. All the evidence disproves this. The glaring face of violence may be seen everywhere now, on stages and screens and in hundreds of millions of printed pages. But where is all the purging? If this theory worked, our streets ought to be safer than they ever were before, our police forces over-manned and not notoriously under-manned. Violence in real life ought to be on the way out, and even drama directors who never read newspapers must know this is not true. Many older playgoers of course are not fascinated by these shows of violence, they simply feel sick. So they very naturally stay away from the playhouse. Who wants to go to the theatre to feel sick?

So far I have been merely negative. Now I will try to make a few positive suggestions, if only to serve as some rough sort of basis for future discussions. To begin with—and this may seem surprising—I would abolish the Lord Chamberlain and his office. There is too much tradition behind them; they are too much a part of the Establishment; and this explains why even now, when they are far more tolerant about sex and violence than they used to be, they are still far too suspicious, cautious, sticky, about politics and religion. (It is clearly absurd that a revue, designed for a small audience, should be forbidden to pillory a political leader, when TV programmes, watched by millions, can do it all the time.) We may need some form of censorship but it should represent not the Establishment but theatrical experience and some knowledge of public taste and feeling.

Bearing in mind our society as it is at present, I suggest what follows. A playwright or manager who wants a licence, to give him complete protection, submits a script to this Censor-Licenser, pays a fee, agrees to delete this or modify that, then receives his licence. After that nobody can interfere with his play, telling him that what might pass in London will not be tolerated in Birmingham or Manchester. If the playwright or manager sharply disagrees with the Censor-Licenser, or has been prepared to go ahead from the first without a licence, then he is at liberty to proceed with his production, but of course without any official protection, at the mercy of local authorities, police, magistrates, outraged Mrs Grundies. If he wants to do exactly what he likes, then he must take the chance of other people wanting to do what *they* like, which may include putting him in the dock or running him out of town. (Remember, the stage is very much a public thing—not private, like reading.) But he can't refuse to apply for a licence and yet demand the protection it would give him; he can't have it both ways; though, of course, that is just how we all want to have it.

Road to Samarkand

IN THE END, though, it was my hat and not my heart that I lost in Samarkand. These hats, which have unusually wide brims, are made for me by Scotts, but even so, they require a year or two's training before the crown is low enough and the brim takes on strange curves. They make me look like something between a folk philosopher and a decayed bandit; an effect of ruffianly intellectuality is what I am aiming at. But as soon as they are reaching their own seedy perfection, these hats vanish. Suddenly they move away from me in some unknown dimension. One left me in Australia, and now this one in Samarkand. Perhaps it shared my disappointment.

Not that the road there was disappointing. Mostly it was a road somewhere in the air, where we sat in big jets, turboprops, or two-engined planes for the short hops in Uzbek. We did only one journey by train, but spent many hours, some of them anxious, in cars, usually high on mountain roads, sometimes being driven in clouds of dust by madmen. I may not look it but I am an apprehensive man. Perhaps that is why the hat deserted me in Samarkand: it was disgusted by the sweat of terror.

Here I must explain—if only because *before* will soon keep popping in—that I spent about three months in the Soviet Union in the autumn and early winter of 1945. Then I was really a guest of the state —there was no other way to see the country—but this time I went as a tourist, paying our way out of some royalties I collected in Moscow. I must add, however, that we were given much help and hospitality from the Writers' Unions, not only in Moscow but also in the capital cities of the smaller republics. In Stalin's time these writers might have made a fuss over me because they were under orders to do so. But not now, when they can please themselves. And how many foreign writers have I ever met—or seen off on a black wet night—at London Airport? Not one. Here we tend to think of writers *qua* writers—I do not count friends—as competitors not colleagues. We attack rather than defend one another, while our huge indifferent public, waiting for livelier gladiatorial combats, yawns as our blood stains the sand.

I did not recognize the Moscow I saw between the international airport and the centre of the city, there had been so much building. And this happened elsewhere, especially in Erevan, which now has a central square that is enormous and magnificent, with an opera house, art gallery and museum. The truth is, in this matter the Soviet people and the British are opposites. They build a tremendous opera house but do not finish the paving outside. We pave very carefully but the street does not arrive at anything likely to uplift the heart of man, unless you have a passion, which I do not share, for immense office blocks. What is their top priority is our lowest, probably not getting into the list at all, and vice versa. So we are all at crosspurposes. A real world civilization, somewhere at the other side of our nuclear imbecility, awaits the end of these crosspurposes, a frank assessment of what is best in both systems. It will be created, if ever, by men and women who are neither Communists, inflexible Marxist-Leninist pedants, nor Anti-Communists, equally inflexible and rather more neurotic, but are sensible citizens of the world.

What impressed me most on this second visit was the astonishing amount of new building, whatever its quality may be, then the tremendous drive towards education in all forms, which no visitor in his senses can doubt, and finally the new atmosphere, not to be mistaken after seventeen years' absence, of comparative freedom and frank talk, with no more looking over the shoulder and lowering the voice. There may still be too many rigid ideas, too much unnecessary censorship (as I told my Russian friends and their Press), too much insistence on keeping the door almost closed when it should be opened wider every year, but this is not the police state it was. And in the arts the thaw is on.

From Moscow we went to Yalta, which I had not visited before. I am no literary pilgrim but I wanted to see the house where Chekhov wrote *The Three Sisters* and *The Cherry Orchard*. We stayed at the Writers' Rest House, beautifully situated and nicely run but perhaps rather too much on girls' boarding school lines for our depraved Western taste. For my part I doubt the wisdom of keeping writers so much together—in their excellent Moscow club, their blocks of flats, their villages, their Rest Houses. They ought, I felt, to be seeing more of other professional men and women—though of course many of their wives or husbands are engaged in other professions—

[151]

and less of one another. But then I do not think of a writer as the state's literary performer, no matter how admirable its financial and other arrangements may be for him, but as somebody brooding apart, owing allegiance to nobody but his readers and playgoers, a seer rather than a kind of civil servant.

The southern coast of the Crimea is very fine in a Riviera style, which is not one I care much about, whereas in Armenia, where we went next, the stupendous and the sublime begin. There is mountain scenery here that would have driven the old romantic painters out of their minds. I tried to get a bit of it down in *gouaches*, which I use as other people use cameras, when I went on expeditions organized so that my wife could see various ruins and sites. On one of them we arrived at the head of a vast gorge—just the location for anybody wanting to film *Kubla Khan*—where there was a cave monastery that had been in use for a thousand years or so, and where some peasants were about to sacrifice a sheep, untroubled by the thought they were now Soviet citizens. Another day we went up to Lake Sevan, a strangely dark lake in a glaring white landscape, and there, in a remote inn, they set before us glorious salmon-trout fresh from the water. We watched with horror as the rest of our party poured vinegar over this delicate flesh, and, mayonnaise being unknown in these regions, we made do with butter. I also watched in some trepidation our chauffeur, who was sitting next to me, drink toast after toast in Armenian cognac. However, he delivered us safely if somewhat dazed in Erevan.

The new opera house was fine, but the Armenian

opera in the Western style, *Anoush*, was excruciatingly tedious, unlike the actual Ensemble of folk dancers and singers, who were delightful. But my favourite character in Erevan—and I trust she will forgive this pleasantry—was the lady who was head of the Tourist and Information Department. She was an extraordinarily handsome brunette, all dark flashing glances, fluttering eyelashes, smiles and dimples, who might have been a mischievous princess in the *Arabian Nights*. There flowed from her red lips a stream of statistics on Armenian metal production, industrial and agricultural developments, available electric current per head of population, and similar topics, while she still looked and sounded as if we were in some moonlit rose garden. By the time she had given us the last figures for copper and cotton, I had imagined a little scene for a comedy. But there is still communication in this mad world, for suddenly, as we were about to part, she looked at us and laughed, squeezed my wife's hand and gave my shoulder an almost caressing rub, as if to tell us that Logos had not utterly defeated Eros. I like to think that at this moment she is telling somebody about manganese production and new hydraulic pressures, her eyes dancing away, every dimple at work.

They missed a sale in one shop in Erevan. I saw a carved walking stick I fancied and, longing to spend some money, went into the shop, a kind of draper's, to buy it. There were two counters, two girl assistants. One counter was being besieged—a familiar sight—but at the other counter the girl was attending only to

her own thoughts. I pointed to the stick. She shook
her head, and made it plain that sticks could only be
bought from the other girl, who had sufficient customers to keep her busy for the next hour. I tried
more miming—I am very good at it and can now
mime a breakfast order for tea, toast, butter, four-
minute eggs, and honey—but it was no use. I mention this trivial incident because the rigid inflexibility
it represents, which may be found in large matters as
well as small, is undoubtedly one of the greatest
weaknesses of the Communist system. At one moment
you see it working with a boldness and sweep you
have to envy, and then the next moment you see it
running an obstacle race against itself, when a little
flexibility and common sense would make everybody
happier.

We made our one train journey from Erevan to the
neighbouring capital of Georgia, Tiflis, rumbling all
day round the mountains, in places running alongside
the Turkish frontier. The coach was wide, comfort-
able, cleaner than most of ours, and still kept the
excellent custom of having a samovar going to serve
free glasses of tea. It was late when we reached Tiflis
—I called it Tbilisi when I was there, but I remember
it as Tiflis from the time when I stared at it in *Chatter-
box*, sixty years ago—but the officials of the Georgian
Writers' Union were waiting for us. (And how many
hours have I spent hanging about Waterloo or Liver-
pool Street waiting to welcome foreign writers? Not
one.) It was the same hotel I had stayed in before, but
now the plumbing worked, unlike the man with a
uniform cap who always stood just inside the door.

He never did anything except look vaguely important, like some people here who are given titles for such service.

Tiflis is a long narrow city, squeezed between mountains. It has built furiously, like the others, but has also kept its leafy, narrow, rather romantic old streets. I am very fond of it, as indeed I am of the Georgians themselves, except when they insist, as they always do, upon drinking toast after toast accompanied by very long adulatory speeches. (It is said that two Georgians can go on making these speeches to each other hour after hour if the wine holds out.) They preserve a boozy ritual of filling and emptying horns that probably began to be frowned upon here about the time of Ethelred the Unready. As their hospitality was prodigious, and I preferred drinking vodka or cognac to wine, and a guest's glass must always be filled, some of these Georgian literary evenings ended very mistily indeed. I can remember reciting Hamlet's dying speech late one night to a crowded dinner table, but have no notion why I did it. (It was at a literary-cum-family dinner party, perhaps the very best we had, given by the poet Shalva Apkhaidze, born like me in 1894—a vintage year.) The men are expansive, voluble, poetic characters; the women are handsome, keep quiet, and pull faces as their husbands go on and on. There used to be far more Georgians in the Middle Ages than there are now; the men died fighting—or drinking—in the mountains, and the women were carried off to harems. But those who are left enjoy life in what is one of the most beautiful countries I know. Sooner or later it will be one of the world's great playgrounds; though I prefer it as it is.

When I was here before I spent a night at the collective vineyard of Tsinandali, in the magnificent Alazan Valley. This has a green and gold floor of vines and dry river beds, with cypresses and poplars for accents there; a near background of russet thickly-wooded hills, like rugs; and a far immense background of the Grand Caucasus, heights of purple and misty cobalt and shining icy peaks. It is almost too picturesque to be true, as if a superhumanly vast opera-and-ballet were about to be performed there. This enchanted region I had to see again, so a two-car expedition was organized for us, with poets coming along, together with the mayor of the province. Going through the mountains on side-roads, on a bright windless morning, the trees on fire with autumn, we had an encounter I hope never to forget. I have a sketch of the scene in front of me now.

Some fifty yards from the road, dark against the grass, the copper and gold of the trees, the amethyst of the mountains, was a group of peasants packed and crouched around a fire. Behind them were three of their pointed covered carts. They were returning, we discovered when we joined them, from a three-day pilgrimage to an ancient ikon in the mountains. They were eating skewered mutton, real *shashlik*, and roasted chickens, tomatoes and raw onion and mounds of the flat Georgian bread; and drinking young wine out of skins and bowls. They insisted that we should eat and drink with them. There were toasts, to which our poet, Josev Noneishyili, made eloquent replies.

Their spokesman, as roughly dressed and leathery-faced as the others but clearly an earnest and intelligent man, spoke to us on the evils of war and the necessity for peace. Food and drink, far beyond our capacity, were heaped before us; packed in between the sun and the fire we were hot, and the onion reek was powerful; but the curious friendly eyes and the crinkling smiles were irresistible. An old man—for these pilgrims were of all ages—began to pluck at some stringed instrument and then improvised a song of welcome to us; a boy of about fourteen began to dance, and he was soon joined by a sprightly old dame, with a face like a walnut shell; and more wine was poured out of skins, either down throats or into bowls for us. Except for our jet-propelled presence on the scene, everything there might have happened at any time these last thousand years. It may have been their eager hospitality and friendliness, the setting of the scene, or even the wine or the onions, but that road-side encounter in the mountains lingers in my memory like a dream, strange but meaningful.

How we feasted late that night at the guest house at Tsinandali and I drank far too much cognac; how next morning, calling up the last reserves, I did a *gouache* of the great valley that I am not ashamed of; how we bumped for miles in a cloud of dust to stare at an enormous ancient cathedral, dazzling and lonely against the mountains; how we lunched, far too late and most unwisely, with the mayor of Akhmeta, the friend and former teacher of our mayor, with both mayors getting gently plastered; how we offended the book-lovers of a town called Gourdzhaani by refusing, out of sheer exhaustion, to break our journey back to Tiflis to eat and drink with them until God knows what time: all these adventures I can mention but cannot describe here. We got back to Tiflis very late, half-dead in limb and body but with our memories blazingly alive.

Georgian hospitality and generosity are on an antique scale, unknown in Western Europe these last centuries. For example, we visited a distinguished Georgian artist of my generation, Lado Goudiashvili, who had a great success in Paris in the '20's. The walls of his big sitting room were covered with his work, mostly large pictures, but he noticed that we particularly admired a small powerful sketch-portrait of a Georgian primitive, now famous, who had lived and died in poverty and misery. When we were going, our host took this picture and put it into our hands: 'I saw you liked this. It is yours.' And ours it is. And if anything of this sort can happen in the studios of senior English painters, I would be glad of a few names and addresses.

Remembering my responsibilities as a literary man, I made the acquaintance—and a very pleasant acquaintance too, for they were mostly enthusiastic and good-looking women—of the teachers of English language and literature at the University and the Institute of Foreign Languages. In both places I faced large audiences of English-speaking students and undertook to answer their questions—'What about the Angry Young Men?'—that sort of thing. I think we all enjoyed ourselves. It happened that the Magazine of Foreign Literature, in Moscow, had just published

a complete translation of a nonsensical story of mine
called *The Thirty-First of June*. One student asked why
I had written it. I said I was nervous of explaining
why, in the Soviet Union and particularly in a university there, but the truth was—'I wrote it for fun'. At
which there was a roar of laughter and applause. Incidentally, what has happened to this story, which I
wrote as a lark and dedicated to my six grand-
daughters, is a good example of the odd twists in a
writer's life. For after I had almost forgotten about it,
the Americans pay a handsome sum for the option on
it as a musical, then when I arrive in the Soviet Union
I find about half a million Soviet citizens pondering
over its little jokes. All this in a world supposed to be
so terribly divided that we are prepared, some of us,
to blow away half of it!

Still accompanied by poets we rode out to the Tiflis
airport, to fly by big jet to Tashkent. These Soviet
airports and the flights out of them seem strange to
Western eyes. They are filled with peasants carrying
babies, bundles, giant watermelons and pomegranates
in string bags. They look as if they are about to climb
into a cart for a five-mile trip into a market town.
But they are all taking planes, many of them the great
jets flying non-stop for two thousand miles. Transport of all kinds is very cheap in the Soviet Union, and
as there are still more roubles than consumer goods to
be had, I suppose these peasants pop off, at nine miles
a minute, to let Grandma or Uncle Nasrulla take a
look at baby. They are good-humoured fellow passengers, though some of them have the alarming habit of
wandering around the cabins long after seat-belts

should have been fastened. Having carried so many
babies and bundles, the planes are beginning to look
rather shabby inside; but they seemed to me to keep
closer to their time-tables than most of our big jets do.
I suspect that the Russians, who largely staff these
services, are wonderfully efficient when the job is
difficult. Easier tasks, such as running an hotel or a
shop, bore them, so they don't bother. They are fine
advanced mathematicians and chess players, but still
use the abacus for simple arithmetic. If you don't find
something appealing in this, something closer to us
than the cold heavy efficiency of the Germans, then
don't go. We did, and were now roaring through the
night towards the Uzbek Republic, which I had never
seen before.

As we spent only a short time in its capital, Tashkent, on our way to Samarkand, but returned later for
a much longer stay, I shall save it, and drop us, in a
two-engined plane and far too early in the morning,
on to Samarkand's rather makeshift airport. If I say
this town was a disappointment, I do not mean that
there was anything particularly wrong with it—
though I would rather have stayed at its Intourist
Hotel when it had water but no taps, instead of a lot
of taps and hardly any water—as if they imagined we
could somehow *milk* the taps. But it was not the place
of my secret dreams, a maze of narrow streets with
camels and caravanserais and green turbans and
glimpses of courtyards and fountains. It is in fact a
spread-out, rather featureless town, with a lot of
lorries speeding along half-finished dusty boulevards.
'Today,' the Intourist booklet declares proudly, 'it is

a city of higher educational establishments and specialized secondary schools with an enrolment of twenty thousand students.' Quite so; but then, so is Wolverhampton, which never set me dreaming and hoping.

Timur, Tamerlane or Tamburlane, the ferocious conqueror, made Samarkand his capital, and is said to have brought into it 150,000 merchants and artisans, together with the best Muslim architects and craftsmen of the late Middle Ages. All that is left of his glorious capital, one of the wonders of the world in the old Eastern chronicles, are widely scattered remains of his and his family's mosques and mausoleums, the famous blue-tiled domes and minarets. I know this blue only too well, for I spent some hot hours—the sun was strong down there—trying to reproduce it, messing about with cerulean, cobalt and dabs of emerald green; and was much relieved afterwards, visiting various Uzbek art galleries, to find that better painters, with more time, had not come much closer to it than I had. Perhaps it was this failure, rather than the fact that I found myself shaving in half a glass of mineral water, or the mysterious disappearance of my hat, that soured me a little on Samarkand. But I have a feeling that, like Wordsworth's daffodils, those elusive blue domes will suddenly rise and bloom again in memory, probably about three o'clock on the darkest February afternoon. I travel, disliking almost every moment of it, for the benefit of involuntary memory and its marvels.

After a few days, we took another plane, again tealess at the crack of dawn, to Bukhara, which is a smaller, even dustier but perhaps more fascinating version of Samarkand. Blue domes and minarets again, but also innumerable fine examples of the *medress*, courtyards surrounded by the ancient cells of Muslim scholars, the town having had at one time a considerable population of these meditative characters, who vanished some time before they could present a problem to Soviet economy. There was nothing wrong with Bukhara, which was all it declared itself to be, and if we cut short our stay there, that was not its fault but ours. Pampered bourgeois types, we longed for baths and clean linen.

We found them in Tashkent, which may be one reason why I took a fancy to this city. There it is, between Asiatic deserts and huge mountain ranges, and from our point of view a hell of a long way from anywhere, and it is bigger—and far more cheerful—than Manchester. Within the new city, which might be almost anywhere, is the old Asiatic town with its narrow streets, markets and mosques, and a place I came to love called *The Old Men's Tea House*. (There you can either order from the kitchen or go and cook the stuff yourself over another fire. Sipping your tea you can stare above the heads of the men squatting on a carpeted dais, playing chess or sharing a hillock of pilaff, and see through the tall windows a semi-circular white bridge and weeping willows.) People from all over Asia seem to have settled in Tashkent, and its headgear ranges from turbans and embroidered scullcaps to our own cuptie wear. There is television, and my new friends, the Uzbek poets, are always reciting on it, at insistent public demand. How long this

[162]

demand will last, as science and technology bulldoze the poetry out of people, I do not know, but at the moment two different worlds meet there, as indeed they do, though less picturesquely, in other Soviet republics.

The people in this odd mixture seemed to me well-satisfied, not labouring under any deep grievances. I judged this from their behaviour in large crowds. For example, on a warm afternoon, I joined 70,000 of them to watch a football match—*Tashkent v. Red Army*. The home team, which played well in mid-field but lost confidence with goals in sight, was defeated 2 nil. The crowd was enthusiastic enough but had none of that bitter fury we know here, where men, with their side a goal or two down, seem to remember suddenly all their frustrations so that every defeated hope comes out howling. If we ever have a revolution here it will probably be sparked off by Sheffield United having a penalty given against them.

We saw much, indeed too much, though again it was astonishingly good-humoured, of the Tashkent crowd on the National Day (a public holiday) on November 7th. We were given the privilege—along with some American doctors and their wives—of watching the grand parade from a small enclosure near the saluting base. As the morning, starting at eight, wore on, and we had to keep standing there, hardly able to move and baked in the sun, we felt less privileged and more dubious, finally making our escape from the endless spectacle, very jolly for the first hour or so, of the banner-carrying, balloon-releasing civilian paraders. Before that we had had the military parade, very well done but in a rigid German goose-stepping style, with generals standing stiffly in cars and looking like belted and be-medalled idols. We even had a long hugely-amplified speech, the only one, from a general. Now I think people who talk—usually in all sincerity—so much about peace should not give such prominence to military displays. Mr Kruschev and his friends, I am afraid, do their cause, their belief in co-existence, much harm every November 7th. No doubt they make these parades of might to reassure their citizens. Our guide and interpreter, an extremely intelligent and civilized young anthropologist from the Moscow Institute, declared that if the Soviet Union abandoned its nuclear arms— 'Next morning the American paratroops would be in our streets'. And there are Americans who look under the bed for Communists. This is what propaganda can do. I suggest, before it is too late, we all lay off for a year or two.

One thing that is happening in the Soviet Union is that the younger painters are really beginning to paint, instead of doing socialist realism posters. It seemed to me I saw more good pictures, all by youngish Uzbek artists, in the Tashkent Gallery than I did a few years ago in the whole exhibition sent from Moscow to the Royal Academy. I could enjoy the painting much better than the singing, of which I heard a great deal, for the felicities of the strangulated Uzbek style, essentially Asiatic, escaped my ear. The dancers were fair, not equal to the best elsewhere, but gradually I paid more and more delighted attention to the men, artists to a man, who played the tambour for them, making a whole dramatic orchestra out of the thing. I rather hankered after buying one—there is an undying twelve-year-old somewhere in me— but was put off by being told that the tambours for sale were far inferior to the instruments I had heard, owned by these masters of the iron-and-velvet finger tips. It was small consolation to buy some of those embroidered skullcaps, which so many Uzbeks wear, even indoors, for not one of them fitted me. Though my pockets bulged with roubles, I bought very little —apart from vodka, cognac and chocolate, good at its best but absurdly expensive—during this long trip, for though there are far more shops than when I was here last, there is still very little a Western visitor wants to buy. The situation I had known so often in my youth, when I had no money and was surrounded by things I wanted to buy, was now ironically re- versed.

We made some small expeditions from Tashkent, one of them to an industrial town, making chemical fertilizer, at the foot of the Chatkal Mountains. Here there was a workers' club that would have driven Arnold Wesker crazy with envy; it had everything, including a cinema-cum-theatre for which I think I would cheerfully give any one of London's smaller playhouses. And all this is in a new town called Chirchik, not even to be found in my atlas, far at the back of beyond, with Afghanistan just round the cor- ner. It was that day we had dinner at the house of a village schoolmaster, a school friend of one of the Uzbek writers with us, a huge leisurely meal in rather cramped but not uncomfortable quarters, just a convivial occasion yet now taking on a dreamlike air. Yes, I liked Tashkent, and I am glad I did a sketch (not good) from our hotel window of the great square, with the high fountain in the middle and the fine new opera house on the other side. And the fact that I can no longer listen to the orchestra there does not worry me at all: it was terrible.

Back to Moscow then, a night flight of over two thousand miles with babies and bundles and all; and friends meeting us at the airport, where snowflakes seemed to glitter in the lights. Too much travelling and sight-seeing; too many toasts at night and none for breakfast; I was beginning to feel rather exhausted. But I was able to meet directors of publishing houses and editors of magazines; to join at their Club writers I had known before, such as Konstantine Fedin, Leonid Leonov, Korneli Zelinsky, Konstantine Simonov; to talk to the British correspondents, who agreed that both regulations and atmosphere were now much freer and easier; and I finally faced a large but very friendly Russian Press Conference. It is a mistake to suppose that Russians will take no criticism. Much depends on the spirit in which it is made, as it does with most women. In spite of its dour representatives abroad, Russia has a feminine soul.

One thing that worried me, which I mentioned, is not peculiar to the Soviet Union, though it may be more noticeable there. It belongs in fact to our age of science and technology and everything for the common man. It is the danger of lowering standards, of debasing the currency of living and the arts, of taste and behaviour, and of forgetting that it is uncommon men who bring common men towards a richer quality of experience, that we are here on earth not to cover it with robots or take dull minds to other planets but to serve *animus mundi* by enlarging and deepening human consciousness. All this I said, and more, asking them, now they are freer and stronger and their youth is stirring, to open the gates a little wider. Stalin is dead—and now, for all those who wait patiently in the bitter wind to enter the tomb in Red Square, he plays Lucifer to Lenin's God—but let us take care not to jeer and snarl and threaten too often or we may resurrect him.

I was glad to get back home; I always am, for this is the country where I can live; but there have been moments, as there were when I used to come back from the American South-West, when I have felt I had left a high and wide adventure to drop into a church bazaar, crowded with too many people quarrelling in too many different accents.

A note about Intourist, *into whose care you hand yourself if you want to visit the Soviet Union. In a moment of exasperation I said it must be being run by the American Secret Service, which offended nobody because it is regarded as rather a joke. Actually, it is not too bad. The brisk young women, who speak some English, are generally efficient, meeting tourists, arranging excursions, getting theatre tickets, and so on. The hotel rooms, though not good in the smaller places, are comparatively cheap. So is public transport, though hired cars are often outrageously expensive. Intourist food is poor, chiefly due to bad catering and an idiotic system that prevents hotels from buying* supplies from local stores. It would be better for everybody if tourists could acquire and spend roubles, as we did, instead of being compelled to use coupons in Intourist restaurants. Solitary touring is possible—we met an elderly American woman cheerfully enduring the discomforts of Samarkand and Bukhara—but not much fun; a large party must often run into difficulties; and I suspect that it would be best to travel with a group of six to eight. A few introductions would be wonderfully helpful; and any meal in any well-run private house or flat puts Intourist where it belongs. While some things, such as luxury foods, are expensive, other things—books and records, for example—are astoundingly cheap. Because Moscow is a big city, you will bump into people there (or they will bump into you) who may seem sour and ill-mannered, like many people in London, New York or Paris. But the average Soviet citizen is more eager to help, to please, to be liked, than most of us are. In this he is extraordinarily like the average American citizen. An odd world, isn't it?

Malaysian Visit

DURING OUR FIRST week in Singapore I don't think we ever saw the sun. Every day it rained heavily, and people were apologetic and said such weather was unusual. But I was quite happy. I sat about and smoked a lot and read old detective stories, and for days not a single idea entered my head. I felt contentedly idiotic, which is what I still feel.

Even when the sun did come out, Singapore—the place, not the community—fell a long way from what I had imagined. It seemed immense, crowded, and featureless, as if parts of Camberley and Wolverhampton had been mixed with a few Malayan Kampongs and a dozen Chinese shanty towns. Even in the bar of Raffles Hotel, still spacious and defiantly Edwardian, the city of Conrad and Somerset Maugham was fading fast. And outside, under the blaze of neon, everybody seemed to be selling or buying elaborate cameras, transistor sets, tape recorders.

In another part of the island is one of the largest housing developments I have ever seen. It is called Queenstown and very soon it will house—vertically for the most part—a population equal to that of Cambridge. It would be terrifying if it were not for the fact that the thousands of families, mostly Chinese, already installed there, hang out their washing on poles, signalling gaily at all heights. The family, these signals announce, has found a new and strange kind of roof, almost in mid air, but is triumphantly itself.

[169]

The poorer Chinese in the city, crammed into narrow streets where they tuck in at all hours at the little stalls selling unimaginable delicacies, are brisk, noisy and cheerful, members of an indomitable race. The richer Chinese, met at dinner parties, are different and rather odd. The men belong to recognizable types—the banker, the successful lawyer, the film magnate—and take on the superficial appearance of their Western counterparts while still clearly belonging to their own race. It is as if a Chinese repertory company were presenting a number of Western stock types.

Their wives are wonderfully elegant, smiling, and fed me at their dinner parties as if I were not a fat old author but a wounded bird. One delightful hostess, after telling me what an honour it was to have me at her table, left me dazed by asking me if my son was also writing in Dutch. The cultural bridge to the West is provided, in these circles, by *My Fair Lady*. Their houses are a queer mixture of the traditionally exquisite—heavenly blue Sung plates and the rest— and the contemporary tasteless.

An even odder mixture was provided by the Indian part of the community, mostly Tamil, at its annual religious festival of *Thaipusan*. Penitent young men go in procession carrying on their shoulders elaborate decorative structures that are fastened to their bare backs by metal hooks sunk into their flesh. They neither bleed nor appear to feel any pain, and when I saw them getting ready for the procession they were being photographed by worried-looking white men who had probably had hooks in their backs for years.

The whole thing seemed to be a fairly typical Indian mixture of piety, tinsel and peacocks' feathers, masochism and orangeade.

In a distant villa overlooking the sea, with a coloured fountain in the garden and flattened palms like gigantic illuminated fans, I was a guest at an elaborately organized Malay evening. It began with iced punch served in half coconut shells decorated with frangipani blossoms, and ended, after dinner and Malayan dancing, with a mock marriage. It was all very charming—the Malays are a handsome and graceful people, making us look like so many glaring horses—but it was also, drinks, dinner, dancing and all, rather lacking in vitality, in drive and guts, in precisely those qualities that other races here might easily supply.

This seems to me an important point. The politicians in Kuala Lumpur, whose speeches regularly make the front page in the two English-language newspapers as if they were all newly inspired, tell us that Malaysia is a viable multi-racial community. And so, I think, it is, and even if its democracy is a bit shaky, it is already something better than a capitalist's stooge or a piece of neo-colonial hocus-pocus. We are right to defend its promising infancy, even though sooner or later we shall have to pull out. And here I must add that I have nothing but admiration for the patience and good sense of the men in command of our Services here. They are behaving like cool wise policemen, not the easiest and most attractive role for fighting men.

Even so, I cannot help feeling that Malaysia is a

melting pot that ought soon to start some melting. As yet its racial ingredients are so many hard unyielding lumps. A successful Englishman, head of an old Singapore importing firm, assured me earnestly that all depended on each race (ourselves included, of course) making every effort to understand the other races, their religions, traditional observances, customs and habits. Clearly this is necessary in a multiracial society, though political and social grievances may remain. Thus, the Chinese join the police but not the army. And outside Singapore, four university places are open to Malay students for every one open to Chinese, even though the latter, as an English teacher pointed out, are much cleverer.

(But this judgement may be unfair to the Malays, who may be just as bright in their own way. The point is that their traditional culture is not literary and bookish—it produces painters, not writers, and prefers dancing to metaphysics—whereas the Chinese are born into an ancient tradition of literature and philosophy and bookishness.)

No doubt the creation of a peaceful multi-racial society is an achievement not to be despised. But it will be a good day for Singapore when at last that melting begins and those racial lumps in the pot are no longer hard and unyielding. It is from a fusion of races, a new mixture of peoples, that an original, adventurous and wonderfully rewarding culture springs. As the centre of such a culture, Singapore could be one of the most exciting cities in the world, an Eastern metropolis of the arts, instead of a featureless huddle of stores and stalls, cinemas and bowling alleys. So far its different races seem to have lost rather than gained by each other's proximity. Instead of turning into a real city, it is in danger of becoming a gigantic supermarket and car park. Its cultural vacuum is being filled by Admass.

I will pass over the absence of first-class bookshops, art galleries, concert halls, to consider the Theatre. Now in spite of its size and wealth, Singapore cannot support one small English-speaking professional repertory company. Indeed, it is a poor patron of visiting professionals or its own amateurs. I may be told that this is an unreasonable grumble, that Singapore is after all largely a Chinese city and the Chinese have their own theatres and touring opera companies. But I can't pass this. Two English-language newspapers circulate widely in Singapore; American paperbacks sell briskly; and the big cinemas show films in English, not always with Chinese subtitles. The truth is, the increasing number of Chinese who understand English mostly pass into the world in which the Theatre and serious books don't matter and the arrival of the film of *My Fair Lady* is the cultural event of the year. And let me add that the British Council (which I visited not only in Singapore but also in Kuala Lumpur and Penang) isn't at fault here: it is doing all it can, within its limited resources. But if the Singapore that turns to the West prefers to go slumming in it, intellectually and artistically, what can a few hard-pressed men do? No, Singapore will rise from an over-blown trading post into a true and magnificent city when at last the contents of the pot begin to melt.

We took a picnic lunch one day over the causeway into Johore. After driving a couple of hours, we turned up a side track, on the way to some abandoned enterprise, and unpacked our baskets on the narrow brow of a hill. Below, so close you could toss a chickenbone into it, was untamed tropical Asia, jungle so thick, dark and infinitely forbidding that you had only to look at it to imagine yourself lost in it, moving no more than a few yards every hour, perhaps at last screaming for daylight and a path going anywhere. And next time 'operations in the jungle' are mentioned, I shall remember that shuddering glimpse I had. Much further north, we have tiny groups of men who crawl through such places for weeks, even months on end, in our service; and we don't even know their names.

We visited Malacca, Penang and Kuala Lumpur. Malacca was rather disappointing, chiefly because it bears one of the magic names of world travel, haunting you in your untravelled youth, and no actual place can live up to such magical associations. (Samarkand was disappointing too.) But we did visit an old Chinese house, owned by a wealthy family. Unlike the hilltop villas of the richer Chinese in Singapore, this house in an older tradition had a narrow front in a narrow street, pretending a great modesty. But once inside we found room opening into room, sometimes with little patios between them, until we had almost forgotten what the heavily barred entrance hall had been like. We also visited a Chinese temple where some kind of service was being held, with two rows of saffron-robed priests facing each other and all

[174]

the accompaniments of gongs, drums, incense and incantations. Meanwhile, another saffron-robed one, speaking some English, was showing us round, explaining this and that, completely ignoring the service, which we felt we might interrupt at any moment. As I have noticed elsewhere, it is the irreligious like us, and not the cheerfully dedicated, who suffer from embarrassment. Malacca was taken by the Portuguese early in the sixteenth century, then by the Dutch in the seventeenth century, then by the British. Whose turn is it next? Or have we, at long last, done with all that?

I found in myself a slight prejudice against Penang simply because one of the unpleasantest sergeants I met in the First War (and I met some stinkers) came from the police there. But this prejudice vanished when we began moving round the island. On the shore to the north there are exquisite glimpses of pink sand striped with dark brown sand and emerald pools and turquoise or glittering sea beyond the palm fronds, and in the fishing villages the nets, most often black but sometimes a lightish ginger shade, were strung out along the sandbanks, and small children, a gleaming bronze, played among the double-pronged black boats—all a painter's paradise. It is all too far away, I suppose, and Soekarno may still be threatening and raving beyond the distant blue shapes that are Indonesia; but a man with an eye, even if he has never mastered any brushwork, might splendidly idle away the worst of our winter there in Penang.

If Singapore seems to be all people and no city, Kuala Lumpur seems to be all city and no people. It has that wide bright empty look that so many rather artificial capital cities seem to have. Some of the buildings, notably the new Parliament House and the museum, are very fine indeed, and often have an unexpected Moorish appearance. Indeed, the railway station, which is at once magnificent and daft, is so be-domed and bedizened that it seems as if some caliph out of the *Arabian Nights* had commanded a station to be built. Within, it is both spacious and soothing, having everything except trains and passengers, a welcome relief in an increasingly noisy and over-crowded world.

We were offered and accepted some very pleasant hospitality in Kuala Lumpur, and admired, with some reservations, the British Council show of modern Malaysian painting. But the best thing we found there was some twelve miles out, nearer the jungle that it serves. This is the hospital for the jungle 'aborigines' (the term is not strictly correct, I am told) that has been run for the last ten years, all on a shoe-string, by a delightful young English doctor, Malcolm Bolton. Whole families of these small, very dark jungle folk are often brought in by helicopter, no other transport being possible, and we saw scores of them in ward after ward. Dr Bolton—a born charmer as well as an enthusiast—has taught former patients, now back in the jungle, to work radio sets, to call him and his helicopters if some Stone Age man or woman, in that green dusk, should go to hospital.

We were enchanted by Dr Bolton and his helpers and his primitive patients and his homely little hospital and everything he was doing. They exist in the world I like best, not that of the old stiff imperialism, nor that of the new Afro-Asian nationalism, with its rather wearisome cliché oratory and over-statements, but that of what we might call individualistic supra-nationalism, which makes one man leave his home and friends and an easy career to go thousands of miles to help other men who need his help. This is the world I want to see, and already we are being given glimpses of it. And the best of the young are being drawn to it, hearing its distant piping in their dreams.

Out of this Malaysian visit, I shall remember long-est, because they seem to me its most significant episodes, first, Dr Bolton and his hospital, and secondly, the dinner after the University party in Singapore. We were invited on the spur of the moment to this dinner, which took place in a small back room of a Chinese restaurant in 'The New World', which is in fact an extremely noisy fairground. Anything further removed from our idea of the silent inscrutable East than this dinner can hardly be imagined. The fairground was noisy and glittering; in the main room of the restaurant a huge Chinese wedding party was drinking its 'Bottoms Up!' with deafening yells; and our back room, with about twenty of us squashed round a table too small for us, and all of us (except the Chinese and Malayan ladies, coolly elegant to the last) getting hotter and hotter, noisier and noisier, messier and messier, while one steaming mound of food succeeded another and more and more tea or beer or whisky was poured out. After two or three hours I for one was a wreck—but a happy wreck.

But in what, you may ask, lies its significance?

Simply in this—that squashed round that table, keeping their cool elegance or turning themselves into happy wrecks, were people belonging to a dozen different races or nationalities. Here, in steamy conviviality, arguing but not quarrelling, was the true United Nations, yet another glimpse of that other world, the only one that has a chance of surviving, in which people are real people, not units of this, symbols of that, but individuals, capable of relationships crossing frontiers and escaping from ideologies. And the fact that their eyes and hair and skins are not all alike adds to the variety and pleasure of their company. Most of the younger British I met out here, mostly belonging to our various public services, already recognize this new world. Some of the older sort, regretting so many changes, never allow themselves a glimpse of it, and are so sad. But I, as old as they are, am not sad, for I know it is with us and growing, and also know it is the only world worth a damn.

Hong Kong and Canton

HONG KONG IS fascinating—but for a reason not mentioned in any advertisement or travel booklet. It is true that Hong Kong occupies a very high place in the imaginary world of JAD, that is, Jet Age Dreamland, where smiling couples, bound for a second honeymoon, are for ever choosing canapés offered them by beautiful air hostesses. It is only in JAD, not in the real world, that nibbling a bit of tired smoked salmon at 33,000 feet is an ecstatic experience.

And certainly Hong Kong is a name of power in JAD. Offer any lady, from Birmingham, Warwickshire, to Birmingham, Alabama, a trip to Hong Kong, and within an hour she will be packing. And she won't pack too much because she sees herself deliriously shopping both on Hong Kong Island and across the water at Kowloon, crammed with exotic bargains, all an enchanting mixture of Sale Prices and Chinoiserie.

Not being a shopper on this level, I don't know whether she will be disappointed or not. The only shopping I have done in Hong Kong has been not for the body but for the soul of man—tobacco and whisky. But it seems to me that it is only at certain moments that the real Hong Kong matches its JAD image. At night, for example, it all looks wonderful. The innumerable ships at anchor are illuminated; the busy little ferries are like glittering water beetles; and on each side of Victoria Harbour there are faerie forests of Chinese signs in red, orange, blue and green neon.

The fact that we cannot read these signs encourages us to believe they are inviting us to fall in love with Suzie Wong's younger sister, whereas they are probably telling us that Tiger Balm is a cure for all ailments.

The place might be described as a rather dull fairy-land, in which one of yesterday's chief social events was a meeting of the Rotary Club. And being a high-powered JAD job, therefore attracting more and more American tourists, it is becoming expensive. We spent the first part of our stay here, before we knew any better, at a new hotel overlooking the harbour, where a bedroom and bath, no sitting-room, were costing us about ten pounds a night, without food. This hotel was so modern that instead of a mere telephone in the bedroom it had a kind of switchboard, so that to try to order a pot of coffee was like helping to run a factory. Often I gave up, afraid that I might end by ordering a yacht, and went out for anything I wanted. But now here, at Repulse Bay, in a pleasant old-fashioned hotel, you ring a bell and somebody comes and you tell him what you want, and there is no danger of dialling the Publicity Manager or the Stenographer when you are trying to ask for a beer, and it is all out-of-date, nice and easy.

Now Repulse Bay, a favourite bathing beach, is on the far side of the island, away from the harbour and the ships, the banks and offices, the stores and the crowded narrow streets of Chinese shops. Yet near this hotel, towering high above it, sending out coloured balconies into mid air, terrifying in this landscape, are blocks of flats that might have been

[180]

fetched from New York's Park Avenue or San Francisco's Nob Hill. And a man who lives near here told me that he went away on leave and when he returned he found the top of a hill had gone and in its place were these monsters, looking down on all the hills, blotting out half the sky by day and adding constellations to it at night.

Now this is what I meant when I began by saying that Hong Kong is fascinating. As somewhere in the JAD world, it is, I feel, rather disappointing. I must have been to at least a dozen places that offer far more beauty, excitement, glamour, Jaddery. The charm of the past hardly exists here. There is little to enchant the eye (in detail as distinct from broad sweeps) or entice the mind into reverie. What does exist here is not the past but the future. It offers us a short trip in a Time Machine. This is what the rest of the world will be like, shortly. Other bays, popular with bathers, will soon be dominated by amazing structures of steel and concrete. Other hills will soon be furrowed with twenty-storey tenements, row upon row upon row of them. For our whole world has this population problem. But in Hong Kong its challenge has been fiercest, most immediate, most urgent.

When I used to live in the Isle of Wight, I think it had a total population of about 90,000. Hong Kong Island alone has now a population of 1,125,000. The total population of the Crown Colony (which includes the Kowloon Peninsula and the so-called New Territories) is 3,600,000, of whom over 99 per cent are Chinese. In one month, three years ago, over 100,000 refugees arrived. I know this is a familiar story. I also

[181]

know that the authorities have made an heroic effort
—not perhaps as good as it was, if only because they
allowed too much material, labour and time to be used
building luxury flats when humbler accommodation
was most urgently needed—to meet appalling demands for housing, sanitation, employment, education. But I can't help wondering what the Isle of
Wight may look like in fifty years' time. And my
trouble is that I can't bring myself to like these sky-
scraper monstrosities, the debris of the population
explosion, and even if I could force myself to enjoy
looking at them, I would still be left wondering how
life will be tolerable, on anything but a robot scale,
when there are just too many people.

This brings me to China, with its 700 million and
lusty babies being born every second of the twenty-
four hours. In Hong Kong you have a chance to take a
peep at China, so we took it, deciding to pay a short
visit to Canton. I started coping with the visa nonsense before we left London, filling in forms and handing over photographs. But all to no purpose. We had
to begin all over again here. There is something in
communism that encourages bureaucratic inefficiency.
The Chinese may be said to have invented bureau-
cracy. They had an elaborate civil service when we
were daubing ourselves with woad, with innumerable
Mandarins-in-office two thousand years before a single
lunch had been served at the Athenaeum. Yet here we
were on the familiar communist official run-around, filling in more forms and handing over newer and even
more villainous-looking photographs. But at last we
were in the train going to Lo Wu Station on the frontier.

You get out at Lo Wu Station, walk about two hundred yards, fill in forms about your luggage and currency, change some money, drink tea, then find yourself in Sham Chun Station, in China. But the day we went, several thousand Chinese from Hong Kong were also going to celebrate their New Year with their families and friends in the homeland. And almost all· these Chinese carried two enormous bundles balanced on bamboo poles. Bowed down but trotting when they moved, sweating with anxiety, they could have been filmed as mobs fleeing some great catas-trophe, whereas in fact they were all off to eat fried duck and sweet-and-sour pork and explode fire-crackers with their aunts and cousins. Few of the bundles seemed to contain food; they seemed mostly composed of bedding, clothing and shining new buckets, which must be scarce in China.

We were now in the great republic of 'workers, peasants and soldiers', where writers are told to go 'to live and work with the masses', but I saw nothing of this austere egalitarianism at the frontier or indeed later in Canton. There was rather more of it back in Hong Kong, where too many Chinese have forgotten their traditional good manners and have not yet acquired any of ours, so do too much pushing and shoving.

The Chinese are very artful at the frontier. Our Western Imperialist Capitalist train, together with all the station buildings is a shabby affair. The Chinese People's Republican station buildings are large, airy, spotless, bright with flowers. The train itself, taller and wider than ours, looks as if it has just been unpacked from some colossal toyshop. Most of its personnel looked like stern schoolgirls in dark blue uniform, and they brought round pots of green tea as if it were medicine. Perhaps it is. Meanwhile, the train made a great show of dashing through the carefully scolloped countryside like a reckless express, but contrived to use up three hours on a journey of no distance at all.

At Canton we were met by an interpreter who was a young man, thin, deeply earnest, reared on the purest milk of Marxist-Leninist doctrine. All communist countries have this young man on hand to interpret for me—no almond-eyed smiling girls for Writer John Priestley—but I must admit that this Cantonese one turned out to be a most helpful and charming fellow. He took us to an enormous new hotel built for the Western trade. It was as gloomy as it was large, had immense halls and corridors with nobody about in them, and seemed like an hotel in some bewildering dark dream. Canton is famous for its food, but the Chinese dinner we ate that night was the same old tired hotel food known the world over. I don't believe any Chinese would have entered that dining room even under threat of torture.

For the honour of Canton, I must report that later we ate in some of its best restaurants and the food was superb, some of the best I have ever tasted. I must also add, for the benefit of those who imagine we ate luxuriously among starving masses, that we caught glimpses of many other eating places, explored food markets, and saw that Canton was bursting with edibles of all kinds. (I am excluding, though they

[184]

didn't, the skinned dogs, snakes, and parts of unimaginable creatures.) Wages are still low; there are
obviously many shortages; but the days of famine are
over, at least in Canton. There were plenty of shops,
from big stores to holes in the wall, all being briskly
patronized but without any long queues anywhere.

One shortage was distinctly pleasing, namely, that
of motorcars. (True, we hired one ourselves, and it
was driven by a careless and arrogant youth who insisted upon turning on piercing programmes on his
radio, and was always in danger of running down
cyclists.) Except for the radio, Canton is an almost
noiseless city of cyclists. Though a very old city, it
has been sacked and burned too many times to be able
to show much of its past, but in its own rather scattered and dusty fashion it has much—a gateway here,
a bridge there—that catches and pleases the eye. It
has far more than Hong Kong has. If they shared the
same political-economic system, I would rather live in
Canton than in Hong Kong. I could be happy, I fancy,
in that Cantonese university we visited, which had no
enormous buildings but scores of pleasing smallish
faculty houses and dormitories in a campus as big as a
park.

We spent one evening in an amusement park. It
wasn't as good as Copenhagen's Tivoli—but what is?
(Nothing we have ever been able to create.) But you
had a choice of acrobats and jugglers, opera, children's
roundabouts and a big wheel, an aquarium, a chess
pavilion, a basketball match, tea houses, and probably
a dozen other things I have forgotten. Possibly the
regime is rather less austere down here in Canton

than it is further north, nearer the seats of power, but certainly this evening I spent strolling round the amusements with thousands of Cantonese and their families did not suggest the human anthill described in so many American articles.

Of course it is hard for a visitor to know when something is compulsory or merely suggested. For example, we were admiring some exquisite specimens of woodblock printing when, without any warning, a loudspeaker high on the wall began screaming at us. It seems that at eleven o'clock every morning government employees do exercises for a quarter of an hour. Then afterwards, we saw nurses and doctors doing 'slow shadow-boxing' on the roof of their hospital. (Our own civil service has been doing slow shadow-boxing for many years, but all behind walls.) Now if it is merely *suggested* you do this, because it will do you more good than harm, then all is well. But if you *have* to do it, because some committee in Peking dreamt it up, then to hell with it and them!

We had time to visit only one commune, a kind of economic self-contained unit, both agricultural and industrial, taking in about forty thousand people. I could see nothing of the anthill about it, and on its agricultural side it seemed to be working well. But on the industrial side, I can imagine that a cheerful sketchy amateurishness might not be very efficient. But this would be preferable to any robot-and-anthill organisation.

For all its clean sweep in the realm of ideas, the Chinese government takes the utmost care, in visual things, to preserve its fine traditions and not to break

[186]

with the past. For which, I feel, we should all thank it. At the same time it is odd that these leaders, cherishing the visual tradition, should dismiss all the ideas held by the people who created the tradition. Why should wisdom have waited for Marx and Engels?

But we should realize, while there is still time, that there is something more than the usual Party line in Chinese anti-colonial bitterness. After all they are an ancient and great people, from whom we in the West borrowed much before we began humiliating them. They are, I feel, intensely aware both of this humiliation and their recent emergence from it. Even if they make aggressive noises (perhaps enjoying the novelty of it) we should try to remain steadily friendly. I am no more a communist than President Johnson is, but the American attitude towards China seems to me completely and dangerously idiotic.

A man told me the other night that America will no longer import shrimps from Hong Kong. The creatures are packed here and indeed are caught here, but they must not find their way into American homes because some of them may have lived for a time in Red Chinese waters.

However, what stays longest in my mind has nothing to do with international relationships. It has to do with babies. I seem to have been looking at millions of babies, mostly carried on their mothers' or older sisters' backs. Babies coming out of the tenement skyscrapers sprouting on Hong Kong Island and Kowloon or out of the squatters' shacks in the New Territories; babies at the frontier; and more and more babies in and around Canton. They are good babies and will soon make sturdy children. But there are too many of them. They frighten me. It is as if that original explosion, which some scientists believe brought this universe into existence, has now taken a human form and is about to break all reasonable bounds. This is World Problem Number One, and we might stop exaggerating our racial and national differences just to take a long hard steady look at it.

These Our Revels

IF THE AUTHOR of *Henry IV* was not born here, in Stratford-upon-Avon, he ought to have been.

The town is so English. Like Shakespeare's own nature and mind (as I read them), it is sharply divided. Its celebrations are the right mixture of the pompous, the foolish grandeur and silliness, not without a flash of poetry. As in the play, Establishment figures occupy the stage, together with clowns and unconscious drolls, dolts and oafs. There have been times lately when I seem to have caught a glimpse of a bearded face, a lurking smile and eyes bright with mockery. Possibly Shakespeare is still around.

But if he still had an address here, I doubt if he would have been invited to take part in our celebrations. I refer now, of course, to the poet and dramatist, not to Shakespeare the British Institution.

There are countries that would take care to associate their own poets and dramatists with a notable anniversary of this kind. But that is not our English Way. It is the fact that Shakespeare was originally an author that makes some good Stratford folk (whose ancestors finally denied the town to plays and players) feel that this Birthday business is a lot of fuss about nothing. The money, they mutter darkly, would have been better spent on a swimming pool.

The revels—if this is not too gaudy a term—began for me on Wednesday morning, with a Press preview of the Shakespeare Exhibition. For some weeks I had been regarding with some curiosity the exterior of its pavilion. It looked as if a large circus had just arrived from Samarkand. The Exhibition covers two-thirds of an acre, contains 200,000 cubic feet of scenery and would require the equivalent of 100 pantechnicons to move it; and it has cost a packet even larger than the £250,000 that was the last published estimate. It goes to Edinburgh in August, to London at the end of October and then, if it is still fit to travel, perhaps to America.

Like all exhibitions, this Shakespeare one was not quite ready. There was still a lot of hammering; many of the lighting and sound effects were not yet working; and I always seemed to be stumbling upon girls with dank hair and thick jerseys standing, with fingers intertwined, beside thinly-bearded young men, waiting to be told to fetch something, perhaps tea.

When everything is in its place and working, this Exhibition will be well worth the 5s. (children and students 2s. 6d.) demanded at the entrance. Mr Richard Buckle and his innumerable colleagues have had the excellent idea of taking us on a picturesque tour of Shakespeare's life and times. Much of this is handled imaginatively; some real artists have been at work.

The actual Elizabethan material, from the large portraits downwards, is magnificent. Some of the glimpses of the London Shakespeare knew are as dramatic as he is. And I much enjoyed a brief visit to an artfully reduced Globe Theatre, where the recorded voices of our best Shakespearean players can be heard. This is perhaps the best of many happy inventions and devices.

But before the Exhibition moves to Edinburgh and

London I beg Mr Jack Lyons (the chairman, and apparently a dazzling ball of fire) and Mr Buckle to eliminate those samples of pop art and cute slang, and somehow to improve the panoramas of the English countryside—not good enough for Shakespeare nor indeed for us. I must confess I never noticed the 'six 18 ft.-high sculptured Beefeaters' mentioned in a memo devoted to Mr Lyons, who incidentally never turned up to talk to us; but I am a man who can get along without 18 ft. Beefeaters. The Exhibition is all right, though. See it.

On Wednesday afternoon the Shakespeare Centre in Henley Street was opened. It is a fairly civilized building and it houses a fine Shakespeare library, but I still thinks it looks out of place in Henley Street. And the opening ceremony seemed far removed from the gentle Bard of Avon. At first it looked as if war were about to be declared against Ruritania.

The mob was sealed off, as it always is when its votes are not being registered. There was a line of soldiers, and the military band was playing. A stand had been erected across the road from the Centre to provide the quality with seats and shelter. Ambassadorial cars came and went, purring or sneering. There was even the beginning of a thunderstorm, probably laid on by Messrs Lear and Macbeth.

The battery of microphones seemed to await President Johnson or Mr Kruschev, ready to abandon nuclear and other collective imbecilities. What actually happened, though pleasant enough, seemed rather an anticlimax to many of us boys and girls of the Press standing herded behind rails and clutching our notebooks and cameras in a chilly grasp. Mr Eugene Black, late of the World Bank and, as I can testify, a genuine Shakespearean enthusiast, spoke briefly and modestly and then cut ribbons and unveiled a plaque. So the Centre is open now, ready to receive all those who need Centres.

Thursday, the great day, the quatercentennial Birthday, opened with more than a glimpse of sunlight and blue sky. We had to be at the Theatre by about 10 a.m. to be marshalled for the procession. As I was not entrusted with any flag-raising this time, I wandered away from the booming voice of the loudspeaker and the sight of Diplomatic First Secretaries holding bouquets, and went out on to the terrace overlooking the river. And there, thank Heaven, was that flash of poetry I mention above.

In that small section of the river I could see, there was no sign of our own time. There was the water with some of the blue and gold of the morning in it; there were swans, idly queening it; and on the opposite bank there were the tender-leafed or budding willows, meeting summer in the spreading green of their reflections. I was reminded for a moment of the riverscapes in the early but entrancing work of Renoir and Monet at Argenteuil. But then I was back another three hundred years for this was the river as Shakespeare must have seen it as a boy, the water and the willows that deposited in his mind, like gold in a bank, so many magical images he was to have at his disposal later, hard-pressed in London. And it seemed as if four centuries contracted to a few moments. Time was a dream.

Then arrangements began again, and we were all more or less put in our places. (Though clearly reduced in status I was glad to find myself well in the rear, among such writers, scholars and actors who had been allowed to take part.) We set out, moving slowly and sombrely with so many black coats and bouquets in our ranks that it seemed as if we had come to bury Shakespeare and not to praise him.

In Bridge Street, we halted. Trumpets sounded from the roof of Barclay's Bank, as if the Rate had suddenly gone up $2\frac{1}{2}$ per cent. A band brayed and clashed. Out fluttered all the flags of the nations, as if the tall poles on each side of the street had by some sorcery been transformed into trees, putting out blue and scarlet fruit, yellow and black leaves. The crowd, fairly thick on either side but by no means jam-packed, murmured and buzzed its pleasure at this sight, but did not roar and yell its approval. Peter Hall and his company any night can better suggest a cheering citizenry.

Walking slowly as we did, up to the Birthplace in Henley Street and then down to the church and its tomb near the river, I had plenty of time to observe the crowd that watched the procession. And I came to a melancholy conclusion.

These people were no more than mildly amused in their detachment. They were not really 'with' us. This procession did not take hold of their imagination, rouse their enthusiasm, release deep feelings of loyalty. It was merely something laid on by and for persons with whom they had nothing to do. There was a gap of only a yard or so between those who officially walked and those who unofficially watched, but within the inner world of feeling and spirit, this was a gap of ten thousand miles.

These people, who stared, smiled, then shrugged us away, were the English of 1964. And the fault is not theirs.

There was one protest, organized by schoolgirls, whose accusing banner read OXFAM CHILDREN BEFORE SHAKESPEARE. I am an Oxfam supporter and cannot be said to be indifferent to the world it is doing something to rescue from starvation. Nevertheless, I think these girls—bless their kind hearts!—are wrong. If we celebrate nothing until the whole world is put right, if we take no time off from brooding over its wide misery, then we might soon find ourselves further away from any solution.

The present plight of the world comes largely from a failure of empathy and imagination. If we celebrate Shakespeare, then we hail in one astonishing man the enduring triumph of human empathy and imagination. Poetry and drama will not delay the arrival of square meals in Africa or Asia; they will bring them closer.

In the church the way to the tomb to which we took our flowers was closely lined with grammar school-boys (less subversive and rebellious than the girls, we must assume), each of them clutching his bouquet and school straw hat. I will confess to being a trifle moved by the sight of these fresh-faced lads, who seemed to bring me closer to the poet than the important personages specially imported by less imaginative arrangements.

One of these, I regret to add, was the enormous

Birthday Luncheon. Its setting was pleasing enough, for the large marquee-pavilion had a striped blue and white roof, with pink and white lanterns, and as the whole thing flapped and billowed a little in the wind I felt as if I were in a gigantic enlargement of a Tissot painting of some shipboard fête.

However, being at my age an impatient and greedy old codger, I hate to sit and wait a long time for routine indifferent food and drink. I am not really an Establishment luncheon or banquet man. I become restive when I hear a toastmaster roll out, more than once, his 'Your Royal Highness, Your Excellencies, My Lord Bishop, My Lords, Ladies and Gentlemen!' I begin to feel that soon I may become involved in one of Peter Hall's excellent historical productions, and find myself trying to cut down Professor Spencer of Birmingham University, sitting opposite, with an immense two-handed sword.

Moreover, I dislike our second toast, which, after The Queen, called upon us to drink to 'The Rulers of Other Nations'. This seemed to me to be carrying this ambassadorial business too far.

There are many rulers of other nations whose health I do not want to drink, even on Shakespeare's birthday. There are some of them I heartily dislike. It is true that Shakespeare—the official dramatist and manager, though not the poet, the creative man—seemed to favour strong, central rule. But it is also true, as he showed us over and over again, that he had a particular detestation of coldly ambitious power men. So I am not sure he would have approved of this Second Toast.

[195]

Lord Avon, tanned and still handsome, smoothly proposed 'The Immortal Memory of William Shakespeare'. He was supported by the Swedish Ambassador, whose cultural background seemed rather too wide and deep for most of his listeners; and then by the High Commissioner for Malaysia, who proved by his presence and his eloquence that our poet held the gorgeous East in fee. And by this time the canvas of our pavilion was straining, flapping, billowing, so hard that we might have been setting sail for Singapore.

I had an argument with a distinguished colleague who declared that Shakespeare would have enjoyed all this, my own contention being that he would have quietly laughed at it. (We use this miraculous man as a mirror for our inner selves.) What is certain quite beyond argument is that he would have clapped his hands at our next move, which was towards the Theatre, where his glory shines. Open Centres and Exhibitions and assemble libraries and arrange lectures and import official panjandrums to propose and answer Toasts if you must, but Shakespeare's Birthday is best celebrated in the playhouse, so blessings on Peter Hall and his enormous, hard-working company!

They did *Henry IV, Part I*, for us, and in spite of Hotspur and Glendower, both excellently played, I wished it had been *Part II*, the deeper drama both in its comedy and tragedy. I could quarrel with this Hall-Barton-Williams reading of the plays, which tends to over-emphasize the careful theatre manager and Tudor propagandist side of Shakespeare at the expense of the poet and rebel in him, which hated these strutting iron-clad princes and nobles and fell in love, so to speak, with Falstaff. (Well played by Hugh Griffith, even though he lacks Ralph Richardson's superb vocal range.) But this is no place or time for that quarrel.

For it was here in the theatre that the real Birthday party was held. It was here in his own place, where we could marvel at the range and depth of this incredible man, who knew instinctively how every kind of character moved and felt and thought and spoke.

The only gift we can bring him—and it is all he would have wanted in the end—is that of our attention and our laughter and our tears. And it will prove the sincerity of our praise of him if we give some of our attention too, a little laughter, at least a few tears, to our own poets and dramatists. Why, one of those rosy schoolboys lining the church might be another master dramatist! So let us, while praising Shakespeare, make sure the playhouses are open and the actors well bestowed.

This was not the end of our Stratford revels. Indeed they go on for months with a bewildering list of commemorative events reaching to September (and the Theatre, best of all, still open long after that). But for the time being I had had enough, not being able to face the Ball on Thursday coming at the end of a long day and determined to avoid last night's banquet, having four close friends at home to dine and wine.

But at about 11.30 on Thursday night, just when we were sleepily turning the pages of our books, I remembered the final item of the Birthday programme—fireworks at the recreation ground in Stratford two or three miles away. So we looked out of a bedroom window, and through the trees we could just see the distant sky exploding into blue and crimson fire, gold and silver rain beyond the branches.

I think Shakespeare would have enjoyed that, after bequeathing to us so many explosions of his own blue and crimson fire, so many sweet showers of gold and silver rain.

Fifty Years of the English

IN 1913 I WAS 18, and already writing after a fashion and eagerly devouring weekly reviews. As we grow older our memories begin to turn in on themselves, as if the path of our inner life was not straight but circular. I remember 1913 better than I do, say, 1948. And 1913 is a year we can easily go wrong about. Thus, readers under 50 must be warned not to think of 1913 in terms of funny old photographs in the family album and those jigging marionettes of the early newsreels. There were real people around in 1913, and very lively some of them were too.

Older readers must be warned—and I have been warning myself—against seeing that time through a golden haze, all faraway and long ago, all sunny afternoons in which a peculiar English genius, reaching indeed one of its minor peaks between 1900 and 1914, blazed like the delphiniums in the borders. The truth is, any Edwardian Avalon there might ever have been had vanished by 1913.

It was in fact a restless and uneasy time, with violence never far away. For example, the militant suffragettes took direct action with a recklessness that makes our nuclear protests seem like apologetic coughs. And the response of the police, the mobs, and finally the government, was more determinedly brutal than anything we have known lately. Again, it was in 1913 that the 'hard-faced men', later to arrive in Westminster, defied the trade unions, which were then busy combining their forces with the massive Triple Alliance at the head of them. Trade was good, but capital was being poured into overseas investments, and any idea of *investing in higher wages*, soon to be tried in America, could not be considered by class-ridden English employers. Why, miners would soon be wanting to buy pianos.

The more aggressive Labour men were being influenced by French syndicalists and the tough IWW agitators, beaten up along the Pacific waterfronts. Tom Mann had gone to jail for inciting the armed forces to mutiny. Ben Tillett taught his dockers to cry in chorus: 'Oh God, strike Lord Devonport dead!' These two extremes of hard-faced employers and loud-voiced union men created between them a kind of Jack London atmosphere, with the Iron Heel not far away. Today's cautious vote-cadging is far removed from the spirit of 1913. It was as if a well-publicized section of the Labour party were now demanding the total destruction of the Establishment. Moreover, this 1913 swing to the left was not without encouragement and support from the more progressive people in the middle classes, especially in the north, where I knew some of them.

There was something else happening then, something that made a deep impression upon me, making me believe—as I still do—that it is the upholders of law and order and tradition, the gentlemen and decent sound chaps, who will, if finding themselves really challenged, resort to lawlessness and violence. Seeing Ulster menaced by Asquith's Home Rule Bill, the Unionist gentlemen prepared for civil war. Distinguished lawyers like Carson and F. E. Smith harangued and reviewed men drilling in the Northern Counties; there was gun-running, possibly with German arms; and finally the cavalry officers at the Curragh threatened to resign their commissions. (I wish they had; a lot of English lives might have been saved later.) Unlike Tom Mann, these officers were not jailed for incitement to mutiny, though it was believed that some of them had spread their views among their men. This whole Ulster business may have been heightened by bravado and tomfoolery, but the German Foreign Office and General Staff would never make any allowance for that, so that Carson and 'Galloper Smith' and their military friends probably brought the war nearer.

Not that any of us really expected it. Most of the people I knew believed that the socialist parties of western Europe, now apparently very strong, especially in Germany, would never allow it to happen. When the war did come, it exploded out of the blue. Nevertheless, I believe that many of us, all young, had a feeling, never put into words, that a time was running out, that *something was coming to an end*. Our world, you might say, seemed a little overheated; we all had a slight temperature; the stuffy people—and there were still plenty of *them*—seemed unbearably stuffy. And there have been worse worlds, before and since, for young men. Though money was scarce on our level, living that included much enjoyment was cheap and easy; a poet who could borrow £50 could live for a year on them; you could have a provincial night out (I often did) on eighteen pence, with Little Tich or

Grock thrown in. It was the brief golden age of pole-
mical writing and eager debate, the great Shaw and
Wells time, when it looked as if everything could be
changed quite soon. And so it could, but not in the
bright conscious fashion they and we imagined.
Already stirring in the dark below consciousness were
the giant tigers, soon to come out glaring and roaring.

D. H. Lawrence really belongs to that time, and
not to the war and afterwards, when sex was not 'in
the head' but all over the floor. In those days it was
very much in the head and going rotten there. Our
popular songs celebrated 'The Girls', those with the
curly curls, all naughty but nice. But who were these
Girls? They were too uninhibited to be the cautious
young women we knew, too merry and careless to be
tarts. They were dream-girls out of frustrated male
sexuality, probably just before it gave half a sovereign
to some dough-faced, yawning slut. In this matter of
sex I sharply disagree with those moralists who think
our society has been sliding to perdition since that
time. Indeed, one of our clear gains among many that
are dubious, is the emergence since then of women
and girls far more attractive, lively-minded and companionable, than their mothers and grandmothers
were. If only women could have transformed our public world, now one-sided to madness in its male
aggressiveness, as they have transformed their
appearance and style of life!

I have described my First World War years elsewhere. Being a soldier I was cut off from civilian England, not being really in it and with it even when I was
back from France. This means that I am a poor judge

of it, though that will not prevent my announcing a few verdicts. Much of that wartime England I disliked. (And when some of its diarists got into print afterwards, I disliked it even more.) There was too sharp, too bitter, a contrast between the innocents who gave all for King and Country—and now I am not thinking of us in the services, but of all those who did two men's jobs on half a man's rations—and the others, the wartime featherers of nests. (Wells reported Balfour saying: 'Our business men are the worst—the *very worst*.') Blood and fat profits made a nasty mixture, no tastier when spiced by the intrigues and the squabbles of politicians, generals and newspaper proprietors. I have no particular affection for the BBC, but I wish it could have been running a news service in 1914–1918, when too many papers were all too often hysterical, irresponsible, silly.

But then I wish now that all the top military brass had been replaced by sensible men who had never been near the Boer War and had a few bright ideas. I also wish we had moved for a negotiated peace in the autumn of 1916, for it might have saved us from most of the horrors we have known since. For that matter I wish now the soldiers returning early in 1919, many of them feeling mutinous, had declared for a revolution. But they would have needed leadership, which would have had to come from the middle classes, from which their junior officers came, and neither then, nor seven years later when the General Strike failed, was that leadership offered to them.

We younger men were too weary and death-haunted to think creatively, even to hope fiercely.

Anxious to get home to the waiting women and to pick up our real lives where we had dropped them, we did nothing but hope vaguely for better things, the old country tarted up a bit for Heroes. We exchanged a new England for victory parades and promises meant to be broken. It was the bad men, still fresh after a cushy war, who had the energy and enterprise. But what about our progressive Lib-Lab elders, who had stayed at home and must have known what sort of eggs that wartime England would hatch? To them we shall return.

That First World War may now seem so much boring history to the young, but they are still suffering from its consequences. It killed a very large number of the best young Englishmen—and this also means that it left a large number of the best young Englishwomen childless widows or spinsters—and these were the very men who might have succeeded in politics, the arts and sciences, invention and industry. So for years our public life was starved of new leadership and boldly creative political ideas. If America's New Deal was swifter and bolder than anything even imagined in English political circles, this was not entirely due to Roosevelt's exceptional qualities as a politician. The kind of youngish men he wanted, to plan and act quickly, were not so many names on war memorials. Revisiting the era of Baldwin-MacDonald-Chamberlain, so petty, so tedious and so stale, we can almost hear it screaming for new blood. But most of that blood had already been flushed down the drain like dirty water.

At least equally important was the effect of that war

on those who survived it. First, there were those ex-soldiers—and I was one of them myself, so I know—who felt they were entitled for a few years to concentrate upon how to earn a living and keep a family. They had apparently saved England once, so let some other people start saving her now. But if we were less sharply political than we had been in 1913, so were our fathers to whom I said above we should return. Unlike the socially highest and lowest levels of our society, still almost brutally tough-minded, our people in the middle were tender-minded, and they were left bewildered, wounded in spirit, deeply frightened by the war. Those who had seen a new socialist civilization rising on a firm foundation now discovered that this foundation itself had collapsed, and from the jagged holes and the dark came the stench of cruelty and evil.

Man was not the easily perfectible being they had imagined him to be. And now terrible stories were coming out of the Russian Revolution. So although more of these people may have given votes to Labour, they withdrew from any revolutionary ideas, dangerous now that the world was revealed as a terrifying place. And because of this shrinking withdrawal, the Left became a working-class industrial movement, challenging employers and hours and wages and not the whole organization and tone and temper of English society, those very influences that reduced Ramsay MacDonald and his friends to impotency. Baldwin may have been an adroit tactician but he owed much of his success to his *persona*, that of an easy unruffled man happy with his pipe and his pigs, a cosy fellow in a terrible world.

[205]

It has been the fashion for some time to be lyrical or nostalgic about the Twenties, especially the earlier, more dashing and devil-may-care Twenties. Those were the days! But were they? (Here, I must add, that perhaps some allowance must be made for my personal history.) English public life was contemptible; the unemployed were beginning to march; and not a new idea was coming to the rescue. That is, of course, at home, for abroad there was the League of Nations to put an end to war. In the West End there was a lot of noise and booze, gin and jazz and sleeping around, a style of life better suited to Scott Fitzgerald's New York than to Aldous Huxley's London. (There is something in the air of London that makes night life seem either soporific and gloomy or squalid.) Young men who had been away at school during the war, probably half-starved, now cut loose, but self-consciously and defiantly, not with any genuine uprush of high spirits. The new bright girls went screaming round the town, mostly looking terrible, the fashion of the time being hideous. We men were treated to an endless exhibition of female legs that somehow all looked unshapely. Homosexuality flourished, beginning its conquest of London's aesthetic life.

It was not the early Twenties but the war itself that rushed through the emancipation of women. Girls who had to drive lorries or work lathes could not be expected to obey the old rules. But it was not only rough jobs and wages, life in digs and hostels, that changed their sexual behaviour. Unsettling them on a deeper level was the war atmosphere, the black casualty lists, the packed hospitals, the leave trains, the excitement that was half-wonderful, half-dreadful; so that towards the end some English towns were like Venusbergs. And then the vote, for which those fanatics in big hats and long skirts had suffered and died, quietly arrived. With what result? Why, more votes went to Labour, because our Jim was out of work and Dad on short time; and more votes went to the Conservatives, perhaps because some of them looked nice in the picture papers. What England has had since female suffrage is life on the dole, appeasement, World War II, the Atom and H-bombs, and now irresponsible advertising-agency politics. I still think women have more common sense than men, but not when they have to mark a ballot paper.

It was in the early Twenties that really *modern* literature and art arrived, mostly direct from Paris. Comparatively few English people may have been directly affected by this invasion of the avant-garde, or indeed have known anything about it, but its social consequences were important. Real literature, as distinct from sociological stuff and popular entertainment, was created by introverts for introverts: the extroverted mob was told to keep out. The development of mass communications and mass standards, which had to be kept at bay, encouraged a haughty aloofness, an inner ring attitude, a sensitivity-on-a-private-income view of life and letters. A certain unselfconscious breadth of appeal, common to established writers and their critics before the First World War when nobody bothered about being highbrow, middle-brow or lowbrow, was lost during these years. And so, to a large extent, was the idea that serious authors should concern themselves with man in society. To writers arriving in these Twenties, whose sharp wits and pens might have done the community a service, anything that suggested sociology or politics was out. And out too was the general reader, who, having been warned off, began to feel that contemporary literature was not for him. So now the English tradition of protest and radicalism in good writing was being forgotten just when England needed it.

The inevitable reaction, coming with the depression, did little to revive that tradition. The new poets from Oxford and the young Marxist critics from Cambridge went swinging to the far authoritarian left, to a communism which, whatever it might pretend, was grimly opposed to any such English tradition. So these clever young men were no help to the Labour party, now a shambles after the split with its leaders. Some of us, who do not pretend to understand high finance, still remain unconvinced, in spite of all the persuasive experts, that that financial crisis of 1931 was genuine. It broke the Labour government, nearly wrecked the party, and that, we believe, is what it was concocted to do. Once again, the upholders of order, decency, the gentlemanly tradition, smelling danger, were ready to play it rough and dirty.

Because of work I had in hand, I saw a lot of that England of the early Thirties and the depression. I said then that the so-called Special Areas, where everybody was out of work, reminded me of prisoner-of-war camps: the men had the same grey drawn look. The dole just kept them half-alive, draining the dignity and manhood out of them. It was a damnable system, wasteful in the worst possible way, filled with the unconscious cruelty of the stupid and unimaginative. When I travelled in America and saw how boldly and imaginatively Roosevelt's New Dealers—all the better able to cope because they were not politicians and brought fresh minds to their tasks—were facing the very same problems, I felt ashamed of my country. It is only when somebody starts firing at us that we really begin to spend money, call in some 'unsound men' and discover a few ideas. Perhaps about 1931 we ought to have declared war on ourselves.

Though not as tender-hearted as we like to think we are, we English are not an unkind people, but through a combination of lazy-minded conservatism, mistrust of any new and bold ideas, lack of imagination among our politicians and bureaucrats, we are forever behaving callously and often with downright cruelty in our public life. (The lack of imagination is very important. For some years in the Thirties I served on a committee that gave grants to people who badly needed them. The only rich man on this committee, a man of enormous wealth, was always trying to cut down these grants, proposing we should give some wretched applicant £75 instead of £100. He could understand the figures but not the difference, in terms of living in a basement with arthritis, the extra £25 might make.) The result is that while we keep on saying what a wonderful country this is, some vast group of innocents is having a hellish time. In the early Thirties it was the unemployed; now it is the old, many of whom would feel better off if they were dogs or horses.

I shall be told that during the Thirties many conscientious and not unintelligent men toiled away at this problem of unemployment, and other problems arising out of it, gradually easing the situation. I know they did. And I doubt if they could have done any better within the limits they were set and in the particular atmosphere in which they worked. It is the limits and the atmosphere that were wrong. If we had still had them in the summer of 1940, we should not have defied Hitler even for 10 days. As it is, in peacetime some large section of us is always being slowly murdered by sound finance and its conscientious public servants. I wonder sometimes if a few economic charlatans, gaudy fellows over-addicted to women and champagne and always lunching well away from the Athenaeum, might not save some of the English from being doomed to die by inches.

Though I used to enjoy visiting Germany, a fine country even if inhabited by people I mostly don't understand, I stopped when Hitler took it over. Like other well-known writers I received cunningly-worded invitations, crammed with culture, to sample Nazi hospitality, but I wasn't having any, and soon my works were banned. As far as Hitler was concerned I took a warmonger's attitude, believing that, however badly armed we might have been, we should —and could—have stopped him much earlier, before paper plans turned into steel and TNT. But while I thought we were desperately wrong about Czechoslovakia, not being an expert I never understood why the Russians and Americans, who would be involved with Hitler sooner or later, thought they had no other duty than to call us crypto-fascists or poltroons. (I must admit that for some years, going well into the war, I found the ringside manner of American correspondents—it was their finest hour—hard to take.) There are mazes of reasons, from the contemptible to the possibly acceptable, why we waited until he was almost fully armed to challenge Hitler, but what is worth considering here is why this brave-last-stand move was approved at once by the English people.

These people are entirely different from those who represent them in world affairs, the foreign secretaries and ambassadors and officials, the cautious double-dealing 'perfidious Albion' types. The popular English imagination is wildly romantic and dramatic, a fact that explains our astonishing literature, almost all of it coming from the people. So it cares nothing for efficiency and success. What it loves are real life epics and dramas, lost battles and glorious last stands, gallant failures. For all his supposed great popularity, it was not Kitchener who got the applause in music halls before 1914; it was Redvers Buller, who kept on losing the Boer War. The secret of Churchill, a much over-praised man after 1941, was that he shared this love of the romantic and dramatic. The broad mass of the English hunger for drama, not now in the theatre (though this is only recent and may be a passing phase), but both in their public and private lives.

One reason why the English resent modern industry, occasionally striking just for the hell of it, is because it is too impersonal, boring and undramatic, without any appeal to this enduring romantic imagination. This explains too why contemporary politics, with their constant small appeals to self-interest, their cadging manner, leave so many of the English indifferent or cynical. They offer nothing to kindle the imagination. There are no backs-to-the-wall, no glorious last-stands. It is because they are bored, with no drama in their lives, nothing for the imagination, that so many of the English rush to spend their new money, out of Security by Affluence, on booze, gambling, and the red-headed woman met in the bus. They make *something* happen.

Most of the English were not bored in the Second World War, where to my mind they cut a better figure than in the First. (This improvement may not continue into the Third.) One feature of this time was a new popular response to the arts. I am not guessing now; I was there in many places where it happened, and in a small way did something to make it happen. CEMA was an impoverished infant compared with our present Arts Council, but it met an eager and unselfconscious popular demand that hardly exists now. Possibly we made too much of this, and certainly some of us were altogether too hopeful about what would happen after the war, when the arts would no longer compete with profit-making amusements on fairly level terms. I admit that I was too optimistic, but I was not deliberately taking a line, and even if I was doing this unconsciously, I don't feel inclined to apologize. I would rather tell people that soon they would be even more lively-minded, enjoying a richer quality of experience, than help to herd them back to commercial exploitation on a vaster scale.

This idea of people wanting the arts and a richer

quality of experience was all mixed up with our politics—as in my opinion it should be—during that election campaign in the summer of 1945. We found ourselves arguing in favour not of this political measure or that but of a whole way of life. Now I genuinely dislike public speaking; I always begin to feel it is somebody else who is talking, and somebody I don't much care for; and during that campaign I was taking this dislike to three meetings a night, sometimes five on Sundays. Nevertheless, I relished the atmosphere of that summer, delighted in the people I met, especially the young enthusiasts who were often devoting their holidays to the service of Labour. There was revolution in the air, a mild and very English revolution, with no heads about to roll, but bent on changing our society. As far as these younger people were concerned, Labour was being sent to Westminster not primarily to give the English security and welfare but to transform our whole society. They wanted—as they said so many times— a different England.

A different England did emerge, but it was not the one those youngsters wanted. Labour did some fine brave things, notably with India and National Health. But the revolutionary atmosphere of those warm nights in 1945 soon thinned away, and though the air was not as cold and sour as a determinedly hostile press maintained day and night, it did much to breed the Lucky Jims and Jimmy Porters of later years. People were given social security and welfare but no wider horizons, larger hopes, creative tasks: they were not going anywhere. The Establishment, essentially

Tory and change-resisting, was never seriously challenged. The Treasury was still in possession of its obviously inequitable system of direct taxation, which left City men alone to enjoy their capital gains while hurrying fiscal thumbscrews and racks to professional men. Bevin, who might have worked wonders at home, threw his weight into a foreign policy that soon made him popular with the wrong people. Then it was very quietly decided that we should make atomic bombs, a fatal decision as we know now, and one about as far removed from the spirit of 1945, and from the humanity and hopefulness of the old socialist pioneers, as a decision to rush critics of the government into concentration camps. Now was that glorious summer changed to the winter of our discontent.

Though the Tory press monstrously exaggerated popular feeling, it cannot be denied that many people did feel that something narrow and grudging, puritanical and life-denying, never absent from one side of Labour, did come out to stop this and forbid that. No doubt controls were necessary, but when they were not accompanied by great positive acts, sudden glorious releases, a sense of living in a bigger and better country, they made Labour seem restrictive, negative, sour. People with any intelligence and insight began to feel themselves to be doubly ringed around, by Labour ministers never saying *Do* but always *Don't*, and by the Establishment still saying *How dare you!* It was too much; one of them had to go; and Labour went.

If you weren't growing old or about to lose your

job, or if you didn't think too much, the consumers' England the Tories created seemed quite pleasant. No secret police hammered on the door at 3 a.m.; no beggars exhibited their sores; almost everybody earned more and spent more; there were scampi on the menu, and smoked salmon if you had an expense account; and finally roulette and strip-tease found their way into the old mill-and-chapel belt. In this England you could apparently make the best of both worlds, for what with everything booming and the bright ads and all that, it was like living in America, but under royal patronage with dukes and lifeguards. Push on in the rat-race, and your girl could be one of next season's debs. The old prizes and the new glittered together and might be won by the same smart Top Type. And not to worry about war, not with that deterrent we had. Not to worry about anything, not with Mr Macmillan in charge, telling us we were all going forward together.

But where were we going? Wherever it was, we didn't seem to be going there together. A general English togetherness seemed to vanish. We no longer appeared to know who we were, either abroad or at home. Suddenly we really had lost face, no longer having any image of ourselves. It occurred to some people that we might be making not the best but the worst of two worlds, America without social equality, dash and energy, traditional England without responsibility and respect for herself, a show for the telly, the admen and the tourists. The young, less addicted to self-deception (the great English vice) than their elders, began to feel dissatisfied and restless, the best of them clearly uneasy in the consumer role allotted to them, unable to find ecstasy among toothpastes, chocs and after-shave lotion. The rebels arrived, and among them were almost all the young men and women gifted with any talent, insight and wit.

Politicians should take time off from the smoking and committee rooms, statistics and Trollope, to read a few novels and to visit theatres not occupied by whodunits and lounge-hall farces. Then they could ask themselves why the more sensitive and articulate young English express so much contempt and disgust, appealing at once to a kind of unfocused rebelliousness among younger readers and playgoers. No matter how hastily contrived, how wilful and wild, this strictly contemporary fiction and drama is important, especially to the politician, because it is news from the hidden centre, dispatches from the invisible front, telegrams of warning from tomorrow.

Even now, in spite of all the pressures and mass-persuasion techniques, youth arrives among us with certain expectations, and some of these cannot be satisfied with money, food, clothes, sex, table tennis and records of pop singers. They want to reach maturity integrated into a society that has a common purpose and noble aims and is not a slobbering mess of irresponsibility, mean devices, and self-deception, where privilege and money can buy honour and once-great names, and parsons preach the H-bomb. There is something in them, through what inheritance we do not know, that recoils from corruption. And this is the most corrupting society that England has known in my lifetime.

[216]

To be fair, however, I must make a pro-English point here. Our astonishing network of voluntary associations, in all their variety and richness, still survives, probably still making a larger contribution to world civilization than the devoted amateurs of any other country. We remain a great people not because we started steam engines working or defeated Napoleon but because we still meet in a thousand places to consider Alpine plants, migrant geese or sixteenth-century madrigals, turning aside from the rat-race to mount our hobby horses. Now the England of the voluntary associations is still with us, and it gives the lie to the notion that the English now lack the energy to play any great part in the world. And perhaps the reason why I have some confidence in the Labour party, now that it is under Harold Wilson's leadership, is not only that he seems to be uniting it, as Gaitskell never did but only appeared to do, but also because he frequently mentions, often as a first objective, 'a release of energy'. For the energy is still here, waiting to be released by politicians with courage and imagination.

A man my age is cut off from many things that delight the young. When they go out to enjoy themselves, he had better stay at home and put on Brahms's Clarinet Quintet. But their dislikes, their growing mistrust, he can share. And now it seems to me that the very best of the young English are on their way out of this official England, spiritually and mentally and often—alas for us—even physically, refusing to set foot towards that Top. They no longer live in the same world as Downing Street, the Foreign Office, the Treasury, the Ministry of Defence, the Central Office of Information, the palaces of Buckingham and Lambeth. And sooner or later, if we don't deter ourselves out of existence, something will have to give and go; either we must risk some honest surgery or become the victims of some chronic and life-devouring disease, choose between some form of social revolution or further and perhaps fatal doses of self-deception. The men largely responsible for this society are not bad men and did not set out to corrupt anybody, but they are incorrigible self-deceivers, realists without any true sense of reality. And this the rebellious young—though they may never mention it—intuitively perceive. So they 'want out'.

Now and again these days something curious happens to me. I find myself among some young rebels; and because we may have had a few drinks or have been sharing our derision noisily, our relation is looser and easier and the years between us vanish; and then, just for a moment or two, prompted perhaps by a look here, a tone of voice there, I feel I might be back again in 1913 with all that has happened between gone like a dream. Such moments can be disturbing. Sometimes I feel a depth of sadness; sometimes a new hope for England, the country I no longer much like yet still must love.

Lectures and Talks

These were designed to be heard and not read. But they make a few points of some importance, and a number of people who heard them demanded to see them in print. So, almost entirely unaltered, here they are.

Lectures and Talks

Life, Literature and the Classroom

During the 1960 Thanksgiving holidays, the American National Council of Teachers of English held a convention in Chicago to celebrate its Golden Anniversary. I was invited to give a special address, which I did in the vast Chicago Opera House. May I add that I have rarely felt hotter than I did after nearly an hour standing in the glare of the Opera House stage lighting or rarely felt colder than I did afterwards when, without respite, without a drink, the use of a towel, or even a chair, I had to stand, drenched with sweat, in a draughty corridor to shake hands with hundreds and hundreds and hundreds of people. They were nice people and I am sure they would have been sorry if they had known I would have to spend the next three days in bed.

MOST PEOPLE ARE secretly afraid of teachers. That is one reason why teachers are given more and more work but not more and more money. This keeps them at home and prevents their getting about and running into people and spoiling parties. If I am not afraid of teachers—and if I were, I would not be here—that is because my father was a teacher and I grew up among teachers. Our front room was always full of them, eating and drinking and arguing. (I am going back over fifty years, remember, to the time when food and drink were much cheaper and argument much safer.) This explains why I have taken care to avoid the teaching profession myself, though in one or two reference books it is stated that I was a teacher once. If I ever had been a teacher of English, I doubt if I would have accepted your invitation. For then I would have been one expert addressing hundreds of other experts—always a dangerous situation —whereas now I can talk to you, telling you your own business, out of the purest ignorance. This means, I hope, you will pity me and not condemn me: 'The poor man,' you will say to one another, 'just doesn't know.'

The best definition of the expert I can offer is an American one, though I am sorry to say I cannot tell you the author of it. This definition runs: 'The expert is the man who avoids all minor errors on his way to the Grand Fallacy.' No doubt I shall stumble into all kinds of minor errors during this address, but I am hoping to keep my back turned to the Grand Fallacy. To me this is the idea, rarely expressed but haunting so many minds today, that Man is nothing but an accident in a meaningless universe. So he begins to behave like an accident—and too often a bad accident. Having almost ruined one planet by his greed and folly, he dreams of landing on another, to see how he can wreck that. Is it not true that the very people who will give no proper attention and thought to the state of this earth of ours, are also the people who are now in a constant lather of excitement about getting out into space, into nothingness, or else arriving on the moon, the deadest thing there is? And what is this eagerness to exchange earth for space, something for nothing, or earth for the moon, life for death, but a despairing attempt to run away from ourselves, always hoping to travel faster and faster so that we will not catch up with ourselves? We are all now in danger of being deluded and trapped by false values and the wrong kind of thinking. And among the notions produced by the wrong kind of thinking is one that particularly concerns us here.

This notion asks us to believe that we come out of our infancy with minds like blank sheets of paper and then find ourselves facing a solidly objective world. Education is then a process not unlike that of the etcher, who brings together, under strong pressure, his inked plate and his blank sheets of paper; and a proud schoolmaster might be forgiven, acquitted of any dubious motive, if he asked a feminine member of the local education committee to come up and see his etchings. But I for one do not believe we arrive with minds like blank sheets or that we are faced with a solidly objective world. Both assumptions are wrong. Just as we have inherited, down through thousands of generations, a physical structure with all its elaborate functions, so too we have inherited, possibly by way of the sympathetic nervous system and the brain, possibly in ways we do not understand, a mental life, a psyche if you like, together with its equally elaborate functions, its patterns of response and behaviour, its emotional demands, its deep-lying fears and hopes, its legacy of dreams. This alone explains, in my opinion, what so many people find inexplicable, namely, the profound dissatisfaction of modern man, who has so many new and wonderful devices to save him time and trouble and to help him to live, and yet persists in feeling restless and disappointed and frustrated, sitting in his bright new home yet suffering from homesickness. The trouble is, he is being asked to accept secondary satisfactions, such as owning a car or a television set, for primary satisfactions, belonging to the ancient human pattern, responding to our very deepest needs. It is as if a woman were asked to exchange a good husband or lover for a washing machine, as if a man had to put in place of the solid satisfaction of doing a good job well the trumpery pleasure of riding in a larger automobile. For we arrive, so to speak, having great expectations. If we came as blanks, it would be all much simpler—though even more disastrous, as a peep into the nearest beehive or anthill might show us. Sometimes I think that if we read the poets oftener, we could do without the sociologists. There is more truth about essential human nature in one line of Wordsworth's *The Excursion* than in some whole libraries of dreary sociological jargon. This line tells us *We live by Admiration, Hope, and Love*. I believe this statement, I trust in it, absolutely. I would be ready to make it the test of any society. When and where admiration withers, hope vanishes, and love is hard or impossible to find, the mental hospitals are over-crowded, the prisons and detention camps are packed, and plans are being made for atomic and biological warfare.

We do not arrive as blanks but we exist from the first in an inner world of our own, although in its deeper recesses there may be nothing peculiar to ourselves. (This is of course Jung's Collective Unconscious, perhaps the most fruitful and liberating hypothesis in the thought of our age.) There we are then, as it were, peering out of this inner world of ours. But at what? At something that is not ourselves, certainly. But is it so solidly objective, after all? Do we not ourselves supply some of the instruments, sensuous or conceptual, that take readings of this outer world? If it appears to have three dimensions, not two or four, that is because we have learned somehow to bring to it a three-dimensional outlook. Unless we suffer from visual defects, we are able to discover in the outward scene a wide range of colours, some of which, we suspect, other men long ago could not find in it. And how much we can be helped here, to discover an even wider and more subtle range of colour, both by some study of the great painters and our own modest dabblings in the art! Then Aldous Huxley tells us how he took mescaline and then stared in wonder at a world he had never seen before, unimaginably enriched and glowing. And it is idle to declare that the world revealed to the mescaline-taker is not the real world. It may be a world less easy to deal with, to take action in, than the one most of us see. The drug may have removed certain inhibitions we have imposed upon ourselves, because we do not want a world of beauty to observe and to admire but one that offers us the maximum opportunity for action. And here I cannot help wondering whether our urban mechanical civilization is not smudging the form and draining the colour out of the world many people see. Perhaps the Irish poet and mystic, A.E., was right when he said we have been disinheriting ourselves. And this again may explain why so many people seem to feel frustrated or disappointed, and clamour for bigger and gaudier spectacles and more violence, cruelty, and blood in their entertainments. Finally, let us remember Blake's proverb: *A fool sees not the same tree that a wise man sees.*

We have now come a long way from any notion of blank sheets waiting for the image of a solidly objective world to be stamped upon them. The blank sheets turn into a whole inner world, which we carry about with us, which insists upon shaping and colouring our thoughts and feelings and creating our dreams. And if we pretend it is not there, so much the worse for us: it will have its revenge, as it has already done with our whole age. Again, the outer world, though not ourselves, refuses to be solidly objective, for it is in part a creation of our inner world, almost a kind of great long dream. Here we might appear to be reducing the importance of the outer world to a dangerous minimum, and we have medical and criminal statistics to show what happens to people who do this. But if our inner world represents a kind of inheritance, then our innumerable ancestors' experience of the outer world, during countless thousands of years, now plays a supremely important part in the life of this inner world. So although these are two very different worlds, the outer has helped to shape the inner, the inner has helped to display the colour and form of the outer. Blake's fool and his wise man do not see the same tree because their inner worlds are different. But they are not so wildly different that one man sees a tree where the other man is compelled to see a lamp-post, though elsewhere Blake, an innerworld man if there ever was one, suggests there can be even wilder differences of recognition. In this instance, however, there is at least a tree substantially there; and by this time, no doubt some of you would be glad to direct me to it and put a rope in my hand. Be patient, please! The mists are now clearing; the main argument will emerge.

We live then in these two worlds, very different and making very different demands upon us, yet inter-penetrating to some extent, just to add to the confusion, to make everything more complicated and difficult for us. This is true for all times of life, once we are out of our early childhood. But as we grow old, either we are able to keep ourselves nicely balanced between these two worlds, do not allow them to be in permanent conflict, in short, achieve wisdom; or we attend to one world and despise and ignore the other, which you may be sure will have its revenge, driving us quietly out of our minds or, as we like to say in England, round the bend. Incidentally, there should be colleges for people who have reached their fifties and need to be taken away, for a year or so, from their work, their usual pursuits, their familiar environment, to learn wisdom and the art of living. The scheme would cost money but nothing like as much money, or grief, as all the mad old men and women, in or out of public life, cost us now. But of course it is much earlier in life when we suddenly find ourselves called upon to face the bewildering challenge of these two worlds. It is during the later years of our childhood

[227]

and in the difficult time that follows them, that of adolescence. It is in fact during most of our school days. It is when, in Wordsworth's phrase, 'shades of the prison-house begin to close upon the growing boy.' This suggests, by the way, that for once Wordsworth and Bernard Shaw find themselves in agreement, for you may remember that Shaw says: 'There is nothing on earth intended for innocent people so horrible as a school. To begin with, it is a prison. But it is in some respects more cruel than a prison. In a prison, for instance, you are not forced to read books written by the warders and the governor.' In our early childhood, when we have not to read anybody, not even Shaw, we do not have to live in two different worlds, know nothing of an outer world and an inner world, because all is one. We exist in a state that a French anthropologist has called *participation mystique*, which we share at that age with some primitive folk. The gates of Eden have not yet closed behind us. The fields we frolic in—and this is one good reason why small children should not be barred from the countryside by leagues of concrete and cement—are still the magical bright fields of paradise. And all this is the lost happiness, the vanished glory, mourned by Wordsworth and many another poet.

Then we no longer live in one enchanted world. We are bewilderingly divided between a world without and one within. These are of course the years of conscious separation from our parents, when we discover ourselves—and insist upon asserting ourselves—as individuals. When what we might call the extra dimension of sex is added, we have arrived at adolescence. Now the whole bewildering challenge, conflict, problem, call it what you like, of the two worlds reaches its climax. Adolescents can easily be regarded as overgrown, difficult, rebellious children, immature minds and temperaments suddenly provided with enormous arms and legs. (As the father of five, now all grown up, with children of their own, I can well remember how as adolescents they were either crazily energetic or suddenly exhausted and sprawling, when their enormous bare legs seemed to fill the room.) But adolescents can also be regarded as men and women still with the lid off, before they have been compelled to come to terms with this life and have settled for less than their first glorious expectations of beauty, truth, and goodness. They do not know yet how many contracts they will be forced to sign with sinister clauses in unreadable small print:

> *Being young you have not known*
> *The fool's triumph, nor yet*
> *Love lost as soon as won,*
> *Nor the best labourer dead*
> *And all the sheaves to bind. . . .*

And remembering the rapturous anticipations of these adolescents, opening themselves to life because they feel instinctively, out of some ancient lingering dream of their inner world, that it must be good and great, I can only condemn our civilization again. For even though we may provide them with a noble education, we do little or nothing to ensure that their environment will not be ignoble. So too often what the school does is promptly undone by the street outside, for somebody's shabby profit. We allow this newly opened flower, the adolescent's expectancy and hope of splendid life, to be tossed into the gutter. And then we wonder why, when we are spending so much on education, there is something wrong with our community.

This evening, however, we must close the school doors and stay inside. We are now surrounded by hundreds of young creatures, bewildered but still hopeful as they find themselves not in one new world but two, though of course that is not how they see their situation. Now there is no doubt in my mind—and here I follow Jung—that the ideal mediator between our conscious and unconscious life, between our outer and inner worlds, is religion. But such religion would have to be both the foundation and the framework of our whole society. It would have to contain us and all our institutions. And this is not our subject tonight. We are now in school and must stay there, still surrounded by these hundreds of bewildered but hopeful young creatures, caught between two worlds, and we must choose the next best mediator, at least a possible guide and friend. And this surely is Literature. If you agree with me that literature is created out of the relation between men's outer and inner worlds, and if you have followed my argument so far without losing all sympathy with it and me, then—you teachers of English—you will not accuse me of flattering you when I declare, as I do now, that the teaching of English is one of the most important tasks that a man or woman can find in an English-speaking country. Perhaps I ought to add that if you *do* accuse me of flattering you, you will be breaking a record that has now lasted many years, during which I have been accused of almost everything except fawning and flummery.

In the rather desperate situation in which we find ourselves today, when the pressure and strain of the outer world meet the mysterious urges and bitter dreams of our inner world, it seems to me that English can no longer be regarded as just another subject, an alternative to geography or history. It has a special significance, outside the curriculum. Language and literature can help us, just when help is most urgently needed, to live with ourselves. The world is filled with people now—they are all round us—who can no longer live with themselves. That is why all they ask is to be taken out of themselves, no matter how brutally, violently, ignobly. This explains the popularity of those television programmes in which people make idiots of themselves for money, and other people enjoy their embarrassment, uneasiness, and fear. We bait people now instead of bulls and bears. And notice how certain sections of the Press, knowing their readers, turn with savage glee to tear down and roll in the mud the very figures they recently held up to be admired. Sometimes I feel our society has only a little way to go, unchecked by any change of mind and heart, and we shall be back to the blood and filth of the Roman Circus. And I need not remind you again that it is your students, the older children and eager adolescents trustfully opening themselves to life, who are most vulnerable, accepting as a gift from the adult world what is often only time-destroying and self-hating. If they are in this situation then, am I exaggerating when I say that language and literature are not just another subject but a rescue team, life-savers?

There is one point, however, that must be made here. We must recognize the fact that language and literature will not work their magic for everybody. We all use words but we do not all respond to them in the same way. Education or no education, human beings belong to essentially different types—and if this truth were always kept in mind, much time, trouble, and misery would be saved—and though we all have to live in these two worlds, we cannot all solve the problem of them in the same way. There are some sensitive youngsters who make a response only to music or the visual arts. There are others who are really educated only when they have thoroughly learned a craft or trade. I do not remember ever meeting a good craftsman who was obviously a fool, whereas many a man glittering like a Christmas tree with degrees, orders, and honours may have neither insight nor common sense. And here I will argue against my own interest—a rare sight on a public platform—by declaring that in education we can easily be overmuch concerned with books and discourse. This does not mean I am now abandoning my main argument. I am merely making the point again that some types remain beyond the spell of literature, and that many of them would benefit most from an education that was not bookish at all.

Some time ago I began to feel that the literary sense, that immediate response to the magic of words,

was weakening, fading, on its way out. My own
family, I noticed, though brought up among books
and fond of reading, eagerly and often passionately
preferred the direct visual image to the word. Most of
their contemporaries, I found, had the same prefer-
ence. The interest of the young in films, art shows,
ballet, reproductions of pictures, illustrated journalism, and finally television, was further evidence of
what was happening. I did not hesitate—I never do, it
is one of my weaknesses—to rush my melancholy
conclusion into print. The feeling for literature, the
old magic of the book, the witchery of fine words,
were leaving our society. But in my impatience to
reach a conclusion—perhaps my worst fault—I overlooked certain things. Because they feel new themselves, the young run to welcome everything else that
is new, believing it to be specially theirs. Now during
all this period, let us say the last thirty years, what
was new was certainly not print, which on the whole
looked worse not better, but the production and
reproduction, in all manner of fascinating forms, of
the visual image. It was all new and exciting and up-
to-the-minute. Moreover, it had another appeal to the
young, who, when they are not tearing around and
exercising their bodies, like to indulge in sprawling
indolence. It was all easier and lazier. They could
stare at these images, in one form or another, while
also keeping the radio or the record player turned on,
again something that was new and exciting. Now I
am not saying we are at the end of this period. Indeed,
there is a real danger that many children brought
up to have their images manufactured for them by

[233]

television will never make full use of their own image-making resources in reading, and as adults will be so much the poorer. I regard this as the only legitimate criticism of television considered simply as a medium. Responsibly and sensitively used it is a fine new medium, a social asset, for it is not television's fault if it is vulgarized and prostituted: we should take it out of the rat race. But though I am not saying that this period of the triumphant visual image is now coming to an end, I am convinced that I underrated the staying power of the book. For example, the enormous production of paperbacks, not all of them filled with dead blondes, suggests an equally enormous number of readers, who cannot be all middle-aged or elderly. I cannot mention paperbacks, however, without giving you one warning. While they do a great service to readers and swell the success of successful writers, up to now, as far as I know, they have not kept a good but still unpopular author alive and working, as many old-fashioned publishers often did.

From these warnings and digressions we must now return to our main argument, that in the outer-world-inner-world situation in which modern man finds himself, the result of our society's negative relation to religion, the task of teaching English to older children and adolescents is one of supreme importance. With certain types of young students, not temperamentally incapable of responding to words, it is, I repeat, a life-saving rescue job. Literature helps to open both worlds to them. It enables them to live with themselves. I am not now thinking of literature

[234]

as a collection of more or less triumphantly-achieved forms and structures, in the fashionable manner of much academic criticism, which seems to regard poets and novelists as word engineers building bridges and skyscrapers. I am taking literature loosely as so much good writing, a record in many different forms, manners, and styles, of man's experience. And of course this experience has gone both outward and inward, and the record of it may relate the most accurate and subtle impressions of the outer world to the strangest and most mysterious feelings rising from our inner world. To all this, it seems to me, intelligent and sensitive youngsters are open and keenly alive. Nor is the reason hard to find. In our extreme youth, but after we have left early childhood behind, we find ourselves, just because everything is so new and strange and exciting, very much aware of the sheer pressure of experience. Now this pressure of experience, felt on many different levels of the personality, is in my opinion the very thing that compels the born writer to keep on writing, irksome and frustrating though it may be. He has to react creatively to this pressure in order, for the time being, to feel free of it. Everything is hitting him harder than it does most people, and he has to do something about it. There is a pretence among men of action and business that the writer is a dreamy debilitated fellow mooning in a corner, probably waiting for the women to make a fuss of him. But if the women do make a fuss of him, it is chiefly because they know that the writer, like them, is wider awake and more alive than most ordinary men of their acquaintance, who are half-asleep, half-dead, turning into blocks of wood. And a writer of any size not only is not moony and debilitated but has more sheer vitality, is more tremendously alive, than all but the very best specimens of other types of men. But being so much aware of things, so open to life, so responsive, he feels the pressure of experience as few other men do. I state this in masculine terms because I believe that women are different. It is the exceptional adult male who feels this pressure of experience, whereas nearly all women know it, but they have not the same deep urge to react to it in a creative fashion. Most women talk the pressure away.

Let us say that a woman has just spent a week end in the country with some rather odd people about whom she and her friends in town are very curious. She returns, bursting with strange things to tell, and her friends gather round and cry, 'My dear, what was it like?' And what she feels at that moment, eager to tell all and yet half in despair because it will be so hard to describe what she saw and heard and did and thought, this is more or less what the writer is feeling a good part of his time. So he writes to escape from this pressure of experience. Once he begins to write, although all manner of technical difficulties may have to be faced, he feels an easing of the burden. Whatever else goes into the creation of literature—and we all know how much else there is—this reaction to experience starts it all off, whether the result is *King Lear* or *Paradise Lost*, *Tristram Shandy* or *Our Mutual Friend*. And now I return to my point that intelligent and sensitive boys and girls, just because everything seems so new and strange and exciting, are in a situation not unlike the writer's. They are perhaps closer to him than they may ever be again, for later they may dull and harden themselves. But now they too are beginning to feel the pressure of experience, and they cannot escape from it as the writer can. One reason why so many adolescents are difficult to live with is that they are artists without art. But literature, which I am still taking loosely as so much good writing, at least shows them that men and women have been experiencing life, just as they are beginning to experience it, for a long time, and that these men and women, in their different ways, have been able to set down what they made of it all, humorously, movingly, beautifully. This may be the mere beginning, but psychologically it is very important. That is why I say the English teacher is not simply dealing with one subject among many.

All this good writing, to which the young student is now introduced—with a minimum of formality, let us hope—is of course itself so much new and valuable experience. And once it is enjoyed and assimilated, taken into the reader's inner world, it begins to change experience in the outer world, which may soon be enlarged and enriched. Just as there is a constant action and reaction between these two worlds, as we agreed earlier, so there is between life and literature. Our reading should offer us a wider entrance into life, together with a sharper eye, a keener ear, and a heightened sensibility. It should take us to a great house and a magnificent company, not down into an air raid shelter. But let me put in plain terms what I am getting at here, before I am led astray by my own metaphors. We must take care not to appear before the young as cosy booklovers, only too willing to let the world go by while we put on our slippers, light our friendly old briars, and prepare to pass the rest of the evening with one of our favourite authors. This is reading as One of the Finer Things, as described by advertising copywriters working for mail order book companies, trying to unload big job lots of the hundred or five hundred or thousand best books. Some of those books you have not read; a few of them, I suspect, nobody has ever read. I remember going without lunch, nearly half a century ago, to buy the Everyman edition of that Finnish epic *Kalevala*. I still have it and after fifty years I have never read it. Now there is in literature and its enjoyment a genuine element of escape from our ordinary life, of consolation for its anxieties and futilities. In his *Office of Literature*, Augustine Birrell observes: 'Literature exists to please—to lighten the burden of men's lives; to make them for a short while forget their sorrows and their sins, their silenced hearths, their disappointed hopes, their grim futures. . . .' This is well said, but it is not meant for the classroom.

I am entitled, if I choose to do so, to accept Birrell's account of literature. For I am elderly and overweight and gouty and am still toiling at my desk when I ought to be tying up a few roses or trying to do a watercolour; I have brought up a family; I have fought in one war and been knocked about by another; I have had most of my earnings taken away from me by the most ferocious system of taxation of all time, chiefly to pay for politicians' mistakes and imbecilities; and so I consider myself entitled to think of literature as a means of escape, a consoler, a burden-lifter, or, for that matter, entitled not to bother about literature at all, simply enjoying myself with *The Case of the Two-headed Brunette.* But in fact this is not my view, as I trust you have already agreed, and it is certainly not the aspect of literature we should present to eager adolescents, who are looking for something better than a substitute, in their later life, for whisky and Nembutal. Still thinking of literature not in terms of its different forms but simply as so much good writing, the true, vital, and haunting record of man's experience, the mediator between his inner and outer worlds, let us consider how we can bring it closer to the lives of these young students. And I mean what they feel to be their real lives, not those hours, passing so slowly before the glazing eye, spent in classrooms. And before you protest against that last statement, allow me to follow it with two confessions. I was supposed to be very good at school, always coming out at or near the top, but most of the time there I suffered from an appalling boredom I have only known since at UNESCO and other conferences. Either I was being told what I already knew, an experience duplicated later, and even more uncomfortably, by the Army, or I neither knew nor cared what they were trying to tell me. This happened, for example, in the physics lab, where two exasperated masters tried to ram into our heads theories that were already being abandoned by more important physicists elsewhere. But none of this was true of English. Yes of course it was my subject of subjects, and, if only as proof that often we start early, I can tell you that the essays I wrote then were kept for years at that school, as models to be admired and imitated, no doubt earning me the dislike of several generations of schoolboys. And I remember when, round about the age of twelve, I produced, in a laboriously fair hand, a whole magazine, which offered the first instalment of no fewer than four serial stories—all by me.

This brings me to my second and happier confession. During these English periods I was face to face with one of the few men whose influence I gladly acknowledge. Yes, he was our English teacher. His name was Richard Pendlebury—a good name and it still rings in my ears like a gold piece on a marble counter—and he died, long before he ought to have done, over forty years ago. He was tall, intensely dark, as handsome and commanding as an ideal Spanish grandee, and if I accepted him then as my model, as a boy so often does, I certainly made a sad mess of reproducing his appearance. His qualifications for teaching English at a high school were officially very modest; he had no Ph.D. for a thesis on the use of the semicolon in the later works of George Eliot; but in truth he had the highest possible qualifications: he loved good writing, and he knew how to communicate and share that love. I think I was already beginning to enjoy my own feeling for literature, but at that age the few personalities we are willing to admire are very important, so that I can well believe that this feeling for literature could hardly be separated from my liking and admiration for Pendlebury. Probably I felt obscurely that literature, the poems and plays and essays he read and discussed with us, had helped to make him what he was, given his glance a flash of fire, had brought a grave courtesy into his manner, had put glints of humour and a cutting edge into his talk. So the teacher took stature and light from the subject, the subject took vitality and significance from the teacher. All this of course came at exactly the right time. When I say this, I am taking nothing away from Richard Pendlebury. I see and hear him again, quite clearly, across half a century, and realize that he must have been an uncommonly fine teacher. But if his influence on me was far greater, as indeed it was, than that of all the professors and lecturers I knew later in Cambridge and the critics I met in London, that was because I sat in a classroom, at the felicitous time, with a teacher who loved good writing. And to any English teacher who, deep in his or her heart, does not share that love, I would say: 'For your students' sake, your own sake, and indeed for God's sake— change your subject!'

No doubt there are many adolescent students who, once they are out of school, regard reading with dis-taste and suspicion. To be content with a book, when a fellow might be shouting and screaming and roaring around with the gang, suggests to them a low vitality. Nevertheless, even these scorners of the printed page are fond of talking. But can they talk? Will they ever be able to talk? When I first began coming over here, thirty years ago, there were a lot of advertisements that said: 'They were surprised when I spoke to the waiter in French.' Now they ought to be equally surprised when he speaks to the waiter in English. Not that we in England, as a people, are any better, and may even be worse. Not long ago I happened to see a number of television programmes in which people were stopped in the street and asked to give their opinions. The people in the South of England were very bad, as if language had just been invented; those in the North of England and the lowlands of Scotland were rather better; and those in the Highlands, where there is still a traditional respect for education and literature, were easily best of all, able to express themselves sensibly, pleasantly yet pointedly. Was it not Robert Louis Stevenson, a Scot, who said: 'Literature in many of its branches is no other than the shadow of good talk'? This is true, but it is also true that much good talk arrives by way of literature. After all, here is some matchless company. No, not matchless, however great and glorious, for we also have as company the persons we love and the friends closest to us. But what are love and friendship without talk? And I should like to say to a class of adolescent lads: 'I'll tell you a secret. It's about girls and women, those mysterious beings who are here with us, sharing our fate, and yet represent the other side of the universe. Now of course they can be impressed by fancy clothes, big fast cars, dinners, and dances. But the really magical thing that fascinates and entangles most of them needn't cost you a cent. For it's talk— but not just jabber and blabber—but fine talk.' Then I should like to cross over to the girls and say: 'Marriage, to which some of you are already giving some thought, has been described as one long conversation.

Again, while *some* of the world's most famous attractive women are said to have been beautiful, almost all of them, we are told, could talk with vivacity, wit, and wonderful charm. The power of talk is not mentioned in the advertisements, which are always bullying you or imploring you to do something about your hair, your skin, your figure, your clothes. Nobody, you see, can make a profit out of your talk—except you, your friends, and perhaps some dazzled and delighted young man.' And then how long would it take you—to connect talk with the enjoyment of literature?

Now where does the enjoyment of literature begin? Surely in the appreciative response to good writing *wherever that writing may be found.* I have stressed those last six words because I think them important and also think that not all English teachers will understand why they are important. Let us suppose you are teaching in Zenith. Now it so happens that the *Zenith Daily Tribune* has a sports writer who is not content simply to shovel into his column the clichés and claptrap of his trade. He has an eye for a character, a feeling for a dramatic moment, and regularly he tries to find some good words to tell his readers what his eye has seen, his mind has felt. This man is *writing*, not just meeting a deadline. What do you do about him? Ignore him, so as not to waste a moment of the time allotted to Chaucer, Milton, or Charles Lamb? If so, you may be missing a chance to do literature a service. This sports column, good writing coming hot from the presses, may be offering your students an entrance into the appreciation of literature. I admit these opportunities are fewer than they used to be. Fifty years ago, when I began reading newspapers, I found in them, as regular contributors, writers like Chesterton, Belloc, H. M. Tomlinson, fine prose served up at the breakfast table. And here, at about this time, that sports writer might have been Ring Lardner. I do not know what is happening here now. There is in your writing, even though it is intended for a large audience, a vitality that may enable it to resist the over-editing, the smoothing out, the standardized finishing processes, all too common now not only in the offices of newspapers and magazines but even in publishing houses. How much comes through alive, and where, I cannot tell you. But I do know this, that every English teacher who pounces upon some topical piece of good writing, to make his or her students aware of it, is doing some service to literature. And a service that is all the more important because it is easy for youngsters to imagine that literature has no more to do with their own uproarious lives than have the glass cases in the local museum, that it is all a lot of dead-and-gone stuff for egghead squares, that your Chaucer, Milton, Charles Lamb, are mummified mandarins, not men who if they appeared among them for half-an-hour could command or enchant them at will. If they like to read crime stories—as most of us do— then it would not be wasting an hour to show them how some crime stories are much better pieces of writing than others, until the point can be made that all our crime stories and gangster films fade into insignificance before the blood and horror and overwhelming darkness of *Macbeth*.

In this search for immediate good writing, for all the sideroads leading to literature, I am afraid the English teacher will not receive much help from the professors and minor pundits of the university Eng. Lit. departments. I may be wrong about this, for I see no records of learned publications, but I cannot help feeling that these university critics now give us too many books about a select few authors, too few books about a great many authors. I could spare some of these analyses, down to the last comma, of Henry James, W. B. Yeats, James Joyce, T. S. Eliot, for example, if we could only have a few more wide-ranging critical studies like Alfred Kazin's *On Native Grounds* or Maxwell Geismar's series on contemporary American fiction. It seems to me that you people, in the front line of the battle for literature, might reasonably complain of a shortage of ammunition. Indeed, you could be excused for thinking that many of the generals and staff officers in the rear seem to have lost interest in the battle you are still fighting. Too much literary criticism nowadays gives us the impression that it has been produced by and for a secret society. Its volumes should carry the sign *For Members Only*. Enjoying a good book, which it warns the general public not to attempt, is apparently more elaborate and complicated than taking part in the Japanese Tea Ceremony. Literature is being fenced in, shuttered up, with critics as police and sentries to make sure only the few with permits are admitted, just at the time when some of us feel it ought to be opened to the public. In these days, when so much of life does without literature, too many people paid to

[245]

profess literature want it to do without life. I realize
of course that such people represent only a small
minority, and that much good work is being done in
Eng. Lit. departments at the university level. Yet I
am not trying to flatter anybody here when I declare
my belief that the work of the high school English
teacher is far more important. My whole argument
supports this belief. It is around the adolescent, preparing for life, that the battle has to be fought. It is
here that English is not just another subject. It has a
special significance because it cuts deeply into life.
With older students, at the university level, the
situation has lost its urgency. Scholarship in English
Language and Literature is one discipline out of many.
I cannot help remembering that the most notable professors of English in my youth—enduring critics like
Bradley, Saintsbury, Ker, Walter Raleigh, Quiller-
Couch—were not themselves the products of Eng.
Lit. departments, which did not exist when they were
students. And I am dubious, not about the detailed
studies the students must undertake, which are
reasonable enough, but about examinations that give
or withhold marks not only for matters of exact
knowledge but also for matters of taste and opinion:

> *Oh cuckoo, shall I call thee bird*
> *Or but a wandering voice.*
> *State the alternative preferred,*
> *Give reasons for your choice.*

Professor Snooks may honestly believe that he is
ready to give high marks for brilliance and originality,
but he is only human, and if Joe Doakes, in his

examination paper, obviously disagrees with everything he has heard in Professor Snooks's lectures, then Joe runs the risk of getting some low marks for not understanding what he has been taught. Yet Joe may be the better critic of the two. I agree that the odds are heavily against this, probably several hundred to one, yet the one chance remains, especially at our older universities where students may be mature adults. There is also the argument, which I have often heard brought forward, that a student taking philosophy, history, or economics may get more out of reading Keats and Shelley for enjoyment than he would if he were grinding away at them for next year's examination paper. From all these doubts the work with younger students is entirely free. I would no more question its value than I would stop a lifeguard, hurrying toward a cry of distress, to ask him if he thought he was doing a useful job.

We have only to take, in film script terms, a 're-verse shot' of our situation, to think about bad writing instead of good writing, and then the urgency is obvious. We live in a smog of bad writing. I am not thinking about split infinitives, sentences ending with prepositions, gerunds without the possessive noun or pronoun, and so on and so forth. I mean the dumping and shovelling out of words as if they were garbage. I mean writing that offers our minds a diet of straw and broken glass. We hear from many quarters that our younger scientists too often cannot begin to report what they are doing, not simply because their research is highly technical and difficult, but because communication in written language eludes them. This suggests that they are no longer with us. They can think in the laboratory but not as fellow citizens, members of the community; which might explain why some of them undertake without protest the most appalling tasks, seeking to destroy all living creatures and the very land that nourishes us. With that comment we will move on, well away from the scientists. Now here, on my study table as I write these words, are three new books that have been sent to me. The first is by an amateur metaphysician; no fool, with some flashes of insight and original thought in his work. I open his book, and this is what I read:

> The success of the ensuing empiricism will rest on how successfully correlation appears to be established. This conceptual bipolarity is equivalent to the predicament between observer and phenomena and is a situation that is always liable to disrupt any dogmatic view of the physical world producing a condition which if fully extended must bring anomaly to the theories of relativity, De Sitter's theory, or indeed to any matrix which, rely-only on certain particular or selective propositions, sets out to say something absolutely non-paradoxically universal . . .

This is sheer horror of course, but after all the author of it is a metaphysician, and an amateur one at that; though it is worth remembering that David Hume was an amateur metaphysician too but never churned out such stuff. The second new book on my table is by a writer of long experience, whose art criticism and aesthetic speculations have brought him a world-wide reputation. So now I open his book somewhere about the middle and this is what I find:

Mondrian's ideal of equilibrium, 'of great importance to humanity', as he says, is not to be distinguished from disequilibrium by the exclusion of feeling: it is merely that the feeling inspired by a sense of equilibrium is distinct from the feeling inspired by a sense of disequilibrium. It might be said, therefore, that the aim of this renewal of artistic volition is to purify feeling, to relieve it of irrelevant or confusing images; in other words, to make identical the Form and Content of the work of art. . . .

I take the third new book, again by an experienced writer, this time an historian and social philosopher, and here is what page 151 offers me:

The argument of 'contingent necessity', usually involving the gravest of risks, together with the systematic building up of elements and areas of potential strength for Armageddon, maintains a 'truce of terror' at the edge of the abyss in pursuance of Elihu Root's dictum that the sovereign right of self-protection includes a nation's right 'to protect itself by preventing a condition of affairs in which it will be too late to protect itself'. When this policy was applied to limited concepts such as the Monroe Doctrine, it had limited risks and seemed a viable policy, but now that the concept has been expanded to include a multitude and wide range of contingent circumstances covering the globe, we have transformed a reasonable policy formerly involving occasional nominal risks into an unrealistic doctrine now involving a continuity of the gravest of risks without reasonable hope of attaining our objectives. . . .

The fact that I agree with this writer, who is trying to say something very important, leaves me all the more dissatisfied with such flavourless and half-dead writing, such a clutter of abstract terms. It is writing that has

[249]

forgotten our living hopeful ears. It is the equivalent in prose not of things carved in wood or hammered out of metal, but of plastics slopped into moulds. And it is part of the irony of our time that all these three men, who are pleading for life in a world of statistics, machines, and death, should offer us writing already losing flavour, rhythm, vital energy, as if statistics, machines, and death were certain of victory. All three of them, I fancy, would have the smallest opinion of— shall we say—Robert Louis Stevenson. So let us dip into him as we have dipped into them; and not the mature R.L.S. but the young man in his twenties with the long hair and the ragged velvet jacket and the affectations that still find their way into his prose.

> It is true that we shall never reach the goal; it is even more than probable that there is no such place; and if we lived for centuries and were endowed with the powers of a god, we should find ourselves not much nearer what we wanted at the end. O toiling hands of mortals! O un- wearied feet, travelling ye know not whither! Soon, soon, it seems to you, you must come forth on some con- spicuous hill-top, and but a little farther, against the setting sun, descry the spires of El Dorado. Little do ye know your own blessedness; for to travel hopefully is a better thing than to arrive, and the true success is to labour.

Very well, it is familiar stuff, and afterwards he wrote with fewer echoes and flourishes and with a more delicate precision; but, even so, this is writing, intended in the old way of prose to reach and haunt the mind through the ear; it is not a mess of verbiage dumped in front of us, cabbage soup in a prison camp.

You know better than I do, ladies and gentlemen, what road you must travel hopefully, what the labour is that will be your true success. What I have tried to do is to connect these daily tasks of yours with some issues that threaten our whole civilization, and how-ever laboriously, long-windedly, faultily, the connec-tion has been made. We have, I hope, established our claim that teaching English is an activity of some im-portance, even urgency. But I do not ask you to re-member any words of mine, inside or outside the classroom. Remember instead that single line of Wordsworth's which I quoted earlier, seven words that tell the profoundest truth about all of us, whether we are hosts or guests, speakers or listeners, teachers or students, young writers who are too thin or old writers who are too fat, even chairmen of the Board or politicians:

We live by Admiration, Hope, and Love.

What about the Audience?

In 1961, thanks to the wise generosity of Mr Sidney Bernstein and his Granada company, Manchester University acquired a School of Drama, and Mr Hugh Hunt, whom I had known for many years and had last seen in Sidney N.S.W. where he had artfully roped me in to lecture, was being installed as its first Professor. He did his rope trick again, so that I found myself giving this talk in Manchester. Really it belongs to my Art of the Dramatist, to which it is a kind of rough-and-ready sequel, but it is more convenient to print it here.

A FEW YEARS ago, I gave a lecture at the Old Vic Theatre that was published afterwards, together with some discursive notes, as *The Art of the Dramatist*. In this lecture I suggested that the Theatre offered us a unique kind of experience, which I called dramatic experience. It was unique because two different levels of the mind appeared to be involved at one and the same time. As members of an audience we had to make a simultaneous double response. We had to respond imaginatively to the play the dramatist had created, and yet had to be aware that we were sitting in a theatre, watching and listening to actors performing. Truly rewarding dramatic experience, I argued, only arrived when there was a kind of balance established between this response and this awareness, between the dream life of the play and the real life in the play's presentation. If this balance is disturbed—if for example we are so completely lost in the play that we forget we are looking at actors on a stage, or if we are so conscious of the theatre, the stage, the actors, that we cannot enter into the life of the play—then this dramatic experience loses its unique quality. The essential balance, the crucial inner relation between play and reality, must be achieved. Then I re-stated the theory in terms of an actress and the part she is playing. Here I quote. Polly Brown, the actress, is playing Annie Smith, perhaps a farmer's innocent but unfortunate daughter. Now if I go, for professional reasons, to observe Polly Brown, caring nothing about Annie Smith and her misfortunes, I reject true dramatic experience. But if I entirely lose sight of Polly Brown and see and believe only in Annie Smith, so that there is no actress but only a farmer's daughter, I am still outside dramatic experience. The genuine unique experience comes from Polly-Brown-playing-Annie-Smith, something to be found only in the theatre. If you doubt this, if you believe as most people seem to do that the actress must vanish in the part, Polly Brown disappearing when Annie Smith is there, then you will find it impossible to explain your attitude towards actors and acting. For the players you like best, calling them 'stars', are precisely those actors and actresses who are always tremendously themselves, recognizable at once, and yet at the same time are very much somebody else, the character in the play. It is above all the great performers from whom we get this important

Polly-Brown-playing-Annie-Smith contribution to dramatic experience.

It is possible that the audiences of stock companies —usually and wrongly called 'repertory companies'— may have been helped not hindered by the fact that everybody on the stage was familiar to them. In the West End, where we preferred type-casting, choosing out of scores of available actors and actresses those we thought nearest in type to the parts, we felt we had left stock companies far behind. We knew they were compelled to do some very rough-and-ready casting, boys and girls, for example, often playing old men and women. Twenty years ago I would not have felt I could work as a dramatist with a stock company, the same people appearing in every play. Now I am beginning to wonder if this would not help average audiences to know dramatic experience. They would be as aware of each actor as they would be of the part he was playing. It might be easier to achieve just the right balance. And after all, theatrical history, down the centuries, has been made by stock companies, arriving at greatness when dramatists of genius, from Shakespeare and Molière to Chekhov and Synge, have worked in intimate contact with a group of players.

But we must return to the audience. I am suggesting that it enjoys itself best, is most richly rewarded, when its mind, at full stretch, has to do two things at one and the same time, on one level responding to the imaginary life in the play, on another level being sharply aware of every detail of the play's presentation. Let me give you a personal example, an occasion in which dramatic experience was raised for me to an almost ecstatic height. Chekhov's *Cherry Orchard* is one of my favourite plays, and when I visited Moscow in 1945 I had already seen various English productions of the play. But there—incidentally it began at noon on Sunday, not a bad time to see a play if you have had a good late breakfast—I saw the Moscow Art Theatre's *Cherry Orchard*. (And here I must add that this production was immensely better than the one the Moscow Art Theatre sent to Sadler's Wells a few years ago.) On this Sunday morning, in 1945, my mind was working at full stretch on both these different levels. Though I only knew a few words of Russian, I was familiar with the play itself, so that language was not a barrier. I felt myself drawn as never before into the profound imaginative depths of the play, into the lives of these people. At the same time I was tremendously aware of the reality of the play's presentation, noting with delight every superb detail of the production, the lighting, the grouping, every move, every inflection of the voices. It was almost as if I had never really been to a theatre before. It was wonderful; almost, I repeat, an ecstatic experience. My mind was not passive but active, you could even say creative. I felt as I do when listening to great music magnificently played. And this is what the Theatre can do when it is at the furthest remove from the familiar English idea of it, a place where two or three hours can be spent idly, with the least possible effort, a killer of time.

On the other hand, I hardly ever sit in the stalls of a West End theatre without feeling that for most people around me the right balance between dream and reality has not been achieved. These people find it difficult to lose any part of their mind in the life within the play, just because they are too sharply aware of the fact that this is a social occasion, for which they have collected a little party, that there they are sitting in the stalls at the So-and-so Theatre, attending one of the successful plays of the season, with this actor or actress giving the performance that has been so much written up and talked about—and wasn't Peter or Derek clever to be able to get seats? Without being priggish about it, I hope, I do believe that the party spirit, the let's-all-have-a-night-out spirit, so common in the English-speaking Theatre, is the enemy of dramatic as opposed to social experience. It encourages the kind of play and production in which you are not expected to lose yourself imaginatively, some familiar and fairly amusing entertainment that provides an excuse for a playgoing occasion, passing the time pleasantly, on a big expense account evening, between an early dinner and the supper at a night club. Nobody, you notice, goes to a remarkable exhibition of pictures or a first-class concert in this spirit, and this explains why so many people, often people in authority, make such a sharp distinction between art and music, on the one hand, and the Theatre, on the other. They insist upon associating playgoing with a frivolous mood, and then dismiss the Theatre for its frivolity. Never having known true dramatic experience, they are quite unaware of the fact that it is a unique experience, of great value, both emotionally and intellectually, to the mind that knows it.

Many people are deficient on both sides of the

balance that has to be achieved. Not enough, we may say, has been put in either of the scales. Let us take first the imaginary life of the play we are asked to share. Such people cannot join in, so to speak, because they hold their minds stiffly against anything that is unfamiliar and not immediately understood. They want to see the same kind of persons in the same kind of place in the same kind of situation. A little different from the last play they saw, no doubt, but not very different. This does not necessarily mean that they must have light comedies of sexual intrigue in lounge halls. The refusal to make any imaginative effort, the deadening effect of convention, can work both ways. We may have audiences now that hold themselves equally stiffly against any dramatic life presented to them in terms of carefully dressed persons in lounge halls and drawing rooms. Unless they are shown tramps and layabouts in dark basements, they may feel their time and attention are being wasted, even though they themselves have never been in such places or encountered such characters. One set of prejudices is just as bad as another. What is wrong is the refusal to open the imagination to the dramatist, to follow him wherever he wishes to take us until he proves himself an unworthy guide; and to demand in advance, so to speak, the kind of life the dramatist must reveal to an audience. One of our most success-ful playwrights has told us that he always has had in mind a certain Aunt Edna, whose tastes and mental limitations must be taken into account. This is com-mercially shrewd, no doubt, Aunt Edna being a notable hostess of little theatre parties and therefore an important person at the box office; but some of us cannot help asking who is Aunt Edna that she should dictate to the Theatre in this fashion, and believe that our drama comes to life when Aunt Edna has to like it or lump it. Let her open her mind and heart a little wider.

Now let us turn to the other side of the scales in this balance, to the reality of the play's presentation, to the Theatre not as a dream world but as a show-case of elaborate and highly expert theatrical techniques. I think most English audiences would gain immensely, coming closer to enjoying the true dramatic experience, if they took the trouble to understand and appreciate these techniques and all that is involved in good production. Too many people adopt a lofty patronising attitude, as if they were so important they could not condescend to notice the difference between a good production and a bad one, superb acting and careless mummery. Others seem to think that actors, who have carefully rehearsed every move, gesture, inflection, are merely playing charades, almost making it up as they go along. Discussing a play, they ask 'Did they do it the night you were there?' This ignorance, often wilful, and not without a suggestion of social superiority—the bane of English life—must be condemned, not only because it is stupid, because it is unjust to the men and women who devote their lives to the Theatre as few other people now devote their lives to anything, but also because it befogs and blunts what should be so sharp and clear if dramatic experience is to be enjoyed. In the Theatre, as in Nature, we receive but what we give. Our English audiences need a little theatrical education. If they were more perceptive and discriminating, in the play-house and in the dining room, the fare they are offered would soon be better and their evenings enriched.

For my part I do not believe that live actors performing on a stage are essential for dramatic experience. We have not shut ourselves off from that experience when we watch films or plays on television. But of course we are more of an audience, capable of achieving that experience at its best, when we are in the theatre. And it is a mistake to imagine, as some people seem to do, that the Theatre is on its way out, just because it is old-fashioned, thinks of its audiences in hundreds not millions, and does not appear quite at home in our new age of technological marvels. The truth is, so long as drama is presented, in no matter what form, the Theatre remains central, the enduring core. Though writing, direction, acting, may have to be adjusted to the new media, as indeed we know they have, the Theatre is still at the heart of the whole matter. Take it away and you would soon see a rapid deterioration in film and television drama. We hear people say that so long as they have their television sets and can pay an occasional visit to the cinema, it does not matter to them if there is not a single stage left in England. But if these people expect dramatic entertainment from their screens, then they should realize that although they do nothing for the Theatre, the Theatre has already done a great deal for them. It is in the playhouse, and nowhere else, that performers and audience come together, and writers, directors, actors, are severely tested, learning if they are wise what is essential in the presentation of drama. I have declared before now that if I were responsible for a large film studio or a television network, and I knew that the Theatre was in danger of disappearing, I would feel it was my duty to subsidize or altogether maintain a playhouse, so that my writers, directors, actors, could face the challenge of an actual audience, coughing when it is bored, silent and intent when it is properly held. And when such writers, directors, actors, had triumphantly survived this test, they would return to their studios refreshed and heartened, feeling closer for some time to their vast invisible and remote audiences. Shrewd experienced performers know that the presence of an audience helps to shape a scene as no expert direction can do. This is particularly true in comedy, where exact timing is all-important. For example, nothing could seem to belong to the world of film farce more than the uproarious scene in the Marx Brothers, *Night At the Opera* where more and more people crowd into a ship's cabin. We think of it as pure film clowning. Yet in point of fact that scene was perfected by being first performed, tried out, for several weeks on the stage, before it was ever played, in its final form, in front of the cameras.

Having acknowledged the central position of the Theatre, however, I must repeat that we have not denied ourselves true dramatic experience when we turn to films or television drama. We are still an audience. We still respond on two different levels of the mind. We can still be rewarded if we can achieve the right balance between dream and reality, between the imaginary life into which the screen admits us and our understanding and appreciation of the performance itself. Good writing, good direction, good acting, still remain good writing, good direction, good acting. But there are of course important differences. We are not the same kind of audience we are in the playhouse. Watching a film, for instance, we feel further removed from it than we do at a play. We know the actors are not there, not with us. I always feel that a play *is happening*, is sharing our sense of present time, whereas to me a film, however engrossing it may be, is always a record of something that has already happened. This has its advantages. If I am there with it, I cannot ignore a bad play; I must either attend to it or leave the theatre. But if a film is equally bad, I sink lower and lower into my seat— not possible in the theatre anyhow with seats as they are—and smoke at the screen and begin thinking about something else. Except for keeping quiet during the serious scenes, a thing many of our youngsters at the cinema cannot do, I do not feel I have any responsibility as a member of the audience, no part to play as I have in a theatre audience. I am altogether more passive, less close in my attention, knowing that the camera will do some of the work I have to do for myself in the theatre. Now and again of course, when a director of genius has made the film, we have to sharpen our attention, and then, just because we are stretching and not relaxing our minds, we may find ourselves enjoying real dramatic experience, feeling as wonderfully alive as we do in a good theatre.

I am not being merely discursive if I say something here about this relaxing business. Modern man, crowded into our huge urban areas, is always being told he must relax. The doctors play the tune on their solitary pipes, the advertisers on their massed brass bands. Relax with this, relax with that, we are told. Now I consider myself a rather indolent and self-indulgent man, and would never have the impudence to recommend a strenuous mode of life, physical or mental. But I cannot help feeling suspicious about all this talk of relaxation. I have noticed that the people who say they must relax in the evening are not as a rule the people who have had to meet most demands during the day; most of them have not really had very much to relax *from*. It is not the hard-pressed professional man, not the educated woman who may be doing a job as well as being a wife and mother, who demands relaxation at all cost; it is—well, other kinds of people, not so hard-pressed in a profession, not doing two women's work. And these other people— we are now back to our subject—are particularly insistent that anything offered them on the stage or the screen must be relaxing. Now in one sense of the term this is a reasonable demand. Audiences rightly ask for entertainment. As a dramatist it never occurred to me that attendance at my plays should be regarded as cultural duty; I began by offering entertainment, first of all, as a better man called Shakespeare most certainly did, though that does not mean that nothing else would happen. But these people who insist upon relaxing in front of the stage or the screen have something very different in mind. They want to be free of any real demand on their attention. They are anxious not to give much of themselves. They are merely killing time. With the ironical result that they are never, as people say, 'taken out of themselves', and because they insist upon relaxation are never able properly to relax, are left still wondering, while the band plays louder and the girls dance harder than ever, whether they ought to have accepted a fifteen-per-cent discount or if Jones is really the right man for the Birmingham branch. And true dramatic experience, from which they shrink, would in fact take them so far from any thought of discounts and Jones in Birmingham, that next morning they would tackle their problems with renewed zest and hope. They might then respond to all those official appeals to produce and export more. Our chief trouble now is not, as some people tell us, that we live carelessly and undutifully, riotously and immorally, but that too many of us English do not really live at all but are content merely to exist in a perpetual dim twilight of worry and vague frustration.

There, in the twilight, the roofs bristle with television aerials and sitting rooms are dominated by illuminated screens. In many of these rooms people are sitting on special television furniture, eating special television snacks. True, the English honeymoon with the Telly is now over; the first excitement is almost forgotten; television is now finding its own place in the national life. But it is a large and important place. Television does not ignore drama, and we cannot afford to ignore television. The size of its audience cannot be grasped, but now and again something happens to give one an idea of it. For example, the morning after some play of mine had been shown on television, I had to visit various shops near where I live when I am in London. In every shop either a fellow customer or one of the assistants made some remark to me about that play. In one morning I heard more public comment than I would have heard during a six months' run of a play in a theatre. This giant has come to live with us; instead of sneering at him, we should try to civilize him. In drama, television is only just beginning to find its own way, refusing at last to turn towards the Theatre on one side, the film on the other. Already there are many youngish directors, actors and actresses who are completely at home in this medium. They know now what it can do and what it never should be asked to do. Working with them, as aware as they are of the virtues and limitations of television, are some writers who owe their reputations to it. They are writers of considerable talent but they will do much better when conditions of performance are improved, when they are made more fuss of, when they are paid about four or five times as much as they receive now. I am not being cynical. Greater rewards would give the writers more time; and if they received more attention, more praise, let us say about half as much as popular comedians receive, they would no longer have the status of studio employees but would come to be accepted as independent creative artists. We writers may not look like flowers, but after a little sunlight and a little loving care we too begin blossoming.

Television drama can not only exist in its own

right, as something quite different from stage plays adapted and simplified, crowded into a small space, then photographed and transmitted on a vast scale; it is potentially a unique and fascinating kind of drama, which might come closer to what our age needs than anything the stage or film can offer. It combines the flexibility of the film—an economy too in presenting a character, suggesting a situation, that appeals to our impatient minds—with something of the immediate impact of the stage play; and potentially it is superior to both the film and the stage play in one highly important matter, namely, in intimacy. Rightly used, it can bring us closer to its characters than they can, putting us in the same room with them, able to notice the slightest glance, the tiniest inflection. I can imagine television drama as closely intimate in its way as the most delicate perceptive fiction; it would be essentially psychological in its approach to life, thereby fulfilling the needs of an age that cannot help but be concerned with psychological analysis. If the politicians, whose outlook suggests they are only just entering this century, began to share this concern, we might stop blundering from one disaster to another. A television drama on politics and politicians might be astonishingly revealing.

All this, however, is potential, by no means an inevitable progress. The television drama I have in mind may never come into existence. It demands certain conditions to which we are no closer now than we were when television began. I am not thinking now about the pay and status of writers. I am back with my subject, the audience. Television drama on a fairly high level must be able to select its audience. It has to break away from family entertainment. It has to ask for and receive a certain quality of attention, taking its audience out of an atmosphere of free-and-easy domesticity, with Dad cleaning his pipe, Mum pouring out cocoa, Sis trying to telephone, and young Bert loudly demanding some other programme. This means, in my opinion, that television drama can develop properly not only where there is a far wider choice of programmes but also when important productions are no longer thrown in with the licence and the advertisements, when in fact they cannot be seen at all except by payment of a special fee. I am not now considering the financial aspect of this move. The separate payment would create an audience, attending properly to what it had paid for. It would take these productions into another atmosphere, unlike that of some vast vague school treat. It would bring into existence a genuine television theatre with its own audience, who would not be accepting what it offered them simply as a cheap and convenient substitute for the stage or film. And these are not impossible demands; our technology is equal to the task of scrambling and unscrambling particular programmes; it is chiefly a question now of finding sufficient people who realize what television is capable of achieving, given the right conditions. But if conditions remain unchanged, no matter how many intelligent and devoted writers, directors, actors, we may have in television, I doubt if much real progress will be made. Television drama able to challenge what is best in theatre and film will be only a dream. The viewer will remain a passive yawning idler, which is what some influential persons, for reasons of their own, would like him to be.

We can now see in our mind's eye three very different audiences. In the centre, with a long tradition behind it, is the audience in the playhouse, looking at and listening to living actors, not images on a screen, and capable of a response that does much to shape and colour the play itself. And this audience can at times be so enraptured by dramatic experience that it never forgets every detail of the occasion, long after it may have forgotten how it came to enjoy something on the screen. Magic may be hard to find in the playhouse but we never go without feeling it might be there. Then, on one side of this central traditional audience is that other audience of the films, people who may still find their way into picture houses to get out of the rain, to spend a couple of hours away from home, to hold hands, to indulge idly in vicarious living, adventurous or erotic, but who, in these days, no longer go out of pure habit, not knowing or caring what they will see on the screen, as they used to do. This is a change for the better, and it would be better still, in my opinion, if we abolished the continuous performance, which has the audience drifting in and out, and followed the Continental custom of having definite fixed performances, bringing the film closer to the theatre. Then, on the other side, really at the opposite extreme even though it too attends to images on a screen, is the vast dispersed audience of television, for the most part consisting of tiny groups in living rooms. This newest of all our audiences is at once the largest and the smallest.

These three very different audiences, however, do share some common ground. The people in the playhouse may be wanting magnificent language and splendid projections of personality; those in the cinema demanding swift movement, changing backgrounds, laconic dialogue; those at home with their television sets preferring a narrowly limited familiar scene and intimate studies of character. But all of them are asking in one way or another for what I have called dramatic experience. Paradoxically they want a heightened reality that they know to be unreal. It is wrong, in my opinion, to suppose that audiences must forget that actors are performing for them. They must be sharply conscious of this fact, technically interested as far as they are able to be, in one part of their minds, while still able, in another part, to live imaginatively with the drama itself. If the work is good, then the more we bring to it, the more we take from it. Returning to the idea of dramatic experience coming from a balance of these two sides, then we can say that the more each scale can hold, with imaginative sympathy on one side, conscious critical appreciation of performance on the other, the more rewarding the experience will be. It is the idle passive acceptance of drama in any form that merely acts like a drug. This is the danger of the routine perfunctorily-acted play, the film composed of stock characters and situations, and, above all, of effortless glazed-eyed television viewing. Audiences that always fail to reach a certain level of curiosity, sympathy, zest, critical understanding, are made up of people busy corrupting themselves; they would be better employed getting quietly drunk. That is one reason—and there are others—why the constant advancement and elevation of drama in any form is a challenge to public spirit and the social conscience. I doubt if audiences can remain long at one level. Either they go up or they go down. If they go up, so much the better for our whole community; if they go down, so much the worse, and even labour relations and trade figures may suffer in the end. I throw that in for the benefit of the self-styled realistic hard-headed types who never seem to understand the interdependence of things in this world.

Our various audiences, watching and listening to the actors paid to perform for them, may seem very remote indeed from the communal worshippers for whom a myth was enacted, perhaps thirty centuries ago, or, for that matter, from our medieval ancestors celebrating a religious festival. We know that drama, whether here or elsewhere, was once rooted in religion. And we assume that those roots were severed long before our time, that nothing could be more secular, almost irreligious, than drama as we know it now, all those painted shows at which clergymen shake their heads. I believe we are wrong to assume this. I believe, strange as it may seem, that those roots were never cut, that the archaic religious foundation of drama has never been destroyed. Something remains, to give a curious sense of urgency, a devotion to their duty, to all players, directors, writers, who have not lost the last whisper of conscience. Something remains too in the audience, when it is not composed of people waiting to die and killing time. Man has been on this earth for many long ages; we are all our ancestors; we have not recently changed our species, as stupid people seem to think, just because we can travel in jet planes and buy frozen food. The ancient myths, with which drama began, may have been banished from consciousness but they are still alive in the dark of our minds. Perhaps we turn unknowingly to dramatic art to renew contact with them outside ourselves. There might be something mystical here, in this dream coming through the multitude of business. I have said elsewhere, describing dramatic experience, that it is unlike any common experience, but that there are certain rare moments in our lives, perhaps when we find ourselves in great danger, when reality itself suddenly turns into dramatic experience, as if the whole world were a giant theatre and all this life a drama, so much play-acting compared with some unknown deeper reality.

The actor worthy of the name, whether on a stage or a screen, makes a double appeal, to our sympathy and to our critical intelligence, to which we in the audience have to make a double response. At one and the same time we take a holiday from ourselves and our affairs, following the fortunes of another human being, and yet, because we cannot enjoy dramatic experience without being aware, alert, sharp-eyed and keen-eared, we are more ourselves than we were before we joined the audience. This sounds like magic, but then deep-down, no matter how often we have been disappointed, we are expecting magic.

Children, poets, wise old men, almost all good women, love drama; it is power-seekers, intriguers, and pompous busy blockheads who despise it. Or they affect to despise it, perhaps secretly realizing that all this mere *let's pretend*, this fancywork of the mind, not only dangerously broadens sympathy but also heightens and deepens men's understanding of themselves. Any man or woman who is a good member of a good audience, hoping to enjoy true dramatic experience, is challenging the worse part of the world in which we live. If there ever was a time when that experience was needed to refresh and hearten men, it is this time of ours, when noise deafens the ears, lights dazzle the eyes, confusion wearies the mind and blurs its judgement, when our very progress in knowledge threatens the human scale, the human values. Shakespeare's Duke of Athens, sitting in the audience, said 'The best in this kind are but shadows'; but we in our audiences, knowing a darkness and despair Athens and Elizabethan England never knew, can find in these shadows a wealth of meaning, movement, colour and living speech, and the faces of our brothers and sisters.

Shakespeare and the Modern World

This is based on a talk I gave in August 1961 to the International Shakespeare Conference in Stratford-upon-Avon. And I have left it in 1961, to which it belongs. But I must explain why the year is important. It is since 1961 that, thanks largely to Professor Kott of Poland, Shakespeare has been dragged, screaming, into the Theatre of the Cruel and the Absurd. Asked to give the Birthday Talk for 1965, I called it Take Him or Leave Him *and protested vigorously against this Cruel and Absurd treatment of our Shakespeare. But I improvised the talk, not even using any notes, and I do not propose now to serve up cold helpings of indignant protests. However, this explains my emphasis above on 1961.*

I AM WRITING this in my house at Alveston, a village just outside Stratford-upon-Avon. I am well situated to report on what is happening to Shakespeare. If I go into Stratford to pick up a book or buy some tobacco, I find the place crowded with visitors, pink, yellow, brown, black, and hear an impressive variety of languages and accents. This, you may say, is mere tourism, but its growth suggests an increasing interest in Shakespeare himself. Moreover, at the Royal Shakespeare Theatre, as it is now called, there is the most successful theatrical company in Britain. From early spring until late autumn the theatre is full. Now the other night I went to see an excellent young actor called Christopher Plummer playing Richard III. Mr Plummer is a Canadian, and has been brought to our Stratford from Stratford, Ontario. Canada has now found its way into the Theatre—through Shakespeare. The most successful recent Old Vic production, of *Romeo and Juliet*, was directed by an Italian. (Romeo will be played here at Stratford by a Pakistani actor.) The most ambitious series of programmes attempted last year by B.B.C. Television was *The Age of Kings*, nothing less than all Shakespeare's historical plays adapted for television. And there was no outcry from the mass audience.

The point, I trust, has been made, and it would be wearisome to pile up further evidence. In this postwar world of ours, not only in playhouses but also in lecture rooms and libraries, far from being neglected Shakespeare is commanding more attention than ever before. We are entitled to feel some surprise. The contemporary world ought to be moving further and further away from Shakespeare. Its own new drama, experimental, off-beat, deeply introverted, is anything but Shakespearean. It has no particular reverence for classical masterpieces, as the nineteenth century had. There is of course a widespread attempt, on the whole fairly successful, to make more and more people realize, in their newly found leisure, the wealth and splendour of our artistic inheritance, so that we have more and more cheap editions of good books, more and more fine reproductions of pictures and music. But this new enthusiastic demand for Shakespeare seems to me outside the general culture drive, the educational process, the vague desire for self-improvement. It is warmer and more personal. Behind it is not simply a recognition of Shakespeare's towering reputation but a new appreciation of the man himself and his work, a feeling on the part of countless contemporary individuals that there is something here that they want, as if they suddenly discovered in themselves a hunger for a certain kind of food.

We are not dealing here with a movement, with anything that lends itself to measurement and statistics. No public opinion poll can take over the job. It is all very individual and personal, this new relation between our modern world and Shakespeare. At this stage, any account of it must be largely based on guesswork. (At last—a man in a review who admits that he is guessing.) But the recent turn towards Shakespeare is a fact, and for that fact there must be some explanation.

One further point must be made. Within the severe limits of five thousand words, certain wide generalizations about Shakespeare must be allowed and some statements taken on trust. To give chapter and verse, to make allowance for every exception, would require not five but fifty thousand words. This is not scholarly practice, but then we are not now concerned with scholarship. We are merely wondering why we men and women of the atomic age should be increasingly fascinated by a dramatic poet who died nearly three hundred and fifty years ago. We may learn nothing new about Shakespeare but may learn something about ourselves and our world.

First, a small visual thing, not important but worth mentioning. Those of us who travel a great deal are beginning to feel that we fly at five hundred miles an hour only to arrive in the same place we left. The old richly confused variety has been bulldozed and then buried under concrete. The same runways go on and on; the same river of steel flows along main highways; the same metal and glass towers rise everywhere; the neon lights may spell different words but their effect is the same: it is all impressive, no doubt, but it is also monotonous, tedious, depressing. Sometimes when we think optimistically about the future—peace assured at last, perhaps a secure world government—we are suddenly visited by an appalling vision of illimitable concrete, of steel and glass forests of office blocks and apartment buildings, of innumerable cities like anthills and termitaries, of what we have already simply multiplied without any real variety a hundred times, the same thing going on and on and on. The comparison may not be fair, but is it not true that if instead of saying 'modern world' to ourselves we say 'Shakespeare' our minds swarm with rich images? Within a second or two we have caught glimpses of forest walks in sunlight, glades in moonlight, trim gardens, moors and heaths shivering in storms, of kings in processions, soldiers going to war, lovers meeting and parting, clowns and shepherds and sailors and murderers, banqueting halls, throne rooms, taverns and huts. There is something wonderfully life-enhancing in this sudden vision of the

Shakespearean world. For a moment or two we feel that almost suffocating expectation, that sense of endless variety and innumerable possibilities, which we knew in childhood.

In this Shakespearean world, no matter what supernatural elements or magical hocus-pocus may be suggested, the basic scale is always human. Terrible things may happen; we may feel that both the poet and his characters are near to madness, to some final darkness we cannot imagine; yet this human scale remains. And no victory is being granted to something anti-human. This greatest of poets *is on our side.* And in this important respect he is in sharp contrast to many of the representative artists of the modern world, men who do not seem to be on our side, who appear to have a contempt for our common humanity, as if they belonged to a fifth column of some new species preparing to destroy us. Everything is curiously *anti*: anti-pictorial painting; anti-dramatic drama; anti-musical music; anti-human humanities. Are machines about to take us over? Whatever may be happening, it is certain that many of us increasingly enjoy slipping away from our own world for an hour or two to ask for some refreshment from Shakespeare.

It has been argued that Shakespeare's scale is all too human. For example, 'AE' (George Russell), the Irish poet, journalist and mystic, criticized him from this standpoint in an essay called 'Shakespeare and the Blind Alley'. He wrote:

> The greatest of Greek dramas leave us with this sense that the characters meet to reveal something greater than themselves. We are almost always waking as a

[276]

Greek drama comes to its climax to a consciousness of some enduring idea. When we waken from the dream we realize how illusionary were the characters and how real the passion or idea. Shakespeare was the first supreme artist in literature who seems to be absorbed in character for its own sake. Nothing before or since has equalled the art by which recognizable personalities are revealed in a few words.

But nothing is revealed in the Shakespearean drama except character. What did the genius of Shakespeare do for literature? More and more since his apparition have dramatist and novelist been artists of character for its own sake; and to be absorbed in character for its own sake is to be in a blind alley which leads nowhere. To the greater Greek dramatists life swam in an aether of deity, and that again bathes all the circumstances of the *Divine Comedy* or of the Indian epic, the *Mahabharata*. We feel as we read that we are in the divine procession, and know ourselves more truly by this envelopment, native to the spirit, than by looking at a mirror which reflects only personal character. We know ourselves as we are known when we are drawn out of our personal reverie and placed in juxtaposition with elemental laws or divinities. When we are absorbed in character for its own sake we are absorbed in our own illusion, and have no perspective such as is necessary for judgment. Since Shakespeare became the shepherd of the artistic soul, dramatist and novelist have been more and more absorbed by this illusion; and we know in reality little more about ourselves when we have absorbed the literature of character than we did before . . .

This will seem to most of us topsy-turvy criticism. It asks that the known should be presented in terms of the unknown. We are surrounded by men and women, by human character, and thus are able to recognize the truth and force of Shakespeare's drama. On the other hand, the cosmos is a mystery, something beyond our grasp and comprehension, as Shakespeare indicates over and over again, unlike those clergymen who talk about God as if He had been at college with them.

There is a remark about a friend by John Cowper Powys—that large-scale eccentric novelist and original genius who has not had the attention he deserves to have—that I am fond of quoting: 'He combined scepticism of everything with credulity about everything; and I am convinced this is the true Shakespearean way wherewith to take life. . . .' The modern world is largely divided between fanatical believers, ready to impose their private universes upon us by almost any means, and people who have closed their minds to any large questions, who accept any convenient twaddle, and live like talking technological apes. Because Shakespeare belongs to neither of these parties, recognizing the riddle of our existence but making no pretence of solving it, he offers us a blessed relief from both the fanatical believers and the incurious and dull-minded. Nevertheless, to suggest as 'AE' does that Shakespeare is entirely absorbed in character for its own sake, perceiving nothing beyond the difference between one man and another, is to do him a grave injustice. Once he reaches maturity as a dramatist he makes us realize over and over again, as I have written elsewhere, that life is a mystery, that man and Nature are symbolic representations, that we can feel if not think our way, through our sense of beauty and goodness, to a reality behind appearances,

[278]

as the lives of the dramatists and players are in a deeper reality behind the shows of the playhouse. It is all there in Prospero's great speech, which it is impossible to regard as a few final touches of character drawing: the poet himself is speaking to us, and no Indian metaphysician or Buddhist preacher can have ever conveyed better than he does here a sense of the insubstantiality and transcience of life in this world.

The mystery is there, and he cannot pluck the heart out of it. He makes no pretence of knowing what that deeper reality is, what remains when all our show of things has faded, who is the dreamer whose dreams we are. The cosmos contains the human intellect, not that intellect the cosmos. When Shakespeare declares in effect that he does now know and we do not know, many of us find this most refreshing. We are surrounded now by people who tell us they *do* know, that this life has no secrets from *them*. Our civilization knows so much that it may soon blow itself off the face of the earth. The danger of hubris has been largely forgotten. But Shakespeare, a sceptical late-comer to the Renaissance scene, was aware of it.

Because he recognized both the mystery and our incapacity to arrive at an intellectual solution of it, he would now be described as 'woolly-minded'. This is a term of contemptuous dismissal in our world, where the steel-minded and concrete-minded are banging and clashing from bad to worse. The astonishing perception and force, the poetry and wit, of Shakespeare's mind hardly suggest anything woolly. But if this is what wool can do, then we should all regard 'woolly-minded' as a compliment. The danger of having a steely razor-edged mind may be that you use it to cut the cosmos down to your own size and leave truth among the discarded fragments. It has been said that the expert avoids all minor errors in his way to the Grand Fallacy. Our modern world is crowded with experts, disdainful of the 'woolly-minded'. It is a relief to escape from them and to return to the other world that Shakespeare offers us, wool to wool.

Only a fool could imagine that in this other world there is nothing but frivolous play-acting, lovers dallying, clowns angling for laughs, good and bad kings and dukes striding across the stage. Some of man's most profound dilemmas are made plain here. Where else has the challenge of power or the relation between imagination and action been more clearly revealed? But one thing has been left out of this poet's world, to the despair of all good Marxists. It is a world without economics. The wine trade of Illyria, the demand for timber in Arden, the imports and exports of Hamlet's Denmark or Lear's Britain, these are all ignored. When so much had to be included, something had to be left out, so there is no place here for economic man. This too is a relief. There are times when we are made to feel that the chief end of our existence is buying and selling, capturing markets, making money. Even ancient myths are explained in economic terms, so that the quest of the Golden Fleece becomes an extension of the wool trade in Asia Minor. True, man cannot exist without some economic activity, but then he also cannot exist without water, yet we do not wait every morning for reports from the Water Board or allow its officials to dominate our lives. And behind our economics are men, not calculating machines, men with a rich variety of character, temperament, motive, not very different from those that Shakespeare shows us. It is at the least a pleasant change to see men outside offices and warehouses, away from profit and loss, grappling with the life that still remains to be lived when economics have had their share of attention.

The modern world honours ambition. Every day our newspapers and television sets show us those men who have succeeded in achieving great power. Never in history, not even when Alexander, Julius Caesar and Napoleon were all-conquering, have men ambitious for power loomed so large in the world's eye. The seers, the thinkers, the artists, noble men and beautiful women, they are all mere pygmies beside these giants. A lad of spirit, growing up in such a world, might well feel that no price was too great to be paid for power, that all the beauties and graces of life, the affections and the decencies, could be sacrificed to ambition. True, we often refer to 'the rat race'. But winners can be transformed almost overnight into benefactors, heroes, the great figures of our time. If there is any grumbling, it is against those young men who do not seem to have enough ambition, not against career-planners and power-seekers. And these are much the same whether they have a capitalist or a communist background. They are all pushing on, hoping for the attention and applause of the modern world.

Again, it is a relief to turn to Shakespeare. If one thing is certain about him, it is that he mistrusted and disliked very ambitious men. No play of his celebrates any cool career strategy, any successful grabbing at power. Our heroes are his villains. Macbeth is something more than a villain, being a genuine tragic figure: he is also a plain warning against sacrificing those beauties and graces, affections and decencies. In play after play we meet a character who has something chilly and withdrawn about him, who refuses to expand in the companionable warmth that Shakespeare creates so easily, and we soon realize that ambition is gnawing at him and that his part is that of an unscrupulous scoundrel. This is entirely personal to Shakespeare himself. Unlike many of his contemporaries he was no admirer of Renaissance Man, self-seeking, arrogant, ruthless, the Cesare Borgia type. Having a share in a playhouse and no taste for martyrdom, he may have occasionally lent himself to what we can only call Tudor propaganda, sometimes overdoing it as if he were giving us a wink (in *Richard III*, for example); but in the world he creates for himself, unlike ours, ambition is not honoured, crowned, celebrated, and men who seek power first are sooner or later doomed. And at least it makes, as we English like to say, a nice change.

His politics of course are not ours. He accepts without serious question a social hierarchy, taking his own stand and viewpoint much nearer the apex than the base of the pyramid. As a dramatist and manager he had to consider his more important patrons, but even so I think we had better accept the fact that Shakespeare was something of a snob, both inside and outside his work. This suggests that what he accepted was already looser than a hierarchy, for it is when one class can begin to merge into another that snobbery arrives. Chaucer, who was higher up the social ladder than Shakespeare, does not condescend to the lower orders but treats all classes alike. Snobbery came in with the Tudors, after the ruin of the old aristocracy in civil war, and it came to stay: we are all snobs in this island.

Not only did Shakespeare not question the inheritance of power, I think he would have defended it against our modern democratic prejudices. It has at least one advantage we often overlook. To some extent it protects society against ambitious men, whose natures may be warped by the desire for power and influence. Birth may put fools in high places but it may also put in those places some easy-minded sweet-natured men, whom we often meet in Shakespeare, men who would never have risked crippling themselves in the struggle for power. We have not to accept this point of view, but a temporary 'suspension of disbelief' in it enables us to enjoy a world very different from the one dreadfully revealed by our newspapers every morning.

In his conscious life Shakespeare was undoubtedly a careful worldly type, taking no risks, a conformist suspicious of rebels. (His belief in order and strong government was something more than a convenient recognition of Tudor rule. A country lad, even in the second half of the sixteenth century, would probably have heard many fireside tales of the horrors of civil war.) But being a full man as a creator, with the unconscious coming into play, he is anything but a careful conformist in his drama. His most famous characters, so wonderfully alive and dominating because so much of his hidden self went into them, are nothing if not rebellious, challengers of all Establishment values. No timid conformist created Hamlet and Cleopatra. Falstaff became so enormous and fascinating, out of all proportion to the part originally allotted to him, that he had to be killed off before he could wreck *Henry V*. True, they all come to a bad end. But it would be a mistake to assume that the modern world would delight in them away from the playhouse and print. To discover people like them we should probably have to search our prisons and mental hospitals. Maladjusted types of this sort are not in favour with us.

One curious little difference between our world and Shakespeare may be noted in passing. The poet's sympathy with, even tenderness for, the individual is common knowledge. He sees every man as a person. Even while hastily sketching some comic rustics, as foils to Falstaff, he can make one of them say, immortally mortal: 'By my troth, I care not; a man can die but once; we owe God a death. . . .' On the other hand, he clearly dislikes the crowd, the mob, the mass, in which individuality is lost in some collective imbecility. And in the modern world we seem to be busy reversing all this. It is not the individual but the faceless crowd, the mass, that is important and must be courted and won, either for votes or for money. In our vast populations the individual seems to vanish, reappearing in a fragmentary and dubious fashion on television screens, in films or the press, ours being above all the age of mass media. Two-thirds of our clever contemporaries meet every day to decide how to amuse stupid people they have never set eyes on, people who must not be expected to make the least effort, who have indeed the collective character that Shakespeare regarded with such mistrust. Conditions of course are entirely different, but all the clever worried men and women trapped in mass media might try giving themselves a holiday with Shakespeare.

It is a holiday too to escape for a time from modern literature and art, almost entirely introverted, and for the most part praised by critics who are themselves equally introverted. We tend now to take it for granted that the genuine artist, the serious creative type, as distinct from entertainers and hacks, must necessarily be one-sided and unbalanced. He may no longer choose to look a freak, as he often did from Baudelaire's time until the end of the century, nevertheless he is still understood to be freakish. He has nothing, it is agreed, to offer the out-and-out extroverts. During the last thirty or forty years we have almost ceased to look for breadth, vitality, a balanced attitude, in literature as art. There we expect to find strangeness, originality, intensity, one-sidedness, all the qualities associated with creation as compensation, often a kind of revenge, the outsider lashing at the insiders. True, in the last resort our society itself may be at fault, men of genius discovering in it appalling stresses and signs of corruption they feel compelled to reveal. But such men of genius are rare, whereas creation and criticism in the fashionable one-sided introverted mode are common enough, so many people keeping in the movement. We can take a holiday from it, and much-needed refreshment, by returning to Shakespeare, as all manner of playgoers and readers are discovering.

For if we take the whole of him into account, not certain plays but all of them, we find in him a welcome balance between the introverted and extraverted attitudes. Now he looks out, observing the world with marvellous swift judgement; now he looks inward, exploring the recesses of his own personality. He goes far out, far inward: this is his greatness. In that magnificently rich nature, the opposites were very strong indeed, but somehow—and there were times when he was nearly over the edge—he contrived to keep a balance between them. Often he swings perilously, like a captive balloon in a high wind, but the rope holding him to earth and our common life never breaks. His creation does not come out of one-sidedness; it is not compensatory, let alone revengeful; it springs from his rich nature, his vitality, his enjoyment of his perceptions, even from an immensely heightened *ordinariness*. (It is this, which his contemporaries noticed, that baffles people who are looking for an eccentric genius in the modern style and so come to believe somebody else must have written the plays.) Without thinking about it all, ordinary people—at least before the mass media began hypnotizing them—feel instinctively that this is the man for them. He out-ranges them, as they well know, often going where they cannot follow him, but they feel, so to speak, he always comes home. 'Be cheerful, sir, our revels now are ended.' There is much of

Shakespeare in that 'Be cheerful': we are home again. All this helps to explain why so many sensible ordinary people, in so many different places and times, have had a special liking for this great master of language and drama. He is their man. And now this is being discovered all over again, often by youngsters who look as if they did not believe anything worth knowing had happened before 1955. It is a hopeful sign, and we need one.

Creation that springs from a rich nature, uncommon vitality, an abundance of energy, has something to spare for friendship, for affection, for tenderness. These are hard to find in the representative literature and drama of the modern world, though of course they exist in life as they have always done. But the one-sided creator, the over-introverted man desperately defending himself against stupid and hostile extraverts, though he may not lack friendliness and affection in his private life, is too hardpressed in his work, too near the end of his tether, to be friendly and affectionate. It is this rather than the fear of being thought sentimental that banishes sympathy and warmth from so much modern writing. Sometimes everything in it seems to be happening among the icy craters of the moon, which contemporary man has such a strange desire to visit. Shakespeare, in certain moods, can be hard, bleak, terrifying, on the edge of eternal night, but sooner or later the sun rises again, to warm kings and clowns, delicate virgins and cynical old bawds.

The breadth and depth of Shakespeare's instinctive sympathy are perhaps better understood by comparatively unsophisticated persons than by the scholars and intellectuals who examine his plays in detail. We are mostly party men now of one sort or another. Our sympathies are at the mercy of our convictions. We fit people into a pattern. We live in a world of propaganda, of deepest black and dazzling white. An ironic comedy like *Measure for Measure* may be difficult, but we make it more difficult by refusing to believe that everybody in it is entitled to his or her point of view, by looking for 'the line', 'the angle', the social or moral judgement. Shakespeare rises above his scene almost like the sun itself. His unique greatness can be discovered not only in his gigantic characters but also, and perhaps more surprisingly, in all the little figures, persons of no particular importance, he brings to life, and a life too all their own, allowing them to declare themselves and to sit somewhere at the feast, with a wonderful tolerance. Such a smiling acceptance of the variety of human life is hard to find in our world. Often we imagine we are being tolerant when in fact we are merely being indifferent. But though Shakespeare is sometimes indifferent to the story he is telling, shrugging away the action when it begins to bore him, his tolerance of people of all kinds —except the cold-hearted seekers of power—is not indifference, otherwise he could not bring them to life.

What we probably find hard to understand—even though we pay the notion some lip-service—is that here in Shakespeare we have a whole kingdom of poetry. This is not quite the platitude it may first appear to be. Poetry and poets exist in our modern world but, we feel, in a somewhat hole-and-corner fashion, catering for special and perhaps eccentric tastes. A few people take to writing and reading poetry as others attempt to sing madrigals or paint murals. We should be astonished if, short of murder, a poet appeared on the front page of the morning paper or headed the news on television. Poetry is up a bypath somewhere, not on any main road. We no longer expect a poet to create, as Shakespeare does, a whole opposition world of poetry, in which the values are not political, economic, social, moral, but poetical. (There is of course some sharing of values, as I have already suggested, but now I must make my point and press on.) These other worlds, threatening our very existence, claim our attention all day and half the night, until we grow weary of them. How refreshing then to leave them now and again for the world a poet has made for us, as strangely different as those distant planets that youngsters now imagine themselves exploring, yet, with this poet, so close to what we know, in the better part of our minds, and feel in our hearts to be true!

Not everything is in direct opposition and the sharpest contrast. There are some similarities, some patches of common ground. There are matters in which our modern world has drawn nearer to Shakespeare, now closer to us in these respects than he was to our grandfathers. There is space for only one brief example. Shakespeare's women, by and large, are modern women. His heroines could step into any good contemporary novel. They are not the romantic wraiths or pretty dolls of the fiction and drama between his time and ours. They want the men they love, and in the service of their hearts they are direct, practical and courageous. Though often lively-minded and witty, they are sensibly realistic, and not, as the men are, always in danger of deceiving themselves. Girls like these, ready if necessary to set out for the Forest of Arden or anywhere else, may be found almost everywhere in the modern world: they are probably its best achievement. But Shakespeare thought of them first.

One last point. While these plays must be read—and indeed many speeches in the later manner cannot be understood at first through the ear—they remain plays, and some time should be seen and heard in performance. (There has been too much criticism of the printed page, not enough of what happens in performance, which Shakespeare always had in mind.) But there are difficulties. Some of them remain even when, at last, we dismiss the scene painters and allow the poet to set our imagination working for him. For example, if we play the long slow entrances properly, so that the 'Look where they come' speeches make sense, we need a production in the large operatic style, to which much of Shakespeare lends itself. On the other hand, the more intimate scenes and the soliloquies would be lost in an opera house size of theatre. As yet we have not the playhouses that can meet these opposing demands. We may be compelled in the end to imitate as closely as we can the Elizabethan stage and auditorium. But the modern world has other resources. To my mind the best of them for this purpose, strange as it may seem to many people, is television, especially as it may soon be developed, using colour on rather larger screens and if possible claiming closer attention by making viewers pay before they look. Good television production could cope equally well with both large-scale production and intimacy, the long entrances or exits and the whispers of their spectators; it could restore to this drama, missing so long on the picture-frame stage, its quick fluid movement; and even in our present, rather improvised and faulty productions, the soliloquies, coming from faces that fill the whole screen, murmured as they can never be in a theatre, are no longer an embarrassment but drama reaching a new intimacy. Here then is hope. And it would be a wonderful stroke of irony, one that Shakespeare would have enjoyed, if the brassiest of our mass media should help us to return to him.

What Happened to Falstaff

This began as an hour-long talk for the BBC Third Programme. (Later, in 1964, an abridged version of it went out on the European and other programmes.) I had in my mind, when I began with Falstaff, six or seven other studies of great Shakespearean characters, enough to make a volume. It may have been sheer laziness or it may have been a distaste for pushing my way into the over-crowded field of Shakespeare criticism, but I found myself reluctant to start work on the other characters. However, I offer this piece on Falstaff without any shadow of an apology. For it is in my opinion (and I could produce some notable supporters) the best thing in this book.

NO SHAKESPEAREAN CHARACTER has received more enthusiastic praise then Falstaff. More ink and print may have been devoted to the enigmatic figure of Hamlet, but it is Falstaff who has turned critics into a rapturous chorus. Among the loudest applauders of the fat knight may be found professors of Eng. Lit. who, after their glass of barley water, have never stayed up later than eleven, and careful men of letters who would no more think of roistering in a tavern than of breaking into a bank. Falstaff is not only wonderfully written in himself but the cause that good writing has come out of other men. But is there anything new to be said about him? I think there is, but only after we have stopped chuckling and clapping, have begun to explore the mind of Falstaff's creator, and have seen both the character and the poet who made him against the widest possible background of English literature and life.

In order to understand what happened to Falstaff, how he was built up and then knocked down, how in this instance the dramatist in Shakespeare conquered the poet, we must first return to some familiar ground. Here we shall keep company not with Shakespeare the poet but with Shakespeare the astute man of the Theatre, anxious to provide his company with plays and to please his large audiences. *Richard II* and *Henry VI* had already been written, and, if there were to be more historical plays, based like the others on Holinshed's *Chronicles*, clearly they ought to fill this gap between Richard II and Henry VI. Moreover, within this gap, waiting for Shakespeare to bring him to life on the stage, was the one triumphant popular figure among all these monarchs—King Henry V. Audiences loved him, for even bad plays about him had proved successful. As a hero-king of drama he seemed to promise everything: first, the madcap youth, the despair of his father; then the gallant prince who helped his father to put down rebellion; and finally the king, now free of all folly, who proved to be a greater man than his father. Such a figure was worth more than one play; there could be matter for two dramas in his wild youth and subsequent gallantry on the battlefield, and for yet another in his reign as king. So Shakespeare devised *Henry IV*, Parts One and Two, and *Henry V*.

The legends of Prince Hal's youthful follies could not be ignored. Indeed, without them there could hardly be a play worth seeing. The serious matter, what could be made out of the rebellions against Bolingbroke, was inferior to that in *Richard II* and *Henry VI*. The scenes containing Prince Hal and his boon companions would be a welcome change from those showing the harsh dry king and his court or the stiff anger of the barons in rebellion. A drama on two different levels was possible here, as Shakespeare saw from the first. (Here I must add, to be rid of the subject, that he accepted the theatrical tradition that Prince Hal's chief boon companion was Sir John Oldcastle. It is generally supposed that the character was renamed Falstaff because Oldcastle, executed as a Lollard, was regarded as an early Protestant martyr. But it is also likely that Shakespeare was glad to give this giant creation a name of his own. And to us he is Falstaff, so that we can forget Oldcastle.) It was a brilliant idea to present the drama of Henry IV and his son on two different levels, dividing it between the court and the tavern, the top people and the riff-raff, and giving the historical play a new breadth and depth. But technically it was tricky. If the comic scenes of low life were not good entertainment, all was lost. But if they were too good, the balance of the drama would be destroyed. Again, if Prince Hal were shown rollicking with tedious buffoons, as the heroic central character he would suffer just as the play itself would. The future hero-king must at least frolic in amusing company. There must be somebody in the tavern, leading him on, more or less his own size and weight. And while this character must be good enough to sustain all the comic scenes, he must not divert any sympathy from Henry when, as king, Henry has to reject him. For unless we are ready, at the end of the second part of *Henry IV*, to join in the cheering for the new young king, soon to be the all-conquering hero of the play of *Henry V*, something will have gone badly wrong. And, as we know, it did go wrong. After Falstaff has been rebuked and rejected, then carried off to the Fleet prison, we stare after him in dismay and cannot do any cheering for King Henry. *Hurray for what?*

It went wrong not because the technical job was altogether too tricky. When his mind was considering every aspect of his work, Shakespeare was equal to any technical problem, no matter how tricky, but often his stagecraft slipped because he was not attending to it properly, not bothering, not caring, just pasting the thing together ready for next Tuesday. What happened in *Henry IV*, however, was not the result of indifference. Here Shakespeare the successful man of the Theatre, the planner of a series of plays about English kings, was defeated by Shakespeare the poet, the creator working out of his unconscious depths. It is the dramatist's experience, craft, talent, that present us with Henry, both as prince and as king; but the character of Falstaff comes out of the poet's genius. This was felt by audiences from the very first, for there are contemporary references to the two parts of *Henry IV* as the Falstaff plays. The fat knight, originally intended as a foil to the prince and so much comic relief, steals both the *Henry IV* plays, and he would have walked away with *Henry V* too if Shakespeare, breaking the promise of the *Henry IV* epilogue, had not killed him offstage. So that the hero-king could live in all glory, Falstaff had to die. In the two earlier plays, Shakespeare does his best for Henry—we can see him working at it trying to keep to his conscious plan—but Henry is overshadowed, almost extinguished, by that huge, triumphant, *effortless* creation—Falstaff.

I repeat—effortless. A character of such size, scope and vitality, a character who seems himself a genius, cannot be sustained by conscious effort. He arrives, pulsing and glowing with life, from the unconscious depths. No writer, not the cleverest who ever lived, could coldly contrive, put together, consciously set in motion, a Falstaff. If such characters seem magical, as indeed they do, that is because they come, like figures in some marvellous enduring dream, from the magical part of man, the innermost recesses and unfathomable depths of his being, the region far within where 'he on honey-dew hath fed, And drunk the milk of Paradise'. These giant characters come unbidden, and when they arrive, they do as they please. Shakespeare, consciously planning his historical series, with one eye on his more important patrons, wanted a useful comic foil to Prince Hal, some fat old fool who would amuse him and us for a time and could then be shrugged away; but what he got, rising magnificently out of his creative depths, was Falstaff, who not only does not fit into the drama's planned structure but finally succeeds, at least for many of us, in wrecking it. At the end of *Henry IV Part Two* we are not ready for a play about *Henry V*—let the treacherous prig stew in his oil of anointment!—but are eager to follow Falstaff to the Fleet prison or wherever he chooses to go, and would echo the cry of Bardolph when he hears that Falstaff is dead: 'Would I were with him, wheresome'er he is, either in Heaven or in Hell!' It is not fanciful to suggest then, as I do again now, that here Shakespeare the poet, the creative man, by conceiving a character so out of scale, so much in excess of what the drama needed, rose up and rebelled against Shakespeare the careful and practical man of the Theatre. It is not unreasonable to regard Falstaff as the retort, the huge protest, of one side of Shakespeare, the inner and hidden side, to the other, the outward, belonging to the smiling and prosperous playwright, already with an eye on some sound property and a possible coat-of-arms.

If Falstaff is much bigger and richer than he was originally designed to be, this is because the life in him was created by an explosion of rebellious energy. Out of this same eruption, which was to be followed soon by the explosions and earthquakes and shuddering darkness of the tragedies, came much else, not offered for our enjoyment now: scorn and disgust and the beginning of horror, all the imagery of disease that increasingly finds its way into this two-part drama of Henry IV and his son. The wretched king, dying by inches, who has sacrificed so much for power and enjoyed it so little; his friends and enemies alike, clanking metallic figures that seem to talk in clanking metallic verse;

the brassy pride, the anger that can be released at a word, a touch, the cold treacheries, the meaningless battlefields still smoking while the next set of pompous lies are being composed and uttered; we are made more and more aware of all these, together with sores, poxes and plagues, as the drama of *Henry IV* moves to its close. The common folk make no better show than the baronial ironclads; they are senile and doting, like Shallow and Silence, or bleating caricatures of common men like those pressed into military service by Falstaff. The bright shield of chivalry is reversed and seems to be crawling with maggots. None of this is realism, simple and direct as it would have been in Chaucer, for example; there are too many diseases, too much scorn and disgust; it is a voice from a man's inner world condemning the outer world of power and glory, to which one side of the man himself may have been too much committed. He is protesting and rebelling against himself. Yeats said that we make poetry out of the quarrel with ourselves; and until his last years, Shakespeare, with his rich but deeply divided nature, was always ready for this quarrel. One half of him, the more outward and conscious half, admired order and detested all forms of disorder; we could fairly describe it as conservative, respectable, conformist. The other half of him, which seized the pen whenever he was being fully creative, was in hot rebellion against the ordered world, and it was the fiery energy of this hidden self that went into his greatest characters, all of them rebels of one sort and another, like Hamlet, Cleopatra and Falstaff.

The secret of Falstaff is that he is masterfulness,

quickness, energy, genius, everything that makes a great commander of men, all in the service not of power and glory but of delight. When we see him on the stage we miss these essential qualities because the over-padded actor is so busy being a fat old man, puffing and wheezing and grunting. But Falstaff wears his years and fat as if they were a comic uniform, using them as matter for more humour, so that all the best jokes about his age and size are his own. We must not be deceived by his sprawling bulk; his eye misses nothing; his mind is wonderfully clear, quick and commanding, working like lightning—but summer lightning, hurting nobody. He is a great man, far greater than Bolingbroke or any of his brawling nobles, but he is a very unusual great man because instead of giving himself to ambition and power, he chooses ease, pleasure, good fellowship, his and our delight. He is the Alexander, Caesar or Napoleon not of battlefields, victory marches and ruined kingdoms but of rollicking evenings and circles of happy faces. If wit, humour and enjoyment should have an emperor, then this is he. And why should not the qualities of a master of men, everything that makes for greatness, serve for once far removed from the standards of ambition, cruelty, death? The triumph of Falstaff down the centuries is not explained by the fact that his scenes offer comic relief from the grim chronicle of Bolingbroke and his adversaries. To go as we do from Bolingbroke's kingdom to Falstaff's is to experience a glorious expansion of the spirit; the glitter of steel is transformed into firelight, candlelight, and the gleams of gold in the sherris-sack; the men of power and war, rigid in iron, all vanish, and we are among boon companions, the enchanted air is filled with 'nimble, fiery and delectable shapes'. Where the two kingdoms come together and clash, as in the battle scenes, Falstaff still commands our allegiance and sympathy. He knows he is ridiculous, therefore there is in him a detached intelligence that demands our respect; the others, for all their pride and high places only like so many brutal boys, are ridiculous without knowing it. In a third kingdom, the invisible but enduring realm of intelligence and spirit, Falstaff is not their butt, he is their master.

His raffishness, his lying and cheating, his astounding impudence, must be accepted, but we are mistaken if we imagine that we have only to add wit and humour to them to complete the character. He is something more than just another lovable rogue. Odd elements, usually opposed and excluding one another, are mixed in him, fused together in his personality. His judgements are absolutely realistic; he is easily the most clear-sighted person in the play; he is entirely free from the common English vice of self-deception; the world in which he moves, so superbly sure of himself, is the real world, where wounds are wounds, corpses are corpses, and cant and nonsense are cant and nonsense. And yet, though he talks prose, Falstaff is undoubtedly one of Shakespeare's great poetical creations; he exists in an atmosphere in which there is an element of poetical idealism; he is almost an archetype, a symbol of the self raised to its highest power of wit and humour, ease and enjoyment; he belongs to some haunting dream, perhaps as old as drink and firelight, of a gigantic wonderful night out, a hell of a party. When we are no longer haunted by this dream, we have finished with our youth for ever. So when Falstaff tells the travellers he is robbing that 'young men must live', or, with sublime impudence, says to the Chief Justice, 'You that are old consider not the capacities of us that are young,' he is not merely making a joke out of his white hairs, for we cannot help feeling he speaks out of a spirit enduringly youthful. When, after seeing through Shallow and Silence at a glance, he says to us, 'Lord, Lord, how subject we old men are to this vice of lying!' we still feel this spirit, dead in them, is alive in him, that his eye is still clear and bright while theirs are misty with age, self-deception and foolishness. That fine critic, Walter Raleigh, in his life of Shakespeare, brings the poet and his creation together here: 'With the passing of Falstaff,' he tells us, 'Shakespeare's youth was ended. All that wonderful experience of London life, all those days and nights of freedom and adventure and the wooing of new pleasures, seem to be embodied in this great figure, the friend and companion of the young.' This could hardly be said better, but we must examine this relation between the poet and the character he created far more closely than Raleigh did.

We have already seen that Shakespeare the popular dramatist, the careful successful man of the Theatre, wanted to write three plays about Henry, first as Prince Hal and then as the triumphant hero-king, Henry V; but he had received from Shakespeare, the poet, the creative and rebellious man, far more than was necessary to keep the story going. Falstaff, a tremendous character, threatened the whole structure of the drama, diverting sympathy from where it was needed, just because he took up so much room and attracted so much attention. And if we follow Falstaff through the two parts of *Henry IV*, we can catch more than a glimpse of the conflict between the Shakespeare who merely wanted to use him as a comic foil and the other Shakespeare who could not help enlarging, deepening, illuminating the character, this figure symbolic of and sustained by his own rebellious energy, his love of a life not found in courts and on battlefields. In the first scene, set in the prince's apartment, Falstaff says some good things but has not arrived at his full stature. Indeed, here he plays the part originally assigned to him, simply as the leading figure among the prince's idle companions. It is of course at the end of this scene, after what we may call the Gadshill plot has been worked out between the prince and Pointz, that the prince, left alone, begins:

> I know you all, and will awhile uphold
> The unyoked humour of your idleness

and tells us that he will imitate the sun, sooner or later emerging from the clouds and then admired all the more. It is a detestable speech, going much further in cold calculation and self-approval than the situation demands. Quiller-Couch, while accepting it, rightly, as Shakespeare's, suggests that it was added to the scene, after the play was written, because the leading actor, playing Henry, insisted upon some speech of this kind, detaching the prince from his low companions. This is possible, but my own view is that the speech is overdone, clumsily losing sympathy, because Shakespeare, already fascinated by the possibilities of Falstaff, is forcing himself to keep the story as he originally planned it. He gives Prince Henry what is at best a tactless speech because he is already beginning to feel divided about him.

Taste in humour is personal. I can only speak for myself when I say that the Gadshill scenes and the long tavern scene that follows them do not show us the great Falstaff, except in a few flashes. My guess is that they were originally planned to keep the prince dominant, with Falstaff his butt, but as the scene in the tavern developed, after the robbery, Falstaff began taking charge of the proceedings. Even so, he is still not quite his richest and ripest self. He reaches this towards the end of Act III, perhaps in that opening speech to Bardolph which concludes with 'Company, Villainous company, hath been the spoil of me'. When we find him at the war he is fully ripe: notably, in his account of how he first recruited well-to-do timid fellows, who immediately bought out their services, leaving him to fill his ranks with riff-raff:

... You would think that I had a hundred and fifty tattered prodigals lately come from swine-keeping, from eating draff and husks. A mad fellow met me on the way, and told me I had unloaded all the gibbets, and press'd the dead bodies. No eye have seen such scarecrows. I'll not march through Coventry with them, that's flat: nay, and the villains march wide between the legs, as if they had gyves on; for, indeed, I had the most of them out of prison. There's but a shirt and a half in all my company . . .

Equally rich are his exchanges with Prince Henry and Westmoreland on the subject of these men—'food for powder, food for powder; they'll fill a pit as well as better'; the famous soliloquy on Honour; and then of course our various glimpses of him during the battle of Shrewsbury. Here, among the *alarums* and *excursions*, he is allowed to make some characteristic observations, as for example: 'I like not such grinning honour as Sir Walter hath: give me life, which if I can save, so; if not honour comes unlook'd for, and there's an end.' But the dramatist, now in charge of these final scenes of *Part One*, takes the opportunity here to raise the prince high above Falstaff. Notice the prince's speech when he thinks that Falstaff is dead:

> . . . Poor Jack, farewell!
> I could have better spared a better man:
> O, I should have a heavy miss of thee,
> If I were much in love with vanity!

Falstaff, shamming death, overhears the whole of this speech and he should have taken better note of the last two lines I have quoted. The business that follows —his taking the body of Hotspur on his back and then pretending to have killed him—is not very happily contrived, at least to our taste, even though Falstaff's account of the matter contains one of those exact details that always suggest a master of lying: 'I grant you I was down and out of breath; and so was he: but we rose both at an instant, and fought a long hour by Shrewsbury clock. . . .' And if, as I feel strongly, there is something unsatisfactory about these scenes that conclude *Part One*, something hurried, forced, over-contrived, I believe it is because the dramatist, as distinct from the poet, has to take charge almost brutally, has to make his points, round off his action, get the thing done. This is a contracting process; Falstaff, like humour itself, is essentially expansive, so he has to suffer some loss.

We do not know exactly when and how these two plays of *Henry IV* were written. Dr. Johnson, and most critics since his time, have not unreasonably regarded them as being what they are described to be, two parts of one drama, divided simply for the convenience of production. It is possible that Shakespeare went straight on from *Part One* to *Part Two*, as if he were writing one long play. But this seems to me unlikely. I think there was a considerable interval between the writing of these two pieces, and that this interval accounts for the fact, as I see it, that *Part Two* is not a mere continuation of *Part One*, even though it shows us most of the same people during the same king's reign: it is a different play. It moves, as all Shakespeare's plays do, in its own atmosphere. Its highlights are brighter than those of *Part One*, its shadows darker; it is both a more comic and a more tragic play. It is divided more equally between public life and private life, between the two realms, the kingdom of Bolingbroke and Prince Henry and the kingdom now triumphantly Falstaff's; and the gap between them is wider until the end, when of course it is brutally closed. It is as if the opposites in Shakespeare's mind and spirit were each given more freedom to do their best or their worst: at one extreme, the politic dramatist bent on celebrating the arrival at last of public order and national unity, represented by Henry V, and at the other extreme, the poet and humorous anarchist who could create Falstaff. These opposites are stronger than they were in *Part One*; but also, here in *Part Two*, we are aware of a third Shakespeare, beyond these opposites: it is the spirit of the man himself, never directly revealed, only to be guessed at, but seeming to many of us to be moving, now at this time, through a darkening world from bewilderment to a loss of hope. There are no droller scenes in all Shakespeare than these in *Henry IV Part Two*; we must not be surprised if they were born of a growing despair. Tragedy, black and raging, will soon arrive; but here, in the dusk, there is still time to enjoy the fireworks of wit, the bonfire of humour, and Falstaff before he is carted away like a felled ox.

Notice Falstaff's first appearance in this *Part Two*. There is now no pretence that he is merely the oldest, fattest, wittiest of the prince's companions. Not only does he exist in his own right; not only is he enormously and victoriously himself; he might even be said to be now more than himself, as if aware of his archetypal nature. For what does he say, a minute after he has arrived on the stage?

Men of all sorts take a pride to gird at me; the brain of this foolish-compounded clay, man, is not able to invent anything that tends to laughter, more than I invent or is invented on me: I am not only witty in myself, but the cause that wit is in other men . . .

Here, in *Part Two*, he exists independently of Prince Henry; in his own kingdom he is now absolute monarch. In all his best scenes—with the Chief Justice and then with Hostess Quickly, with Doll Tearsheet and Pistol in the tavern, with Justice Shallow, the recruits and Master Silence—he is not seen here with Prince Henry. Again, tastes differ, but to my mind the long tavern scene—with Doll Tearsheet's immortal 'Come, I'll be friends with thee, Jack: thou art going to the wars; and whether I shall ever see thee again or no, there is nobody cares'—loses far more than it gains by the entrance of the prince and Pointz, in disguise and playing the last of their uninspired farce tricks. But there is one remark by Pointz that should be remembered: 'My lord, he will drive you out of your revenge and turn all to a merriment, if you take not the heat.' What a wonderful gift this is, to be able to drive any man, or any combination of men, out of any thought of revenge and turn all to a merriment! A Falstaff at the United Nations would be worth all the billions we spend on arms.

The scenes in and around Justice Shallow's house in Gloucestershire, on or off the stage, have perhaps never been equalled since in any English comic writing. Shallow and Silence and the rustic recruits may be broad caricatures, rapidly sketched by the hand of a master; but no man who has spent any time in the remoter parts of rural England, and has kept his eyes and ears open, would agree they are caricatures of types that have long ceased to exist: they are all with us still, down to this day, and only Falstaff— alas—has vanished from the scene. And even among these hearty drolleries there are flashes of truth and deep feeling: for example, the confusion of past and present in the old men's chatter of Shallow and Silence; or in Feeble's sudden manfulness: 'By my troth, I care not; a man can die but once; we owe God a death: I'll ne'er bear a base mind.' For my part I could sit for hours after dinner in Shallow's garden, over the wine and apples and caraway seeds, listening to Master Silence being so unexpectedly merry 'in the sweet o' the night'. Somehow we are made to feel that behind the hiccoughing and belching, the jokes and drunken snatches of song, there is the enduring poetry of the English rural scene. This poetry is exquisitely suggested in the pastoral interlude towards the end of Elgar's *Symphonic Study, Falstaff*, a work too-little-known, perhaps his masterpiece, certainly superior to his familiar *Enigma Variations*. Across the centuries a lantern lit by Shakespeare's mind illuminates and inspires the Edwardian composer's score.

We have been asked, fairly enough, to notice how Shakespeare, in these last scenes, compels Falstaff to put himself in the wrong with us. We know very well of course that Falstaff will get what he can out of this silly old Shallow—that is his way and we have come to expect it—but his winks and nudges, being forced, are too gross. In the same fashion his expectation of power and influence, now that Hal is king, is deliberately pitched too high and given an ugly sound: 'Let us take any man's horses; the laws of England are at my commandment'. There is *hubris* here, asking to be toppled down; but it is not quite Falstaff as we have come to know him; we feel he is being pushed and hurried by the dramatist, now busy preparing us for the rejection scene. But before these sinister preparations have reached their height, we have had the most elaborate of Falstaff's soliloquies, ostensibly celebrating the virtues of sherris-sack. It follows, we must remember, an encounter with the cold and correct Prince John of Lancaster, who has just put down the rebellion by an appalling act of treachery. As he goes, Lancaster says:

> Fare you well, Falstaff: I in my condition,
> Shall better speak of you than you deserve.

To which Falstaff, alone now, retorts:

> I would you had but the wit: 'twere better than your dukedom.—Good faith, this same young sober-blooded boy doth not love me; nor a man cannot make him laugh: but that's no marvel; he drinks no wine . . .

We are then told by Falstaff how a good sherris-sack—

> . . . Ascends me into the brain; dries me there all the foolish and dull and crudy vapours which environ it; makes it apprehensive, quick, forgetive, full of nimble, fiery, and delectable shapes; which, deliver'd o'er to the tongue, which is the birth, become excellent wit . . .

This may be wine at work but it will do very well too for the imagination, which our Prince Johns, bent on power and a career, then and now, prefer to avoid: they find it no help in the rat race.

It is this same Prince John who has the last word, after the King has cried, ' I know thee not, old man:

fall to thy prayers' and all the rest of it, banishing Falstaff, on pain of death, 'not to come near our person by ten mile'. Prince John re-enters, with the Chief Justice and his officers, who carry Falstaff and his followers to the Fleet Prison; and it is he who cries, 'I like this fair proceeding of the King's,' and later adds, to round off the play:

> I will lay odds that, ere this year expire,
> We bear our civil swords and native fire
> As far as France . . .

To which we can add that this native fire, after consuming a hundred castles, villages, towns, crowded with folk who only asked to be left alone, put a torch to the faggots under Joan of Arc. So Henry, turned away from his former self, is now in the saddle, with brother John at his elbow; and Falstaff we never see again. The play of *Henry V* could not have contained him; so he has to die off-stage. Shakespeare can no longer trust himself to do two contrary things at the same time, to give equal play to the divisions in his own nature; the furious creative energy that went into Falstaff—and is nowhere to be found in the drama of *Henry V*—must now wait for the great tragic figures, who arrive when the lid comes off and history and politics are forgotten. The poet gives a shrug, as the dramatist insists upon taking charge; and Falstaff has to die. A character having the same name and appearance and a trick of speech copied from the original Falstaff finds his way into *The Merry Wives of Windsor*, a farce so uninventive that it yawns in our faces, though I shall take care it never yawns in mine again;

indeed, we do Shakespeare's memory a service if we refuse to produce this botched hack job. We see the last of the real Falstaff, being carted off to prison, at the end of *Henry IV, Part II*. Perhaps the offstage character who repents and dies in *Henry V* is no more our Falstaff than that fat buffoon at Windsor, for the one we treasure is both unrepentant and immortal.

The rebellious poet in Shakespeare created a better man than *Henry V*, but the other Shakespeare, the Globe Theatre playwright and 'sharer', the careful man, felt compelled to sacrifice him to Henry. The patriot hero-king must have his play to himself. The English nation, so desperately warring against itself in so many of these historical plays, must now be seen united behind a strong popular king, almost as if the Tudors had arrived. But this unity of Crown and People, this appearance of the English nation, and this common understanding between Establishment and mob, all represented by Henry's change of heart and mind, his rehabilitation, his welcome into the ranks of sound decent people in authority, can only be achieved if Falstaff is denounced, banished, jailed. When, earlier, Falstaff and the Chief Justice met in the street and fought a duel of words, Falstaff won handsomely. He did it in his own harmless fashion, not having the Chief Justice carted off anywhere but simply making him forget his anger, luring him into wit and humour, turning 'all to a merriment'. But now King Henry, reassuring the Chief Justice, has said to him:

There is my hand.
You shall be as a father to my youth:
My voice shall sound as you do prompt mine ear;

And I will stoop and humble my intents
To your well-practised wise directions.

And one of the first of these well-practised wise directions is to have Falstaff taken to the Fleet Prison. The Chief Justice, not as Falstaff left him at the end of their duel, tolerant, indulgent, humorous, but in all the intolerant bad temper of the law lord, can claim complete victory. Falstaff is out. The nation unites, Crown and People find themselves in harmony, the Establishment waves and smiles as the mob cheers; and Falstaff, together with all he stands for, is very firmly—we might say even ruthlessly—rejected. England goes her way without Falstaff.

Now of course there is a great deal in this disreputable character that will not do at all, and that we English, then and now, are better without. Idleness, gluttony, drunkenness, lechery, lying and cheating, cannot be approved. Shakespeare deals very honestly with us here. He never forgets that these historical dramas are taking place in a real and not an ideal world. Oberon and Puck have already had their turn; Prospero and Ariel have not yet arrived: here among these chronicles of kings, though dramatic liberties may be taken with men and events, our feet are kept to the ground, no magical tricks and transformations are allowed, causes inevitably bring effects. If Shakespeare shows us plainly what the desire for power can do to a Bolingbroke or an Earl of Northumberland, he also makes it clear that irresponsibility and the lusts of the flesh can turn Sir John Falstaff into a lying old toper, ready to swindle any senile acquaintance foolish enough to trust him. This is not a pleas-

ing picture. As King Henry says in his notorious
rejection speech:

> How ill white hairs become a fool and jester!
> I have long dream'd of such a kind of man,
> So surfeit-swell'd, so old, and so profane . . .

No doubt this is what is being banished. Both King
Henry and his brother, John of Lancaster, tell us that
Falstaff must reform himself before the Court will
consent to set eyes on him again. 'All are banished,'
says Lancaster, 'till their conversations'—and by this
he means not just talk but general manners and behaviour—'till their conversations appear more wise
and modest to the world.' But a Falstaff who appeared
wise and modest to this cold-blooded young prince
would not be recognizable as Falstaff; in fact, he
would not be Falstaff at all. He could then no more
'turn all to a merriment' than Lancaster himself
could. We would not waste five minutes listening to
such a character. On the other hand, the unreformed
Falstaff, the one who has to be banished, has been
applauded by three centuries of critics, many of them
sterner moralists than I can even pretend to be. So if
official England, represented here by Henry V,
totally rejects Falstaff—for this is what is happening,
because a reformed Falstaff, acceptable to Lancaster
and the Chief Justice, would not be a Falstaff at all—
then this England deprives itself of the whole Falstaffian quality. It may want to have its cake and eat
it, but in fact it rejects what is good in Falstaff as well
as what is bad. And as we have already seen, there is
much in Falstaff that is wonderfully good. But let us

take a closer look at what is being dumped overboard from the ship of state.

To begin with, though capable of uttering the most gigantic lies, most of them never intended to be believed, Falstaff is remarkably free from the vice of lying to himself. He may deceive others, although he does that only rarely, but he never deceives himself. Instead of deliberately befogging his mind, as so many of the English do, especially when they are in authority, Falstaff keeps his mind clear, open, marvellously perceptive. His judgements, as I pointed out earlier, are absolutely realistic. When he talks nonsense, he knows he is talking nonsense, and is indeed turning 'all to a merriment'. What he does not do is precisely what the official English have been accused of doing for hundreds of years—that is, talk a lot of cant, solemn and dangerous nonsense, born of hypocrisy or elaborate self-deception. England has produced mountains of it, which Falstaff would have seen through at a glance. If an example is needed, there is one in the passage already quoted from King Henry's speech reassuring the Chief Justice. Here it is again:

> There is my hand.
> You shall be as a father to my youth:
> My voice shall sound as you do prompt mine ear;
> And I will stoop and humble my intents
> To your well-practised wise directions.

I think that is cant. To quote Shakespeare for once against himself, it represents 'that glib and oily art / To speak and purpose not'. When King Henry promises 'to stoop and humble' his intents to the directions of the Chief Justice, then if he believes what he is saying he is deceiving himself, and if he knows he will never keep this promise, then he is being hypocritical. Either way he is talking cant. One glance from Falstaff would have shrivelled this solemn humbug to a wisp of smoke and a nasty smell. That is one good reason why King Henry had to banish Falstaff, and why Shakespeare, who may or may not have known that a lot more cant was on its way, had to kill him off.

Ever since then, we English have had no more Falstaff but an ever-increasing load of cant. Over a hundred years ago, Peacock's Mr. Crotchet grew warm on this subject: 'Where the Greeks had modesty,' he says, 'we have cant; where they had poetry, we have cant; where they had patriotism, we have cant; where they had anything that exalts, delights, or adorns humanity, we have nothing but cant, cant, cant.' If there has been much improvement since Mr. Crotchet's time, it has not been noticeable. We now have cant from the pulpit, blessing hydrogen bombs. The reputation of the English Establishment and its admirers for smug self-deception, hypocrisy and perfidy, has long had some notoriety in the outside world. We are famous for our pious treacheries. King Henry, John of Lancaster and the Chief of Justice lead an immense procession of personages, heavily titled and glittering with orders, all saviours of the nation, all masters of cant. Now, after print has reeked of it for three centuries, the air is filled with it. But it is only fair to add that the banished Falstaff has had his followers too, keeping alive and bright the perceptive eye, the unfogged open mind, the realistic judgement, the humorist's temperament. In their different ways, Swift and Dr. Johnson, Fielding and Sterne, Hazlitt and Carlyle, Dickens and Peacock and Meredith, Wilde and Shaw and Wells, to name no more, all spoke out against cant, risking—and sometimes suffering—banishment of one sort or another. After all, Falstaff and the poet who created him were Englishmen too. The antidote grows in our island as well as the poison. But now I hope it will not be thought utterly unreasonable to discover something symbolic in that final scene of *Henry IV, Part II*, with its rejection of Falstaff. It is as if there floated into Shakespeare's mind, which must have broadened like some vast spreading flood when he was at work, a vague precognition of what was to happen to England and the English down the centuries. It is as if he were given access for a moment to 'the prophetic soul of the wide world dreaming on things to come'.

If we turn now to the more positive side of Falstaff's personality, then the symbolism of his rejection, in the light of what has happened since in English social history, is still more striking. Here let me repeat what I said earlier: the secret of Falstaff is that he is masterfulness, quickness, energy, genius, everything that makes a great commander of men, all in the service not of power and glory but of delight. He is a very unusual great man because instead of ambition and power he chooses ease, pleasure, goodfellowship. A large and influential section of English opinion, from Shakespeare's day to ours, has felt that this attitude of mind should be discouraged. No empires can be founded on it, no fortunes made out of it, no power hunger satisfied by it. That a formidable character like Falstaff, with a kind of genius, at once perceptive, commanding and ingratiating, should leave the highroad for the byroads, the court and camp for the tavern, profit and power for merriment, seems a shocking piece of treachery. Banish the fellow, jail him, hurry him out of sight and hearing, so that the solid business of the country can go on, Parliament be summoned, money be raised, and France invaded again! Remember—*My lord, he will drive you out of your revenge and turn all to a merriment, if you take not the heat.* This corrupting spirit must be resisted: there are fortunes to be made, great positions to be won, French villages to be burnt and peasants to be hanged. Falstaff, who would keep us loitering and laughing in taverns, *must go.*

Already, while Shakespeare was writing 'I know thee not, old man: fall to thy prayers', a dark suspicion of all enjoyment was common in England, spreading and gathering force. Falstaff, we might say, was being rejected and carted off to jail every day. For example, we like to think of this as the Glorious Age of Elizabethan Drama, and even our politicians, after an exceptionally good dinner, have mentioned it favourably. But already the suspicion of all enjoyment was at work on it. The City Fathers, the London Council, disliked actors and playgoing so much that the theatres were built just beyond the city bounds and their control. Attending the play was denounced as an 'unthrifty waste' of money. When Shakespeare was a boy in Stratford-on-Avon it had been visited by various companies of actors; but about the time he was making his hero-king banish Falstaff, the Stratford Council was banishing the Drama itself. Here it was only following, as it said, 'the examples of other well-governed cities and boroughs'. Jumping forward to our own time, the years since the last war, I must add that during these years no fewer than 175 theatres have been closed in Britain, not through any fierce puritanical opposition but because of public indifference and neglect, people preferring now to sit at home with their television, staring at advertisements of detergents and tooth-paste. Incidentally, which is worse—to condemn actors because you believed, as the old puritans did, that they were 'fiends sent from their great captain Satan', or to neglect them in the Theatre because you would rather see them in advertisements pretending to be ecstatic about lubricating oil and mouthwash? Give me the old puritans, for something can come out of people who can talk about the 'great captain Satan', and something did—Cromwell and Milton, for example; whereas out of the imbecilic prey of advertising agencies nothing can come but more advertising agencies and more imbecility.

We know that from the early years of the seven-teenth century onwards England acquired a reputa-tion, the reverse of her former character as Merrie England, for being peculiarly joyless, taking her pleasures sadly. Foreign visitors increasingly left our shores shrugging their expressive shoulders, de-lighted, in spite of the terrors of the Channel passage, to turn their backs on the dreary island. Now this is generally attributed to the influence of the puritans. But puritanism is to blame only if we take it in its very broadest sense, in which it has little to do with what was thought and felt by the genuine old puritans, with their vision of an angry God and an ever-busy and infinitely artful Satan. Here, with Falstaff still in mind, we must discriminate. After all, Henry V, John of Lancaster, the Chief Justice, were not puritans. Shakespeare, who created Falstaff only in the end to humiliate him, was like all the dramatists and actors an enemy of the puritans. Yet Falstaff has to be knocked down and carted off. Why? Because he represents something anarchic, ungovernable, outside the pattern of power, property-owning, social standing, mockingly critical of all solemn official cant, just as the playhouses themselves did to the mayor and aldermen of the City of London. What happened to him symbolises, almost as if Shakespeare had caught a glimpse of his country's future, a strange division in the English national character and life, in which Falstaffs are being for ever created only to be rejected. The negative side, the rejectors, the haters of ease and merriment, wit and humour, are not God-haunted salvation-seeking puritans, comparatively only a few. They are all those, from the top men of the Establishment down to the crowds outside their gates, who want anything from supreme power to the greyest respectability that is darkly suspicious of candour, an open mind, and merriment. Falstaff must go. We cannot afford him. This spirit, suspicious and sullen, can be discovered at work among the merchants and empire-builders, behind the black horrors of the

Industrial Revolution from which every foreign visitor shrank appalled, in the elaborate hypocrisies of the Victorian Age detested and denounced by every great Victorian writer. It is still with us, this Falstaff-rejecting spirit. For example, to this day, as all our friends from abroad realize with astonishment, at an hour when in other capital cities the glasses are being filled again, on behalf of merriment and goodfellow-ship, in London the glasses are removed and tavern lights begin to be extinguished. Our legislators, who have their own glasses filled at all hours, are afraid that Falstaff might walk in again and take command.

Given time and space I would undertake to show how this negative spirit, this suspicion of enjoyment, this fear of Falstaff, has come between England and her men of genius, often darkening their lives. It has happened time after time, one age after another. But there is a place here for only one example, that of Oscar Wilde. Now Wilde talked and wrote a lot of solemn and often tasteless nonsense about art, to which, in fact, he was too idle and self-indulgent to devote himself properly, as an artist should. What was real, what was good, about this over-dressed, curled and scented giant was his genuine Falstaffian quality, the ease and merriment, wit and humour, that made him irresistible in all companies. All we know about him proves him to have been generous and compassionate; he corrupted nobody but was the easy prey of youths other men had corrupted; the pederasty, for which he was jailed and broken, was so common in London that he might as well have been arrested for using *eau de Cologne*. The cold ferocity of the Law, the

[320]

orgy of cant in the Press, the jeering and yelping of the crowd, revealed the English, high and low, at their worst. Wilde was really a victim of this negative drive, this suspicion or envious hatred of gaiety, colour, brilliance, whatever refused to serve the power motive or broke the drab pattern of respectability and conformity. Falstaff was rejected and banished again. The prophecy latent in that final scene of *Henry IV, Part II* was being fulfilled, as it has been over and over again, in ways too numerous and various to be listed here. But in all this we are keeping to the shadow side of the national character and life; after all, Shakespeare is English and so is Falstaff too. All that immortal ease and merriment, the wit and humour, are as English as the apples in Shallow's orchard. The shadow in us, which I think was there in Shakespeare, may condemn and reject these qualities and gifts, but the sunlight in us, when it has not been kept out by power drives or a timid conformity, welcomes and cherishes them. So these days, more and more English people save their money, consult the innumerable travel agencies that have sprung up in all our towns, and then go abroad for a summer holiday, anywhere from Norway to southern Italy. Why do they do it? Partly, I think, because being English they secretly hope for a magic hour somewhere abroad to turn all to a merriment, so fine, so gay, so careless, that there will be in it a kind of poetry, all those nimble, fiery and delectable shapes. Perhaps some of these people, knowing him to be immortal, are looking for Falstaff.